GW00832932

FORTY YEARS IN PURPLE

Forty Years In Purple

David R. J. Evans

DE

D. J. ELLIS

PULBOROUGH

2022

Copyright © 2022 D. R. J. Evans

David Richard John Evans has asserted his right under the Copyright, Designs & Patents Act, 1988, to be identified as the Author of this work.

ISBN 978 0 9554944 2 0

Acknowledgements

I would record my especial thanks to:

- Valerie Raybould, P.A. during my six years in the Bradford Diocese. She was responsible for the initial typing and filing of several thousand letters;

- Mary Rollin, who was my last P.A. with SAMS. She actually typed the manuscript for this book from my almost illegible scrawlings;

- Robert Lunt, who manfully undertook to proof-read and edit the final version;

- Bishop Henry Scriven, who wrote the Foreword. He and I have had remarkably similar trajectories in our ministerial lives;

- The Rawes family and especially Tess, a granddaughter, who coloured the cover for this book.

First published December 2022

Published by

David J. Ellis

Fernwood, Nightingales, West Chiltington
PULBOROUGH, West Sussex, RH20 2QT

British Library Cataloguing-in-Publication Data

A catalogue record for this book
is available from the British Library.

Printed and Bound in Great Britain by Lanes (South East) Limited, Broadstairs, Kent

To my family,
my wife Dorothy and three children, Hilary, Caroline and Peter
in recognition of my frequent absence on long journeys

and

to many I have been privileged to know and serve around the world

CONTENTS

FOREWORD

by BISHOP HENRY SCRIVEN

As I write this I am about to mark 25 years as a bishop in a variety of situations. So it is an immense pleasure to write this foreword for a book celebrating 40 years of episcopal ministry.

David and I share several things in common, like working in South America and in England (with the South American Mission Society, later part of Church Mission Society) and especially as General Secretary of EFAC (the Evangelical Fellowship in the Anglican Communion); you will find out more about it by reading the book!

It is very refreshing to come across a book like this which is not just the story of a life, interesting though I am sure that can be. But David here shows his gift as a teacher by drawing out themes that are relevant to the ministry of a bishop but are also shared by every committed Christian. We are all called to mission and pastoral work of some kind, not always in other countries, but surely always with an awareness that we are but a small part of God's family. There is much we can learn from reading this book.

It has always been difficult for the Church to hold to biblical teaching on doctrine and ethics in cultures that increasingly move in a very different direction. I often tell young people that it is much more difficult to be a Christian in this age of social media and countless pressures than we ever experienced as young people. It takes courage and the young need encouragement. Here is one resource that will help Christians of all ages to be faithful and steadfast, however difficult life might be.

Thank you, David, for your faithfulness and for what you are passing on to another generation. May the Church be blessed and strengthened by reading your words!

x

1
INTRODUCTION

I was consecrated bishop in the Church of God to serve in the country of Peru, South America on 14th May 1978. My life of 80 years at the time of writing, therefore, splits neatly into two periods of 40 years.

In my other autobiographical book, I majored on the large number of journeys I have been on. The title was *Have Stick Will Travel—Mainly South American Journeys*. The first much shorter part (39 pages) covered my earlier life, though still from the perspective of journeys.

I don't intend to repeat material I used then. But to clarify my own writing and your reading now I offer the table below, which divides my life into seven sections.

1 1938–1965 Schooling and education in the U.K. leading up to ordination, and three years (1965–68) as a curate at Christ Church, Cockfosters

2 1969–1977 Missionary service with SAMS in Argentina, South America

3 1978–1988 Bishop in Peru and Bolivia

4 1988–1993 Bishop in Bradford, U.K., and International Coordinator for EFAC (Evangelical Fellowship in the Anglican Communion)

5 1993–2003 General Secretary of SAMS (Sussex and Birmingham) and International Coordinator for EFAC

6 2003–2010 House for Duty Priest in Alderminster and Assistant Bishop in Coventry

7 2010–2018 Retirement in Warwick and Assistant Bishop in Coventry

On reflection I notice that in every geographical location I have had working responsibilities in two areas at the same time. Even as a young curate at Cockfosters, learning the ropes of ordained ministry, I was also the Student President at national level of the InterVarsity Fellowship. Later in Argentina I was involved in helping the local diocese to move from a traditional English-speaking chaplaincy mode into a Spanish-speaking one. But also I was the National Secretary of the Argentine Biblical University Association (A.B.U.A). In Peru I was involved as Chaplain at the English-speaking Good Shepherd chaplaincy and Bishop of a young and growing diocese. When I arrived in Bradford I had potentially full-time responsibilities as a stipendiary bishop under the Diocesan Bishop Roy Williamson. However, he said every bishop could be expected to have up to a month every year of extra-diocesan responsibilities, so I accepted the job of International Coordinator for EFAC, which involved a lot of overseas travel. Then the move to Maresfield, Sussex, and Birmingham as General Secretary of SAMS with the EFAC job continuing. In Alderminster as house-for-duty priest my commitment was Sundays and three other days. I was quite able to tie that in with being assistant bishop in the Coventry diocese.

2
CELEBRATING FORTY YEARS
Pentecost Sunday, 13th May 2018

At the morning service of celebration at St Nic's, Warwick, I had been invited to preside and to preach. This was in recognition that Pentecost Sunday 2018 was the 40th anniversary of my being consecrated a bishop in the church of God. That had taken place in the Cathedral Church of the Good Shepherd in Lima, Peru. We were so grateful that 17 special people were able to be present with us in 2018. People who had been present or very closely connected with us in 1978, forty years before.

Not only were there two occasions on Pentecost Sunday. A further 40 years back in 1938 I had been born, also on a Pentecost Sunday. That was in Dar-es-Salaam in Tanganyika. So, the feast of Pentecost linked my birth in Africa with my consecration in South America 40 years later and a 40th celebration of that in the Coventry diocese in the U.K. That spans 80 years, which is declared in the Bible to be a good length of life! Amen to that.

40th Anniversary, Consecration Cake, 13th May 2018

The special visitors present in 2018 included Caroline and Peter, two of our three children, Bishop Colin and Barbara Bazley with their daughter Libby.

Page from Spanish Bible, 1978

Colin had been Presiding Bishop in 1978 and I remember him telling me to enjoy the 1978 ceremony. SAMS missionaries included Paul and Esme Russell, who had worked in Chile, Peru and later Bolivia; Steve and Di Lee of Crosslinks, active in shanty town and middle class work in Lima; Peter and Brenda Duffell, faithful and very long term supporters from my curacy days in Christ Church Cockfosters, (who donated for my episcopal robes, which I still wear!); Philip and Rosemary Tadman, long term and faithful SAMS home staff; Rosemary Kelly from Ireland, who worked with her husband Wilbert in Lima with Crosslinks; and the Revd Juan Sedano and his wife Lis, a school teacher. Juan was one of the very first Peruvians whom I ordained. In celebration of this he helped in the Holy Communion service wearing his Peruvian poncho. We sang the Peruvian Gloria (in English) and I gave the blessing in Spanish. It was a splendid occasion with a marvellous cake to eat afterwards. It had been made by a church member with great skill—an open Bible shape with decorations as in the special title page of my Spanish Bible.

This beautifully produced dedication was written in the Spanish Bible which had been presented to me by the people of Christ Church Cockfosters for my service there as curate from 1965–1968.

An explanation of the border of the document:

> In Exodus 28 we read a description of the vestments of the high priest, worn when he served in the tabernacle in worship of God. The high priest had a garment called an ephod. It was blue and around the hem had a very special decoration: "and beneath upon the hem of it thou shalt make pomegranates of blue, and of purple, and of scarlet, round about the hem thereof; and bells of gold between them round about." (Exodus 28:33 *KJV*).

The golden bells may be taken to represent the fruit of the Spirit. They are sweet in flavour and attractive in colour, and are loaded with seeds, and thus not only remind us of fruit, but of fruitfulness. The gifts of the Spirit, the golden bells, are balanced by the fruit of the Spirit.

The gifts of the Spirit again, are wisdom, knowledge, discerning of spirits, faith, miracles, healing, prophecy, tongues and interpretation of tongues. The fruits of the spirit are: love, joy, peace, patience, gentleness, kindness, faith, humility and discipline.

In order for there to be a "golden bell and a pomegranate" as the Scripture says, around the robe of the priest, there would have to be an equal number of each. There are, of course nine gifts of the Spirit and nine fruits of the Spirit in the preceding lists. In order for the golden bells to ring clearly, harmoniously, without clashing into one another, there must be fruit between each one.

Gifts brought through lives that are lacking in fruit and motivated by a desire for self-esteem and a wish to be noticed will be about as uplifting as so many clanging tin cans. The gifts of the Spirit are given "without repentance"—that is, God does not take them back because they are misused—and so they may function through lives that are un-consecrated, and through persons who need to make restitution to God and man, but these would be nothing more than ear-shattering brass bells to those who have discernment. This is what the Apostle means when he speaks of "sounding brass" and "clanging cymbals". Our bells should not be brass or tin, but pure gold. Golden bells represent lives that are in tune with the Lord and the brethren, and whose central desire is to lift up Jesus Christ, as they manifest the gifts.

It is significant that this pattern of the alternate bells and pomegranates carried into the New Testament, since between the two great chapters on the gifts, 1 Corinthians 12 and 14, is found the beautiful chapter on the central fruit of the Spirit—love.

The above is taken from The Holy Spirit and You *by Dennis and Rita Bennett.*

Peter and Brenda Duffell, our son Peter, and Philip and Rosemary Tadman

A local restaurant accommodated the 19 of us for an excellent Sunday lunch and a good number stayed on for a walk and tea in our home to continue sharing memories. It is remarkable how different people remember different details and have varied memories of the same events.

The following week was filled with pastoral visits, sometimes taking pieces of the 'episcopal cake' to different homes, especially to the members of the midweek Holy Communion group, who virtually form another house group from our church. They are particularly friendly. The celebrations didn't stop there, however; on Sunday 20th May I had been invited by Bishop Christopher Cocksworth to preach in Coventry Cathedral and help him in a Pentecost confirmation. It was planned as a more informal occasion, mainly because of a number of immersion baptisms and a liberal sprinkling of water over the congregation of several hundred! Nearly 50 were confirmed in all; we did half each. They included a member of the Coventry football side destined for Wembley within a week and a Syrian lady just 12 months resident in the U.K. Before the service a huge cake was produced for the confirmees to commemorate my anniversary. It was black, white and scarlet, the colours of a traditional Anglican bishop's robes, of surplice, rochet and scarf. The decoration was a mitre and a flock of llamas! I was very moved at the end of the service. I was due to give the final blessing. Bishop Christopher Cocksworth handed me the Coventry diocesan crozier to hold as I gave the blessing. A lovely gesture on his part and a fine end to a week of commemoration and thanksgiving for the call to episcopal ministry and acknowledgement of the Lord's faithfulness. As my first Vicar, the Revd. Kenneth Hooker wrote in my first Spanish Bible as I left Christ Church Cockfosters in 1968 as a 'humble' curate, "if the Lord calls you . . . you will be able."

With Caroline and Peter at Warwick [Hilary was in the USA], 13th May 2018

3
CONSECRATED A BISHOP IN 1978

I reproduce here the report in the LIMA TIMES of May 19, 1978 concerning my consecration as bishop.

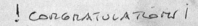

2 — LIMA TIMES · May 19, 1978

Anglican bishop consecrated

THE REV. David Evans, chaplain of Lima's Church of The Good Shepherd, was consecrated and enthroned as bishop of the Anglican diocese in Peru on May 14 at The Good Shepherd Church.

The consecration was performed by three bishops — Colin Bazley, Bishop of Chile and Bolivia and presiding Bishop of the Anglican Council of South America; Douglas Milmine, Bishop of Paraguay; and David Leake, Bishop of Northern Argentina.

The two-hour ceremony was attended by more than 250 members of the Anglican English and Spanish speaking congregations in Lima and representatives of the Roman Catholic and Protestant Church in Peru. The main part of the service was held in Spanish.

Bishop Evans' pastoral staff, which is of local craftsmanship, was presented to him by the Church Council.

Bishop Evans, 39 was born in Tanzania, where his father was employed as a mining engineer and was taken to England the following year. He read theology at Cambridge University, served in a Middlesex regiment in Cyprus and was curate at Christ Church, Cockfosters, England from 1965 to 1968.

Before coming to Lima in July 1977 he was co-pastor at the Holy Trinity Church in Lomas de Zamora, Buenos Aires (see also page 9).

The newly consecrated Bishop David Evans of the Church of the Good Shepherd.

The Rev. David Evans, chaplain of Lima's Church of The Good Shepherd, was consecrated and enthroned as bishop of the Anglican diocese in Peru on May 14 at The Good Shepherd Church.

The consecration was performed by three bishops — Colin Bazley — Bishop of Chile and Bolivia and presiding Bishop of the Anglican Council of South America; Douglas Milmine, Bishop of Paraguay; and David Leake, Bishop of Northern Argentina.

The two-hour ceremony was attended by more than 250 members of the Anglican English and Spanish speaking congregations in Lima and representatives of the Roman Catholic and Protestant Church in Peru. The main part of the service was held in Spanish.

Bishop Evans, 39, was born in Tanzania, where his father was employed as a mining engineer, and was taken to England the following year. He read theology at Cambridge University, served in the Middlesex regiment in Cyprus and Germany, and was curate at Christ Church, Cockfosters, England from 1965 to 1968.

*Before coming to Lima in July 1977 he was co-pastor at the Holy
Trinity Church in Lomas de Zamora, Buenos Aires (see also page 9).*

LIMA TIMES · May 19, 1978 — 9

Left to right: The Bishop of Northern Argentina *David Leake;* Bishop of
Paraguay *Douglas Milmine,* and the Bishop of Chile and Bolivia *Colin
Bazley.* Photo: D. Gillespie.

THE consecration of **Bishop David Evans** at The Good Shepherd Church was attended by a wide variety of people of all creeds and nationalities. The Church, apart from visiting Anglican Bishops (above), was also represented by Monseñor **Federico Richter Prada,** Archbishop of Ayacucho, representing the Roman Catholic Bishops; two representatives of the Maryknoll fathers, the British Benedictines, Mother Teresa's sisters, the Cenacle Sisters, the Director of the Summer School of Linguistics, Lutheran pastors and representatives of other Protestant churches. **Dr. Merino** represented the prime minister's office (see also page 2).

Lima Times Press cutting, 19th May 1978

*The consecration of Bishop David Evans at The Good Shepherd
Church was attended by a wide variety of people of all creeds and
nationalities. The Church, apart from visiting Anglican bishops (above),
was also represented by Monseñor Federico Richter Prada, Archbishop of
Ayacucho, representing the Roman Catholic Bishops; two representatives
of the Maryknoll fathers, the British Benedictines, Mother Teresa's
Sisters, the Cenacle Sisters, the Director of the Summer School of
Linguistics, Lutheran Pastors and representatives of other Protestant
churches. Dr. Merino represented the prime minister's office (see also
page 2).*

This article appeared in *La Prensa* on the 15th of May, the day after the ceremony. It showed considerable interest in what actually went on in the service, which would not have been familiar in a "Roman Catholic country". One detail was very wrong! It was stated that there were 100,000 Anglicans in Peru. The real number would have been less than 1,000! It also mentioned specifically that there was a Peruvian pastor Pompeyo Vargas Palomino present. Unfortunately, he didn't have a happy career with us. Unbeknown to us he had had to leave the Roman Church. He seemed like a gift, or at least a foretaste of a future indigenous priesthood. Our ways parted after a few years.

I propose now to share with you excerpts from letters of congratulation I received in 1978. Reading quite a weighty file I was intrigued to notice the variety of phraseology to describe the process of becoming a bishop. Even the Book of Common Prayer is not sure! The text of 1662 reads The Form of Ordaining and Consecrating of Bishops, Priests and Deacons. Historically a deacon is *made*, a priest is *ordered* while a bishop is *ordained* or *consecrated*. The traditional prayer is; "Receive the Holy Ghost for the office and work of a Bishop in the Church of God". The letters I received revealed an even greater diversity — I was congratulated on my bishopping, my preferment, my appointment, my promotion, my elevation, my election, my consecration! 1 Timothy 3:1 reads "This is a true saying, 'if a man desire the office of a bishop, he desireth a good work.'" The *New International Version* of the Bible translates: "Here is a trustworthy saying: If anyone sets his heart on being an overseer (traditionally bishop) he desires a noble task." Both translations emphasise that there is work to be undertaken and a task to be performed, rather than a privileged position to be occupied and enjoyed, with everyone bowing and scraping! But it is envisaged that a person have a genuine sense of vocation and a desire to oversee, which, of course needs to be tested by the Church. In truth most people would be put off by someone suggesting "I think I would make a good bishop." Some betting houses have been known to run episcopal stakes—normally with very poor results for the punters!

Several times I have been asked: "Can you apply to become a bishop?" The answer is still No, I believe. But the selection process has come out a lot from behind closed doors. Advertisements are posted in the church press. The meetings of the Crown Appointments Committee are no longer secret in date and location. It is more widely known that each diocesan bishop is asked to produce an annual preferment list of clergy

La Iglesia Anglicana del Perú consagró y entronizó ayer a un nuevo Obispo

Desde ayer, la Diócesis Peruana de la Iglesia Anglicana Episcopal, cuenta con un Obispo que residirá en Lima. Su consagración y entronización tuvo lugar en una ceremonia especial realizada en la Iglesia del Buen Pastor de Miraflores.

El Obispo consagrado es el Rvdo. David Richard John Evans M.A. La ceremonia fue presidida por el Rvdo. Colin Bazley, Obispo de Chile y fue asistido por los Rvdos. Douglas Milmine, Obispo de Paraguay y David Leake, Obispo-Asistente en el Norte Argentino.

Al acto asistieron autoridades eclesiásticas de diversos cultos como el Arzobispo de Ayacucho, Mons. Federico Richter Prada; pastores luteranos y representantes de otras Iglesias Cristianas.

La ceremonia resultó trascendental para la Iglesia Anglicana Peruana, considerando que recién en noviembre del año pasado se creó la Diócesis Peruana y el Obispo que la presidirá ha sido consagrado precisamente en una Iglesia Peruana.

El nuevo jerarca eclesiástico es británico de 39 años. Casado con Dorothy Parson con quien tiene tres hijos.

La Iglesia Anglicana Episcopal del Perú cuenta con aproximadamente 100 mil fieles. En Lima existen 6 Iglesias dirigidas por un igual número de clérigos.

La Iglesia del Buen Pastor está destinada al culto con los seguidores de habla castellana y el clérigo que la dirije es precisamente el único Pastor peruano y que por coincidencia es periodista: Pompeyo Vargas Palomino.

LA CEREMONIA

El acto de consagración es netamente ritualista, donde el pueblo asistente participa activamente en la ceremonia.

En la primera parte, el Obispo que preside el acto presenta al Obispo electo por quien los fieles oran. Más adelante y después de haber dado lectura a la Epístola y al Evangelio, y ofrecido el sermón correspondiente, el Obispo electo es examinado respecto a su disposición para ejercer el cargo.

La consagración propiamente dicha empieza cuando el nuevo Obispo se viste con los hábitos episcopales ayudado por los obispos consagrantes.

El momento más trascendental lo constituye la llamada "Imposición de Manos". Los obispos colocan sus manos sobre la cabeza del consagrado, con lo que simbólicamente le otorgan la gracia del Espíritu Santo para el Oficio y la Obra de la Iglesia Anglicana.

Luego le hacen entrega de una Biblia recomendándole su lectura para su meditación, así como una serie de normas morales y humanas que deben caracterizar su conducta en el futuro.

La entronización está simbolizada por la entrada física al templo después de haber tocado la puerta por tres veces. El Obispo que preside la consagración lo declara instalado en su nueva Iglesia después de haberle hecho entrega del Báculo (símbolo de autoridad).

La ceremonia culmina después que los fieles asistentes comulgan con el pan y el vino.

Aspecto del momento más trascendente de la ceremonia de consagración del Obispo Anglicano: la Imposición de las Manos. (Foto: Tomas Matta).

Prensa 15 de Mayo 1978

Prensa Press Cutting 15th May 1978

in his diocese, who could have potential for more senior and responsible posts. These lists are sent to the two central appointments' secretaries of the Church of England, one representing the Prime Minister, the other the two Archbishops. These lists used to be secret. Clergy can now ask to be informed whether their names have been included or not. But they can't suggest themselves that they should be considered! Of course, any sense of call has to be tested and recognised by the appointed church authorities. The episcopal appointments committee is a well-balanced group of local diocesan and national figures, under the chairmanship of the archbishop from the other province that is not looking for a new bishop. The membership is elected partly by General Synod and partly by the local diocese needing an appointment. The State is involved only by the P.M.'s secretary for appointments. Though later of course the monarch is approached and can technically not choose the recommended first candidate on the list of three. It is understood to only be very rarely that our present Queen has not agreed to the first choice being ratified and that person proceeding to 'kiss her hand'.

Three Consecrating Bishops outside the door of the Good Shepherd Church after the service, May 1978 —Bishop David Leake, myself with Peruvian Crosier, Bishop Douglas Milmine, Bishop Colin Bazley

In Peru of course, procedure was much easier! I had been asked to move from work in Argentina to work in Peru, a nascent diocese. It was understood that the move across the Andes might involve my future candidacy for bishop. I understand that my name had been discussed among the bishops of the province of the Southern Cone. When Bishop Bill Flagg retired to the U.K. from Peru an episcopal selection committee was formed in Peru. Two names were presented. When mine was chosen it had to be ratified by the bishops of the province. I could then be approached — except that I was in bed with hepatitis! Eventually I recovered and discovered that I had a noble task on my hands.

I produced a short article for the South American Mission Society years which sought to respond to the question:

What are bishops for?

They must be for **mission**. To help forward the mission of the church. Spearhead Episcopal Missionaries they have been called, especially in South America. If they are not, then they can be a hindrance, as the title of a lecture I have been asked to give in Birmingham implies: "Leadership in mission: Bishops, help or hindrance?"

But also, they are for **maintenance**. I remember a diocesan bishop in England remarking how hard he had to work just to keep the show on the road and the wheels turning. Not dramatic of course. But back-room work is not to be despised. It is not just administration but also pastoral care.

Also, they are for **unity**. To be a visible sign in their person and office that helps to give identity and a sense of cohesion across a diocese. When you have a long vacancy between bishops one is made more aware of the importance of this role, which can easily be taken for granted.

And also, they are for **representation**, both inside the diocese to other denominations and outside the diocese to the Anglican Communion. Our Church's foreign ministers in fact.

Remember bishops cannot be bought at a supermarket. They are people who first have to be evangelised, then discipled, then called to ordained ministry. They have to become holier in community with us, they have to be prayed for. So, we all have a part in producing bishops. I hope you are praying for yours, the present one and the future ones.

4

A KALEIDOSCOPE OF LETTERS
OF CONGRATULATION, 1978

In this chapter the 90 letters from which I quote extracts provide a range of snapshots of quite a lot of my life up until this 40th year at the time of my episcopal ordination. They illustrate what a public and indeed international event a consecration is. The listing is only related to their order in my correspondence file and has no other special significance. Putting this together has, however, been quite an emotional journey. Not least because a number of the writers have already moved on to heaven.

A good number of them refer to situations and events described in more detail in my book *Have Stick—Will Travel: Mainly South American Journeys.* If you want to skip to Chapter 5 please feel free!

Letter 1

A card from Salta in Northern Argentina signed by Rachel Leake and her three children, Judith, Andrew and Philip. Rachel's husband David was one of my consecrating bishops. It shows a procession of 'gauchos' on the Virgin Mary's Feast Day! A text from Jude (v24 & 25) reads "to Him who is able to keep you from falling and to present you before his glorious presence without fault and with great joy . . . be glory through Jesus Christ."

Letter 2

A card from a number of Argentines from Northern Argentina including Iris and Humberto Axt. I was to be present at his episcopal consecration on 25th May 1997.

Letter 3

A card from Gerald and Antonia Vincent. Gerald had lived for several months with us in Buenos Aires, while he finished his school exams.

Letter 4

A letter from the Archbishop of Kenya, the Most Revd Dr F. H. Olang'. The airmail lettercard had an engaging picture of a young warthog on it! I don't think it was meant to be significant! Though at 39 I was the third youngest bishop in the Anglican Communion at the time.

DIOCESIS DE LA

Iglesia Anglicana

EN EL NORTE ARGENTINO

MITRE 364, SALTA
T. E. 20370
FICHERO DE CULTOS N°. 301

CASILLA DE CORREO 187
SALTA
ARGENTINA

Embarcación, 28 de abril de 1978

Sr. David Evans
Iglesia Anglicana
Lima, Perú

Querido David:

Estamos aquí en una reunión de nuestra diócesis y habiéndote recordado en la tarea que pronto emprenderás junto con tu familia, queremos enviarte nuestro saludo fraternal y la seguridad de nuestras oraciones para el domingo 14 de mayo y los días venideros. Queremos en representación de nuestros hermanos en el Norte argentino dejar contigo 1 Tesalonicenses 5:24 " Fiel es el que os llama, el cual también lo hará. "

Un abrazo fraternal:

OBRA INICIADA EN LA ARGENTINA 1844

Diocesan Signatories from Northern Argentina

Letter 5

A card with love and prayers from all at Woodchester Parish Church, one of our most faithful prayer supporting groups.

Letter 6

A beautiful card with 17 signatures of the members of the Bethany prayer group at Christ Church Cockfosters, our home church. We are in contact with most of those still alive today. Especially Peter and Brenda Duffell, whose daughter Lucy later visited us in Peru.

Letter 7

A letter from the Roman Catholic Archbishop of Ayacucho †Federico Richter F. Prada, who also came to the consecration service. He commented graciously that it had made an impact on him and he offered prayers that we might go forward perfected by an authentic Christian faith and an openness to the ecumenical contacts proposed by the Second Vatican Council. I was later able to visit him in Ayacucho, which became a centre for the terrorist organisation 'The Shining Path'.

We sat together throughout the three-hour service on Good Friday in the R. C. Cathedral and shared a light lunch afterwards.

Letter 8

A letter from Richard Kadege, who at the time was chaplain in the university of Dar-es-Salaam, Tanzania. I had met him at a young people's summer camp at West Runton, Norfolk years before. He was later principal of a theological college in Tanzania and I was able to visit him there.

Letter 9

A letter from Harold and Eileen Satterley, a church warden at Christ Church Cockfosters while I was a curate (1965–1968) there and for many years afterwards. (A tape with numerous personal greetings had also been sent.) We spent Christmas Day with them in 1966, when Dorothy was heavily pregnant with our first child, Hilary. However, she didn't arrive until January 4th, much to the Satterleys' disappointment. Their daughter Christine later married Bruce Chanter. Between them they still run a prayer newsletter for those who were members of the Sunday evening Youth Fellowship. So once again contact continues over the course of many years.

Letter 10

Quinton Benz was the organiser of a Scripture Union Bible Study Group in Seaford, Sussex. I joined this during vacations from my time in Cambridge and enjoyed it immensely. I was however called to the office of the Archdeacon of Lewes and 'reprimanded' for not joining in more with the parish church, as an Anglican candidate for ordination. Did that help to give me the conviction that the Holy Spirit of God doesn't confine himself to neat ecclesiastical boundaries? As mentioned elsewhere, my Christian service has always included contributions to Christian work outside denominations — interdenominational university work in Cambridge, the national organisation of the I.V.F. in the U.K. and A.B.U.A. in Argentina (The Argentine Biblical University Association). Even now, my association with SAMS, CMS, CMJ and EFAC are non-ecclesiastical, but of course deeply missional with separate organisational structures from the C of E. Thank you, Quinton Benz, who uncharacteristically I never saw again after my student days.

Letter 11

A telegram came from the Fellowship at Emmanuel Church, Northwood, "wishing that God's Spirit would strengthen and fill you for your great task" (Joshua 1: 9 "do not be discouraged, for the Lord your God will be with you wherever you go"). The church in Northwood was another special church for us. My wife Dorothy's father had been Vicar there. Because of that we were married there in 1964. Subsequently I visited to preach on a number of occasions and a happy relationship developed with the Revd Richard Bewes, who went on to be Rector of All Souls Langham Place and Chairman of the Evangelical Council of the Church of England, where our paths crossed again in later years.

Letter 12

Dr P. S. Sanson wrote a very newsy letter about his family and Cockfosters. He was also concerned about my health. I had been suffering from a pretty severe attack of hepatitis B, which meant I was in bed for a month. The episcopal selection committee had gone ahead and chosen me for the episcopal role, but sensibly waited to invite me to take up the office until I had recovered, and I could stand on my feet again!

Letter 13

Alan Wood wrote a lovely spiritual letter. He was one of the

Pathfinder leaders at Cockfosters, where I had oversight. He remained single and in youth work all his life. We have exchanged letters at Christmas every year since 1978. A faithful prayer supporter.

Letter 14

Mary Tipler's regular prayer support dates back to my life in Seaford, Sussex. She was also involved in Quinton Benz's S.U. Bible Study. Her letter of the 21st March 1978 to me reads:

> The post came just as I was leaving for Lewes, so as soon as I reached my office, I phoned David's parents to share with them in their happiness, only to find that they hadn't heard!! I was sorry about that; but they were thrilled with the news and not at all upset that I was the bearer of the glad tidings.

Letter 15

The Revd Nigel and Delia Bennett were also Pathfinder leaders at Cockfosters, or rather, Delia was before she married Nigel and they began their ordained service together in Tonbridge.

Letter 16

Pamela Richardson (neé White) wrote from Turkey and a very small Christian community. We had worked together in the Cambridge Christian Union. She wrote:

> May the Lord grant to you both and for all of you as a family the extra resources of wisdom and graciousness and interruptibility and capacity to handle well every conceivable sort of person that you are obviously going to need.

What a prayer!

Letter 17

A wonderfully graciously expressed letter of congratulation arrived from the Venerable Bernardo Merino Botero, President of the Standing Committee of the Episcopal Church in Colombia. Within a year or two I was able to visit him in Bogotá and enjoy hospitality in his home after he had also become a bishop.

Letter 18

A fellow theological student at Clifton, Bristol, Paul Hunt, wrote from Isfahan in Iran where he was serving as Chaplain to the Bishop of Iran, Hassan Dehqani-Tafti. We had been neighbours in college and then, sent to different parts of the world, we exchanged views on the challenges of contextualisation. "Only today I have been listening to criticism by a gringo missionary of a fellow Peruvian pastor, criticism based largely on a failure to understand cultural differences." As Paul hoped, I did meet his bishop at the international Lambeth Conference in 1978. I also met him in London later when he was preaching at a church where I was baptising a nephew. Later still I invited Paul to lead an ordination retreat in the Diocese of Bradford, when I was acting diocesan bishop. Then I discovered on retiring to Warwick that his last 'job' had been as vicar of a local rural parish in the Diocese of Coventry.

Letter 19

David Jackman had been Vice-President of C.I.C.C.U. when I was President in 1963. My wife Dorothy was the Treasurer of C.I.C.C.U. He also did me the honour of being my best man at our wedding in 1964. His letter of 12th May was very warm with offers of hospitality, etc. However, surprisingly in the following decades our paths have not crossed, though I followed his work at Southampton and then with the Cornhill Trust in London.

Letter 20

A letter arrived from Mrs Ostik from Warsaw in Poland, a lovely Christian lady who had known Dorothy's parents when they were working in Poland. She had some connections with Argentina, so I asked her to consider the possibility of 'dropping in' to see us in Peru afterwards on her way back north, should she revisit Argentina.

Letter 21

Emilia Tejada, Director of Peruvian Industries of Good Will wrote with her congratulations and offer of continuing help and cooperation.

Letter 22

A great and welcome surprise was a letter from Arnold Dodds from Buenos Aires. Very much part of the Anglo-Argentine community in the southern part of B.A. and a staunch supporter of the work in Spanish in addition to the English.

Letter 23

Chua Wee Hian, the General Secretary of IFES (The International Fellowship of Evangelical Students), wrote from the U.K. He expressed concern for the political situation in Peru, as well as pledging extra money for the University work in Argentina, with which I had been very closely associated. I have always remembered a seminal talk he gave with a long historical perspective on the dynamic relationship between church structure mentality and para-church organisations. Having had a foot in both camps all my life I found his observations very meaningful. There are of course, many tensions, but the underlying problem, I think, is when either side assumes that the Holy Spirit is working only through them.

Letter 24

Maurice Sinclair, later to be its bishop, wrote from the Diocese of Northern Argentina. He particularly mentioned the challenges of urban mission, with which he was concerned.

Letter 25

There was a very moving letter from Gwenever Miller, the leading light of the Cockfosters Prayer Group for missionaries. A service was held in Christ Church at the same time as the consecration service in Lima. She had been the dynamism behind the idea of funding the purchase of my episcopal robes from Wippells in London and then getting them out to me via British Caledonian "in the diplomatic bag". I still wear the same robes today 40 years on! They are very well travelled, and a bit worn I must say, but they will see me out for work here on earth. A white robe of righteousness is provided for celestial responsibilities! I note that Gwenever Miller wrote about the whole prayer group being "tickled pink" in their involvement with my ministry—not just the robes or the ongoing prayer and financial support but having had a hand in knocking me into some sort of acceptable shape through the three years of curacy training!

Letter 26

Peter and Brenda Duffell remain close friends from Cockfosters days. Their first child Lucy visited us in Peru; we have stayed in their house while on furlough and Dorothy is godmother to Lucy, who is now ordained. On the wall of my study I have an antique map of Peru, Bolivia and Chile with the pre-War-of-the-Pacific (1859) national boundaries. It shows the Bolivian corridor to the Pacific coast, later divided up between Peru and Chile. This was a present from Peter and Brenda.

Letter 27

Eddie Gibbs was Church Programmes Manager of the Bible Society. Previously he had worked in church planting in Chile and later in theological and mission education in the U.S.A. He welcomed the setting up of a diocese in Peru and also wrote:

> You will be interested to know that last week (March 1978) I stayed the night with Bishop Richard Hare, who told me that he had passed on to you a pectoral cross whilst he was at Allen Gardiner House (The SAMS U.K. H.Q.), saying that he thought you might be able to use it sometime in the future! He certainly seems to have a prophetic gift.

Bishop Richard was a big figure in the early days of the charismatic movement in the U.K. He was also the brother of the businessman in Seaford, Sussex who first put my parents in touch with Christ's Hospital, where I went to boarding school from 1950–1957.

Letter 28

My aunt Phyllis Vaughn Harvard from Weston-Super-Mare wrote a very gracious letter. She and her doctor husband, Richard, were staunch Roman Catholics. I imagine they might have questioned the presence of a nephew in Peru and a bishop at that. However, they were gracious and went to tea in Locking near Weston-Super-Mare where Dorothy's parents lived in retirement.

Letter 29

My training vicar at Christ Church Cockfosters, the Revd Kenneth Hooker, wrote a lovely letter to congratulate me "on saddling up for the episcopal stakes"! He also apologised that he had not replied to my letter to him of good wishes for the C.I.C.C.U. Centenary celebrations in June 1977. He wrote

> I was able however to pass on your greetings and also mention you and your work in a sermon at Holy Trinity Church on the morning after the celebration in King's Chapel attended by 1700 people.

Both he and I were much involved with C.I.C.C.U. and the famous evangelistic sermons held each Sunday term time evening in Holy Trinity, the central Cambridge church closely connected also with the notable preacher Charles Simeon. I still have a well-known copy of four black-and-white woodcut drawings of Charles Simeon of 1818 showing characteristic gestures from the pulpit as he faithfully expounded the Scriptures and preached on the urgency of the Church taking the Gospel to the whole world. He became one of the founding fathers of the CMS (Church Mission Society).

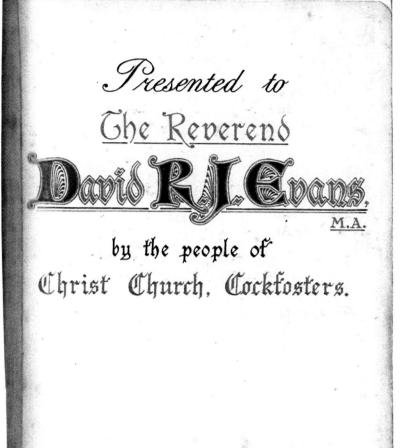

Page from Spanish Bible, 1968

On the left is the title page from the Spanish Bible that Kenneth Hooker presented to me on our farewell from Cockfosters en route for our work in South America.

A further two pages of the same Bible are filled with signatures from some of those present on 14th May 2003, when the 25th anniversary of my consecration was celebrated in the Good Shepherd church in Lima, now itself the Cathedral of the Diocese of Peru. Bishop William Godfrey led the celebration. Among faithful friends from 25 years before were Luis and Teófila Villalobos, Pat Bygrave, Peggy Massey, Julio and Norma Montoya, Susy Tapia, Helen Dors, Ada Vivar, Gail Griffith Lozano, Pedro and Josefina Jáuregui, Antonio and Agueda Centenio, Eleonor Zuniegi, Martha Rivera, Lillian Zapata, Guillermo Fallaque, Philip and Bess Muna. They represented the total cross-section of Peruvian Society the Anglican church was reaching.

Letter 30

The future Bishop of Northern Argentina, Nick Drayson, wrote to say he was delighted with my "bishopping". At the time he was much involved in the translation of the Bible into Chorote and ministering to the Indian peoples of Northern Argentina. He wrote challengingly about the vast gulf between the rich and the poor of the world and the agonising reality that many don't care and that others actually profit from it. He commented that the spiritual wealth of some of the poor is immeasurable.

Again, a longstanding relationship with Nick continues. We first met in a meeting in Keble, Oxford. Later Nick came out to Buenos Aires to teach at St Albans. Then he was called to work in the north. One factor in his call was that he had come with me and others from B.A. and St Albans on a summer trip around the Chaco area. Always a memorable if not life-changing event!

Letter 31

A surprising letter from Tony Sparshot. He had been a member of the Good Shepherd English congregation for a while. He wrote from Stowe School as a language teacher (his Spanish full of Peruvianisms!). The headmaster of Stowe School was the father of Nick Drayson. He was a keen supporter of SAMS and in that regard invited me to visit the school and preach in their chapel. Tony Sparshot had left by then.

Letter 32

A letter from Northern Ireland brought good wishes from the BCMS home team, now Crosslinks, with greetings from Brian Herd, Bishop of Karamoja in Uganda. This was a gracious letter because Wilbert Kelly was the other candidate to be bishop in Lima. He was supported by BCMS Ireland with his wife and five children. We remain good friends to this day with his widow Rosemary. Wilbert was the only person I 'canonised' during my time in Peru. I think he appreciated it!

Letter 33

A letter from the Provost of Portsmouth, Michael Nott, was rather special for various reasons. He had been Vicar of St Leonard's, Seaford during my school days and having made friends with my father persuaded him to be confirmed from his Presbyterian background. Because of these family connections he took part in our marriage in Northwood in 1964. My parents visited him at Lambeth Palace where he had a post as Chaplain to the Archbishop. He wrote (from Portsmouth): "I always thought something like this would happen to you though I confess I hoped it might be in England!" That may reflect my parents' hope that I wouldn't stay in South America for too long. We did stay nearly 20 years but returned to the U.K. well before either of my parents passed on.

Letter 34

A long four-page letter came from Argentine friends and members of Holy Trinity Lomas de Zamora in Buenos Aires. It contained much affection; the desire we should return to Buenos Aires as their bishop; some very funny stories; some family news and a splendid poem about God's life in his children — Marjorie, Bela, Helen and Teresa were all among the first members of the Spanish-speaking congregation at Lomas.

Letter 35

Gerald Vincent is an Anglo-Argentine who lived with us in Lomas de Zamora for a time in order to complete his studies. We are still in touch with him. He now lives in Scotland (recently moved to Spain) and has always been keen on sharing the Christian faith with others. After Argentina he went to Spain and inaugurated an institute to teach English to Spaniards. This was a slight amusement to us because his

English in Lomas was very Spanglish. In fact, his letter of congratulation started off with the words "Hello! How are you all? ¡Tanto tiempo!" This might be translated as "Long time no see!" We have met up in England. We visited them especially in Zaragoza, Spain. He is very active on Facebook now. He is a real link with the younger Anglo-Argentines with whom we spent much time, especially as I taught religious knowledge and debating in St Albans every week. Gerald is a faithful Christian, though he is into a second marriage and his parents also had a divorce, one going to Brazil, the other to Spain.

Letter 36

Ella and José Luis De Piero were key totally Argentine members of the Spanish-speaking congregation in Lomas. They were great friends, though they are not good correspondents. However, when we visited Buenos Aires in 2016 they came to a lunch in a central hotel, which was great. They were from a Brethren background but got really stuck into the church work. When José Luis was elected onto the church council for the first time, proceedings had to be held in Spanish. A big cultural change, symbolising the new direction of the congregation. Their letter was pretty exuberant—"¡Arriba David—felicitaciones al Flamante obispo y a la obispa Dorothy!" Together with Mr Hortis they formed a music group for the church with six guitars, three flutes, one accordion, two trumpets, one drum and one triangle! This last was played by Gabriel, their son whom I had baptised. They also sent a letter of congratulations from the young people's group signed by 13 of them.

Letter 37

Carlos García wrote a kind letter on behalf of the First Baptist Church of Lima. He was one of the leading evangelical pastors in Lima and our paths crossed on a number of occasions. I like their church motto: "La iglesia en el corazón de la cuidad, con el corazón del evangelio, para el corazón del hombre". (*The church in the heart of the city, with the heart of the Gospel, for the heart of humanity.*)

Letter 38

In his May newsletter John Stott added a personal note: "Congratulations and best wishes on your 'elevation', David! May the Lord continue to guide and bless you. Love, John." As so many evangelical Anglicans over the past sixty years, I owe a lot to John's wonderful international ministry. I hadn't joined C.I.C.C.U. when I arrived in Cambridge in 1959 (to read Modern Languages—French and German), but an unknown C.I.C.C.U. member invited me to a Freshers' sermon preached by John. I didn't actually go to this sermon, but on a follow-up visit the faithful C.I.C.C.U. man passed on a phrase from it which started me seriously on the road to a Christian commitment.

As President in 1963 of C.I.C.C.U. I was responsible for hosting John in Tyndale House. He had preached at another Freshers' sermon with many undergraduates responding to the Gospel invitation. I sat up late at night (in fact, into the early morning) typing out on an old machine the long list of names and addresses for him. I popped this list under the door of his room next to mine. At breakfast he thanked me and commented that I had been busy during the hours of the night like an owl. I enjoyed his ornithological expression of thanks! When I was General Secretary of A.B.U.A. (The Argentine Intervarsity Christian Union) we invited him to be a speaker at our summer camp. He was, of course, excellent, with Dr René Padilla being his interpreter. We have a

John Stott and our Family at a Student Fancy Dress meal in Argentina

photo of him and our family at a fancy-dress meal at that A.B.U.A. camp.
My wife Dorothy in the photo was dressed as 'Night and Day'. John
excused himself from our frivolity but more than made up for it on a
coach journey when he led the whole group singing in Latin the medieval
musical round of *Non nobis Domine* (Not unto us Lord . . . be the glory).

It is appropriate to mention here that Dorothy and I had met at
Cambridge through C.I.C.C.U. We worked together on the C.I.C.C.U.
Executive Committee, and were engaged to be married before we left
Cambridge. Dorothy's father, Revd Martin Parsons, had been a member
in his own day (see his letter and photo on page 38).

Later in Peru John stayed in our home. Actually, we hadn't yet moved
into our missionary quarters and were temporarily staying in the home
of the Canadian Consul, who was on leave. The house had two maids, one
of them a large and wonderful black nanny, Persian carpets on the walls
of the corridors and very superior living conditions indeed. John Stott
threatened to tell SAMS supporters back in the U.K. how their sacrificial
money was being spent!

I also had a lot of contact with him when I was asked to be the
International Coordinator of EFAC (Evangelical Fellowship in the
Anglican Communion). We met on EFAC business in various countries of
the world, not least in Manila in the Philippines for the Second Lausanne
Conference. I was delighted to be able to participate in his huge
memorial service in St Paul's Cathedral.

Letter 39

Maud Bedwell from Chile, who served many years in Latin America
with SAMS, sent me the following:
"Over me" Song of Solomon 2:4
"Round about" Psalm 34:7
"Underneath" Deut 33.27

Letter 40

Irene and Sister wrote from Locking in their retirement. They had
worked with Dorothy's father in Emmanuel Church, Northwood. He also
had retired to Locking, near Weston-super-Mare. She wrote:

> Do wish you could have seen the joy on your father's face when he told
> us. Your mother, Dorothy, was not with him when he told us, but her voice
> on the phone sometime later was just as full of joy. The Lord's love-touches
> along life's way are very precious.

Letter 41

Ray Smith was the minister of the Santiago Community Church in
Chile. He wrote to offer the Church's promise of prayers. It had been in
that church building at a midweek prayer meeting that I first offered up
a prayer to God in Spanish! This was between our language study in
Mexico and a brief stopover with the Bishop of Chile, Ken Howell, on our
way to Buenos Aires.

Letter 42

Peter and Grace Huntingford wrote from Christ Church Cockfosters.
For years he was the church treasurer and both were faithful members of
the prayer group for missionaries who had been members of the
congregation.

Letter 43

I was very moved to receive a letter from my housemaster Johnny at
Christ's Hospital, where I studied from 1950–1957 as a boarder. The
relationship with Johnny prospered because my brother Michael
overlapped with me for one year in the same house, Lamb A, and of
course continued with my parents after I had left. He was a confirmed
bachelor dedicated to the best education he could impart. He taught me
German privately so that I could jump up a year in the school and study
languages. He wrote:

> I hope you will allow me to say that I am delighted that you have
> received this recognition and that I and everyone else who remembers you
> at C.H. will share in this feeling, no doubt at the same time nodding their
> heads wisely and declaring that nobody is a bit surprised.

That was very gracious of him, as my student days at C.H. were not
without one or two disciplinary problems! No details! But I was one of his
house captains!

Letter 44

My brother Michael wrote: "I always knew I was born into the right
family. A bishop for an elder brother!" My parents had visited us in Lima
just beforehand. In fact, we had all been together in the Andes on holiday
when I went down with hepatitis. They were able to take back a first-
hand account of life in Peru. Michael was very keen to come to visit us as
well. However, he never did, although as a journalist he covered even
more countries of the world than I did. We had a competition once

counting them up and I think he just won. He did visit the Falklands in his capacity as Defence Editor of *The Times*. But he didn't make the mainland of South America.

Letter 45

Cecelia and Ricardo Maseratti were one of the young couples I married at Holy Trinity in Lomas de Zamora. They wrote with family news and good wishes.

Wedding Group at Holy Trinity Church, Lomas

Letter 46

The Revd Graham and Molly Dow wrote from St John's Theological College in Nottingham. Graham had been President of O.I.C.C.U. at the same time as I had been President of C.I.C.C.U. That created a bond. He wrote

Warmest good wishes at your episcopal appointment. I've been expecting it for a few years. May the Lord endow you with great wisdom and boldness in proclaiming the Gospel of Jesus Christ. Remember to obey God rather than men and let nothing stand in the way of your supreme loyalty to him. But may the Lord give you, in particular, such friendship with him as will enable you to know what he is doing in your diocese and corresponding discernment to see all the wiles of Satan and expose them.

Very wise words. Graham subsequently was elected Bishop of Carlisle, where he had a hard time since he was a virtual prisoner in Rose Castle on account of the surrounding foot-and-mouth disease and epidemic.

Letter 47

Mary Nixon wrote from New York, where she was on a business trip. She was sad to miss the Consecration. She had been a member of the Episcopal Selection Committee, so partly to blame for my election! Mary had been a very efficient and experienced secretary and indeed personal assistant to a Peruvian Prime Minister. She continued in a private capacity to his family. She kept the minutes at our Peruvian diocesan council in apple pie order. A great asset and faithful Christian.

Letter 48

My 'sis' Ruth wrote to her "smashing brother a Bishop!" from Stockport, where she then lived with her husband and family. Nick Clarke was one of the Dallas Boys who had a well-known musical group. They did once play as a backing group for Cliff Richard! Ruth's career as a dancer took her abroad as did Nick's as a trumpeter and drummer. Their careers took them to many fields not often visited by bishops. I remember especially one comment of Nick's: "Never criticise a full house!"

Letter 49

It was quite emotional for me to come across separate letters from my mother and father filed away in my consecration folder of 1978. I didn't know whether I had filed them or not. My mother wrote her letter from her desk, which had four photos of me on it (which I still have today). One of me at 2 years old with her, another one at 19 in my army officer's uniform, a third as a young curate at Cockfosters, and a fourth of the family in Buenos Aires (me with a beard). Her comment was "we still like you best without a beard!" My mother occasionally wrote poems—here is a short passage from one she sent to me in 1978. She wrote it in a prophetic style with "God speaking".

Your Son David born to you upon this earth
My son created by Me in you
To do the work of My will
He is a branch of My vine
Spreading out in that other place
Far from the country of his birth
A vine in a dry desert that will flourish
With the living water of My Holy Spirit
With the water of the Holy Spirit, all things are possible.

It was totally fortuitous that my parents had been able to spend a few weeks with us in Peru in 1978. Exactly the time I went down with hepatitis, which coincided with the work of the Episcopal Selection Committee. The delay in asking me, in order to make sure I recovered from hepatitis, meant my parents had already returned to England.

My father's letter referred to the distance between Peru and England:

> I wish the intervening miles could be reduced to a reasonable hundred or so! Then my last real gesture as your father would be to *ensure* that you delegate a substantial number of those routine duties so that you can feel free for more important work related to your new appointment.

Letter 50

The Revd Richard Kew wrote from Massachusetts as Chairman of SAMS USA. Already in the pipeline for coming to serve in Peru from SAMS USA were John and Sue Haward, busy in raising their supporting salary. John was special for me in that I ordained him deacon on 15th September 1979, together with a Peruvian, Pedro Jáuregui. John has now gone to be with the Lord, but we are still in touch with his wife Sue in the USA and our daughter Hilary stays with her from time to time, when visiting one of her daughters at a nearby boarding school. So, Richard Kew and I met up on a number of occasions as SAMS USA took larger commitments in the new Diocese of Peru.

Letter 51

In March I received several letters from Bishop Colin Bazley. He was the President of CASA (The Anglican Council for the Southern Cone). He was writing to the Peruvian Selection Committee to inform them that the Anglican province had ratified my election and that they could proceed to organising the consecration. A few days later he wrote again, in English this time, to pass on to me very kindly a letter he had received from Mario Lorenzo Meriño, the ancillary Bishop of Northern Argentina.

Mario was the first Mataco, or as we now say, Wichí, bishop in the province. We had got to know him when he stayed with us for a night in Buenos Aires to attend the consecration of David Leake. He was a very humble, deeply pastoral man who had what proved to be an irreplaceable ministry among those of his own tribal background and beyond. He wrote:

† Mario Meriño and DRJE, Ingenerio Juárez, 1997

We are so joyful that brother David Evans can be a bishop for the Lord's work in Peru. We pray that it will be by God's hand and we will continue in prayer. Receive thousands of greetings and love for you all, and may God bless your work in the Lord. I am yours in Christ.

One of my fondest memories of Mario is drinking maté with him in the Chaco of Northern Argentina, sitting in a wicker chair on the balcony of his house in Ingeniero Juarez as the sun was setting and heralding very welcome cooler air.

Letter 52

A beautiful greeting from the Convent Sister of the Cenáculo in Lima. I had been included in their book of spiritual partners and 9 masses a month were to be offered for me!

Letter 53

Frank Martin from Buenos Aires, an Anglo-Argentine businessman, wrote to congratulate me on my nomination and to commiserate with me over the bout of hepatitis. I had forgotten — before re-reading all these letters — how connected my consecration had been with the attack of hepatitis. I think it must have motivated more people to pray more for such an ailing specimen!

Letter 54

Philip King, the then General Secretary of SAMS U.K. phrased his letter slightly strangely:

I was very thrilled to hear from Pat Harris a few days ago that the Diocese of Peru have elected you as the new Bishop. Assuming the information is correct, I write on behalf of the Society to say how delighted we are and to assure you and Dorothy of our support and prayers in your leadership in the future. It has been exciting to see how the work in Lima has developed so well, and although there will inevitably be demands and pressures, it should be a very stimulating and exciting task. It may be that the Lord allowed some of the trauma in B.A. as part of this preparation, but I hope that experience will not be repeated.

1978 was well before the introduction of internet connectivity. Bishop Colin Bazley's letter to Lima of the confirmation of my election was dated 6th March. Philip's letter to me was dated 8th March ... I can only imagine that Pat Harris (Bishop of Northern Argentina from 1973–80) had telephoned England. Some news did travel quickly even then. Fortunately, it didn't turn out to be fake news. Philip added a P.S. "We will not publicise the election unless and until we hear something officially." That careful letter bears witness to Philip's legal training and to being in the vulnerable position of having sometimes to hold on to interesting news without the freedom to pass it on to others.

Philip King was at the Bluecoat School of Christ's Hospital as I was. He was four years older than me, so we didn't meet then. But this was made up for later on many occasions, not least when we visited South Africa together with his wife Margaret.

Letter 55

Philip and Edith Blakely from Cockfosters, but retired to Norfolk, wrote a newsy letter. Philip had been our local doctor and had oversight of the births of Hilary and Caroline while we were in the diminutive headmistress's cottage by the C. of E. church school playground. It had been called affectionately 'Pot Cot'. It had been the home of several curates. When we left, it was demolished. We had a great demolition party, which attracted a good deal of publicity.

Letter 56

Denise and Leslie Webster wrote from Northwood. They of course knew Dorothy's parents well and had met my mother at a SAMS Parents' Day in Tunbridge Wells. Their daughter Esme, who had married Paul Russell, had moved to Peru from Chile and they were very active missionary partners in the diocese.

Letter 57

The Worthingtons wrote from Huancayo in the Andes mountains. They were serving with the Peruvian Methodist Church. They majored on the hepatitis rather than the consecration; "We unfortunately lost a missionary here in Huancayo a few years ago with that complication. Would hope to see you under better conditions soon." Amen to that!

Letter 58

We enjoyed good relationships with a succession of British Ambassadors over the years. Bill Harding was the first one. We enjoyed receptions in his embassy on several occasions. Various members of his staff were regular members of the English-speaking congregation at the Good Shepherd. He was very good at tracking down and visiting older members of the British community.

Other ambassadors we met were the Canadian, the Indian, the South African consul, the Israeli and the North American—I once was asked to introduce a new British ambassador for Bolivia to the shanty towns of Lima, as part of his induction process to South America. Quite a responsibility! However, it was deemed safer for him to come with me in a VW than to appear with a number-plated car. I also was personally asked to look after the Canadian ambassador's wife, who got involved in

BRITISH EMBASSY,
LIMA.

29 March 1978

The Reverend David R J Evans
Church of the Good Shepherd
Av Santa Cruz 491
Miraflores

Dear David,

I was delighted to receive news from the Episcopal Selection Committee of your appointment as the new Bishop of the Diocese of Peru. May I offer you my warmest congratulations on this notable elevation, which I am sure reflects the general appreciation of your parishioners for the work you have done over the past months as their Chaplain, with Dorothy's notably tactful and effective support. I hope that when you require the support of the Embassy in your work, you will not hesitate to let me know.

With warmest regards to you both,

Yours sincerely,

G W Harding
HM Ambassador

Letter from British Ambassador

social work projects, especially a soup kitchen in the shanty towns. Her first-hand experience of locals unfortunately motivated her to remove all the smaller ornaments from their public rooms when they had them there for a reception! The ambassador was very supportive, however, and on one occasion the social work programme in La Paz, Bolivia benefited considerably from funds remaining in his annual budget for local social work. Our last British Ambassador was John Shakespeare. I met up with him quite recently in Salisbury Cathedral at the memorial service for a long-serving British businessman. We both gave tributes to him, Ken Eckett, for his work in Peru. However, John Shakespeare's son achieved even greater publicity through his literary career especially the publication of a book about Abimael Guzmán, the notorious leader of the Shining Path terrorist movement in Peru. It turned out that he had been living for some time incognito above a Ballet School in an area of Lima next to where we lived in Barranco! As far as I know, Guzmán (ex-university professor in Ayacucho) is still alive in prison in Lima today. My closest friendship, however, was with the New Zealand ambassador, with whom I played numerous games of squash. I was even able to visit him in New Zealand years later.

Letter 59

Don Churchman, the Vicar of Christ Church Cockfosters, wrote a letter and added a warm invitation to visit the church during my visit to the U.K. for the Lambeth Conference of 1978. Also, David Bryant writing in a circular letter to Cockfosters missionaries on behalf of the church. Gwenever Miller wrote on behalf of the Prayer Group, offering to help with my episcopal gear! It turned out to be my consecration robes for which the money was raised very fast apparently. "Everyone is thrilled to bits for you! The memo has gone around like wildfire!" I replied that the main garments should last all my life. "I shall feel sealed with the Christ Church Cockfosters 'stamp' for the whole of my ordained ministry."

Letter 60

Penny Avann, Editorial and Youth Secretary of SAMS, wrote, and of course asked for a copy and photos of the Consecration.

Letter 61

I was moved to find a letter from Kenneth Howell, former Bishop of Chile, Peru and Bolivia, then living in retirement in Hampstead, London.

A letter from me had arrived to congratulate him on his re-marriage, which was to take place the day after my letter arrived. This was his second wife, who was a good companion to him in his latter years. Ken Howell of course knew the whole situation in Peru and had visited the Miraflores Chaplaincy church on many occasions. He was delighted to learn of the plans to develop into a separate diocese. He also mentioned two members of the church of the Good Shepherd—Jack Harriman (Mr Great Britain, as some called him), who had been on my Episcopal Selection Committee and the person who physically spoke to me and conveyed the decision of the committee; and Fred Buchner, who had been the Austrian Consul in Peru, a very dear friend of mine. I took communion for years to his widow in Lima and have on the wall of my study as I write now, a painting by him of the Good Shepherd church interior. It shows clearly the chair 'cathedra' in which I was seated after my consecration. On my bookshelf still I have a beautiful Chilean silver maté, donated to me by the Howell family when Bishop Kenneth died. All these marvellous connections make me feel quite emotional — the weaving of a wonderfully rich web of memories and mementoes.

Letter 62

A typically different letter from the Revd Colin Buchanan on behalf of Grove Books, then at St John's Nottingham. The first and longer paragraph is about some money I apparently owed them! The second reads:

> I doubt if I would have written just for this, but the church press tells me that you are becoming a Bishop—indeed *the* Bishop. It could not happen to a nicer man! We do warmly congratulate you, wish you God's richest blessing and hope that now you have come into your kingdom you will not forget Grove Books or St John's College. The Lord bless you.

Colin himself subsequently became a bishop. He also wrote a Grove Books biography of my father-in-law Martin Parsons. We meet up still every two years for a gathering of retired bishops hosted by the Archbishop of York in Bishopsthorpe. Bishop Colin is on the front row at the extreme right (see page 230 for photo).

Letter 63

The Revd Jose Valenzuela from Bogotá, Colombia, was in contact with me sending occasional contributions to the small production *Misión Urbana* that I edited and circulated around South America. He had read of my election in *Rápidas,* which was a continental magazine to exchange

news amongst all the Anglican dioceses of Spanish-speaking South
America. Onell Soto was the editor, who became Bishop of Cuba later
and whom I visited in New York. I have an orange-coloured candlestick
behind me in my study now as a memento of that visit and contacts with
the dioceses north of the Southern Cone of South America.

Letter 64

A letter from the Revd Martin Parsons, my father-in-law, is very
special. He wrote:

> We rejoice together. I feel it is a matter for rejoicing, even though it
> means shouldering a heavy burden, and taking a position which could be
> lonely. Paul tells Timothy that 'to reach out after the office of a bishop is a
> good work'. A good comment on that is: 'It was a good work which they
> neither coveted because it was gain, nor shunned because it was work, and
> work of a specially arduous kind.' Hugo Latimer in his great sermon to the
> negligent bishops of his day said: 'If it is a good work it is work; ye can
> make but a work of it.' We pray very specially that you may have strength
> for the task, and wisdom to keep within your physical strength.

The Revd Martin Parsons and his two sons, David and Robert, and me

Letter 65

Samuel Escobar wrote from Córdoba in Argentina. I had invited him
to be present. This was impossible for him with his multiple speaking

commitments throughout South America in the whole area, principally of university students. We had been together in student camps and training sessions in various countries. In fact, I had first met him in the U.S.A. at a Nyack-based conference where more than anyone else he opened up the challenge of the field of Latin American universities to receive the Gospel. He, René Padilla and Pedro Araña were the three outstanding leaders of work among university students. It was a huge privilege to have known them all and worked alongside them on occasions. Years later in Peru, Samuel invited me to assist in his ordination as pastor in the Baptist church. One of the few Baptist pastors anywhere, I think, to have had episcopal hands laid upon him at his ordination!

Samuel Escobar, Rene Padilla and Student Leaders
Lima, February 1971

Letter 66

Marco A. Achoa was Bishop of the Peruvian Methodist Church. We had a good deal of interaction over the years. The U.K. Methodist Church doesn't have bishops but the U.S.A. one does, and the Peruvian branch had been founded by Methodists from the U.S.A. Marco Achoa and I felt a certain affinity, in that in 1978 we were the only two non-Roman-Catholic bishops in Peru! We were also the only two married bishops in Peru! So we had a certain rarity value! In some South American countries now, other Christian denominations have adopted an episcopal system of ministry, especially in the numerous Pentecostal groups. When Peru returned to a democratic government from a military one, Marco Ochoa and I were asked to sit on a Parliamentary committee to advise on policy about government censorship of films and books.

Letter 67

Jeanette Grenfell, ex- Christ Church Cockfosters, very faithfully undertook the printing and distribution of our quarterly prayer letter to individuals and prayer partners. She did this for over 20 years extremely efficiently and being responsible for the cost of it herself. Each time some 200 letters were regularly sent out. At the time of writing Jeanette is in her retirement home in Worthing and still in touch. The Lord will surely honour her work behind the scenes for such a length of time. Any 'success' in spiritual work can often be traced back to faithful 'prayer warriors'.

Letter 68

The Revd Walter Barker was General Secretary of the Church's Ministry among the Jews. He wrote: "Every ministry has its own particular disadvantages as well as compensation. But I imagine the task of a Bishop overseas is one of the most arduous and demanding." I write elsewhere of my long relationship with the CMJ which continues to this day.

Letter 69

W. Weller of the Peruvian Evangelical Lutheran Church wrote a formal congratulatory letter. At a later date I was invited to participate in the ordination of one of their pastors in the Andes.

Letter 70

Bishop Cyril Tucker, my own bishop, who had originally invited us for work in Buenos Aires back in the late 60s, wrote from his retirement in the U.K. He and his wife were connected with us for a long time. When we arrived in Buenos Aires in 1969, we stayed with them in their penthouse flat in Palermo for a whole month until a home could be found for us. Many years later we visited his wife Kathleen in retirement in Cambridge after Bishop Cyril's death. I was asked by the family to take Kathleen's memorial service and preach; a great privilege. There are biscuits that Dorothy often cooked which we always called Aunty Kathleen's biscuits from our time in their B.A. home, when also our two daughters Hilary and Caroline discovered Kathleen's oil paints and decorated themselves and the bedroom walls!

Buenos Aires Clergy, 1970s
Bishop Cyril Tucker in the centre

Letter 71

I was pleased to receive a letter from Pablo George, who wrote on behalf of Certeza, the Argentina Christian Publishing House, who had commissioned and published my book for university students on intercessory prayer. His letter included, in Spanish of course, the following telling phrase: "God makes love a constant miracle of our lives, which in turn generates miracles around us." A nice idea!

Letter 72

David Gooch, in the name of the Parish Council of Holy Trinity Lomas de Zamora, wrote to convey sincere congratulations. Not all on the council perhaps would have been 'totally' sincere. Not all had approved of the move from English into Spanish in the church! However, the church survived into the new era and now has an Argentine pastor. David Gooch himself moved to another church in Buenos Aires and had an effective ministry as a layman and still does, in another of the Anglican Spanish-speaking congregations.

Letter 73

Again from Lomas de Zamora church a letter from Tina and Sergio Martini with congratulations, I had married them. They wanted to tell me of the birth of their first child on 19th January 1978 and their desire that I should baptise the little boy, Alejandro, had I not been so far away. Tina was an active member of the young people's group that got going at Holy Trinity, several of them, like Tina, who went to school at either Barker's for the girls or St Albans for the boys. They were independent private bi-lingual schools. I taught a bit at both. The debating classes with the girls were the more successful, or at least the easier. The Scripture classes with the boys were the more stressful.

Letter 74

The headmaster of Stowe School, Bob Drayson, and his wife Rachel offered congratulations and best wishes on my 'elevation'. As mentioned elsewhere Bob Drayson was on the SAMS Board of Trustees, and was the father of Nick, who became the Bishop of Northern Argentina. Bob invited me to preach in the School Chapel. More recently, since his death, I have played golf several times in some of the school grounds which are hired out as a private club. It is only a nine-hole course. Main features include a magnificent lake, an obelisk, a mock Grecian temple, a 'golden statue of Andromeda, a huge urn — all of these are to be avoided while playing golf. I got very near the statue of Andromeda once!

Letter 75

The Revd Ted Pratt and his wife Jo wrote from their parish church in Mackworth, Derbyshire. We are still very much in touch with Ted.

After the death of his first wife, he has married again, an old friend of the family. She is a good companion for Ted as he has serious problems with his hearing. Ted taught me to drive a car while I was at theological college in Bristol in 1964. I passed the test the second time just weeks before our wedding! We meet most regularly now through his expertise as a botanist, a hobby he shares with Dorothy.

Letter 76

Another lovely letter from my father-in-law Martin Parsons. His writings and publications were always inspiring. He was a notably good biblical expositor. Through his chairmanship of the Charles Simeon Society he came into contact with a large number of preachers and bishops. This letter included the following:

> We are continuing instant in prayer for you and Dorothy (though she is not consecrated she will be commissioned by God and given the grace sufficient for the task) and for the Consecration and Enthronement Services. If people congratulate us on your 'promotion' I try to explain that it is the call of God to a particular office of rather particular difficulty. In a way you are to become the leading foot-washer in the Diocese. Is this promotion?

Letter 77

Mary Coles from Locking Church wrote: "We can't send you any flowers but just a touch of England in May." Her letter was embellished with a lovely vaseful of red tulips. Another very faithful prayer partner.

Letter 78

Ralph Matthews was the pastor of the Union Church of Lima. This church ministered in English and mainly to the North Americans working in Peru. Geographically it was quite close to the Church of the Good Shepherd in Miraflores. The main time I can remember is when both churches jointly sponsored the ministry of Marney Patterson for an evangelistic campaign with English-speaking people in mind.

Letter 79

The Diocese of Northern Argentina sent a letter with a biblical text and signatures from their diocesan council. David Leake was to be one of the three bishops needed to make a consecration valid and he would travel over the Andes to be present in Lima, and also lead a short retreat for pastors beforehand. Many who signed the letter in 1978 have now gone to be with the Lord in glory. We rejoice that Bishop Maurice and Gillian Sinclair, Michael and Virginia Patterson, David and Rachel Leake are still with us. We still enjoy fellowship with them.

Letter 80

Bishop Colin Bazley, our Southern Cone presiding bishop, wrote me a reassuring letter about episcopal garments etc. As the chief consecrating bishop, he wanted to ensure that I was suitably uniformed:

> Apparently the tradition is that you wear a black (rather than scarlet) chimere for your consecration. I have never worn one since my consecration! However, I do possess one that used to belong to Bishop Daniel Evans (from the time of the undivided Diocese of Chile and Argentina). I could bring that with me for the consecration.

(In the end I used the scarlet one from Wippells in London through the generosity of the people of Christ Church Cockfosters and have been wearing it now for 40 years.)

Colin added with his fine sense of humour to diffuse any sense of over-formality: "You'll need a ring for the fourth toe of your left foot too!" In fact, I didn't have an episcopal ring at all until I returned for ministry in the U.K. Wearing a gold ring with an amethyst stone didn't seem appropriate for the Peruvian shanty towns. It might have been dangerous too.

Letter 81

"Don't take Mary away from me."

Edmundo Montaigne wrote from California in the U.S.A. He had married Susan Griffiths (an Anglo-North American) from the Good Shepherd Church. He was Peruvian, a cousin of the Roman Catholic Cardinal of Peru! Before leaving Peru, he was very high up in running the Peruvian Railway System. He, with Susan and a number of other Peruvians, came to a Thursday evening Bible/discussion group that I led. He found it particularly helpful. He liked the emphasis on the centrality of Christ, I remember. But also, he did once say to me:

> This devotion to Mary was caught up with the female figure from pre-Christian times, Pachamama, the earth goddess venerated in Inca culture. It also reflected the emotional need for a sympathetic figure for worship, to compensate for the austere, rather remote suffering Christ portrayed in so many pictures and statues.

Without regular reading of the biblical picture of Christ, something of a caricature and an unattractive portrayal could be given. The son of a Presbyterian, Juan Mackay wrote a very significant book called *The other Spanish Christ*. In this dialogue about the true nature of Christ, one can begin to understand the huge loyalty to Mary, so prevalent in

South America, especially during the centuries when any sort of biblical/protestant representation was resolutely forbidden. The Spanish Inquisition operated effectively in Lima well into the 20th century. Edmundo and Susan Montaigne joined an Episcopal church in the U.S.A. when they moved from Peru.

Letter 82

The Roman Catholic Maryknoll fathers not only sent greetings but also a cheque for work among the poor in Lima, together with the expression of joy and happiness on the day of my ordination as Bishop of Peru.

Letter 83

Ricardo Cutts, the Anglican Bishop of Argentina in Buenos Aires, sent a telegram of prayerful good wishes. After Bishop Cyril Tucker, Richard came from experience in South Africa, but he had the decided advantage of being Anglo-Argentine. He spoke good Spanish, which was a great advantage after Bishop Cyril Tucker. But Cyril Tucker was the bishop who pushed forward the strategy of the move from English into Spanish in the Southern Diocese of Argentine; he was the bishop who boldly first ordained native Argentine Indians into the priesthood; also he supported and paid for me and my family to have a crash course in Spanish in Cuernavaca, Mexico before touching South American soil; but he never mastered Spanish himself.

Richard Cutts was also sympathetic to the Charismatic movement, which fitted well with the South American religious climate.

Letter 84

I was so pleased to receive a letter from the Revd Chris and Marjorie Idle in Limehouse, East London. We had been at college together. He made a big impact in the area of hymn writing and publication. We visited them on our first furlough, and I was hugely impressed by the challenges of Christian work in the Tower Hamlets area of London. He and Marjorie did this without the glamour of being sent abroad with a missionary society and hundreds of prayerful mission partners. When he wrote in 1978, he had had 18 months in Limehouse:

> I sometimes think that the main ministerial skill is 'handling interruptions', or rather turning interruptions into opportunities, as Jesus did. It seems that when occasionally I do get a clear stretch of work, I don't know how to handle it—I am geared to ten-minute spurts!

Letter 85

A surprising letter (in fact amongst many) was from Alec Clifford from Córdoba, Argentina:

> Please accept my sincere congratulations: I really mean it, in spite of my Plymouth Brethren prejudices! May the Lord bless you richly in your Peruvian ministry. You are certainly missed in Argentina. Our current magazine (*Pensamiento Cristiano*) is running your excellent article on Liturgy.

In my reply, in Spanish of course, I wrote:

> A strong embrace from a 'naturalised' Englishman very much missing his adopted country of Argentina.

Letter 86

The Revd Michael Cole from All Saints Vicarage in Woodford Wells, a SAMS stronghold, wrote an encouraging letter from his wide experience in the evangelical Anglican scene of the U.K. He knew Bishop Bill Flagg, my predecessor in Peru, and was very much part of the 'forward move' of SAMS promoted by the then General Secretary, Canon Harry Sutton. This had come from the 1958 Lambeth Conference, when Anglican bishops worldwide accepted that South America was a legitimate area for mission work. The door had 'officially' been closed after the 1910 Anglican Missionary Conference in Edinburgh.

Letter 87

The Bishop of Pontefract, Richard Hare, wrote:

> I was so delighted to hear the news of your appointment and have a note to pray for you specially on Whit Sunday. It is good to know that the cross which the Lord prompted me to give you was so prophetic a gift! Incidentally I have found that it is better to shorten the cord considerably: it then becomes a pectoral, rather than an abdominal cross!

Richard Hare was very much associated with the Charismatic movement and for that reason was interested in church development in South America and the ministry of SAMS.

Letter 88

Very appropriately in my file follows a letter from Bishop David Pytches, the former Bishop of Chile, Bolivia and Peru, who had taken over from Bishop Ken Howell. He indicated that for some time there had been plans to separate Peru from Chile and Bolivia. He had sent Bishop Bill Flagg to Lima to begin the process, but he wrote:

We discussed the possibility of your succeeding him there as inevitably his days were numbered. Obviously in making plans of this kind one has to be ready to see the Lord over-ruling in surprising ways and things developing in surprising directions, but your appointment seems to confirm that we were getting the pattern right.

As a family from Buenos Aires we once spent part of a holiday in the Pytches' home in Viña del Mar, while they were on leave in the U.K. We always remember the notice on their fridge "Alleluia Anyway". Much later when we were rather struggling to find a suitable person to take over leadership of the newly-to-be-formed Diocese of Bolivia, I did write to him on the off-chance that he might feel a call to return to South America; in fact, as he commented, to a third part of his original diocese! He declined.

Letter 89

Jorge Foweraker Villalón, General Secretary of the Peruvian Bible Society, sent the Society's greetings and well wishes. I later had the opportunity of serving the Society in an honorary capacity.

Letter 90

A letter from the Bishop of Edmonton was a nice surprise. He had been apprised of my appointment by Don Churchman, the Vicar of Cockfosters, in the episcopal jurisdiction of Edmonton. Bishop Bill had also had Bishop Ken Howell (ex-Chile, Bolivia and Peru) in his area as an assistant after he left South America. He wrote:

> I can truthfully say that I have never been happier in my ministry and have found in the episcopal office great demands, but great fulfilment, and pray that God may grant you the same in a very different part of the world.

So, in summary as an overview, these 90 letters sketch in something of my first 40 years of life before becoming a bishop.

The next section will provide another overview of the following 40 years living and working as a bishop in South America and in the UK.

5
SEVEN FACETS OF EPISCOPAL MINISTRY, 1978–2018

In Shakespeare's *As You Like It,* Jaques declares that:–
All the world's a stage,
And all the men and women merely players:
They have their exits and their entrances;
And one man in his time plays many parts,
His acts being seven ages.

There follows the marvellous depiction of those seven ages, from "the infant, mewling and puking in the nurse's arms" to the "second childishness and mere oblivion, sans teeth, sans eyes, sans taste, sans everything."

As I look back over the last 40 years of my life on the episcopal stage, I discern development and different emphases. I'm not going to overdo the similarity to Shakespeare's inspired poem! Although in early days I was referred to as a baby bishop! But it provides a way of summarising these years of ministry. So, very broadly, seven facets of episcopal ministry in different spheres:–

A Bishop as an Apostle	Peru and Bolivia
A Bishop as a Strategist	Province of the Southern Cone of South America
A Bishop as an International Agent	Anglican Communion
A Bishop as a Pastor	Bradford, U.K.
A Bishop as an Evangelical Leader	EFAC
A Bishop as a Missionary Executive	SAMS U.K. and International
A Bishop as an Assistant	Retirement in U.K.

5A
A BISHOP AS AN APOSTLE: PERU AND BOLIVIA

When I was consecrated bishop in the Church of God by Colin Bazley of Chile, Primate of the Southern Cone, David Leake of Northern Argentina and Douglas Milmine of Paraguay on the 14th May 1978, I entered what some people call the apostolic ministry. I was given a copy of my episcopal 'ancestral tree' showing the continuity of consecration through bishops right back to apostolic days. Every consecration ceremony needs a minimum of three bishops to safeguard its authenticity. This is known by some as 'manual apostolic succession'.

Others will place more importance on the transmission of the apostolic faith than the actual imposition of duly accredited episcopal hands. But the long historical episcopal tree is impressive. In my case that long list of three names for every consecration stretches back to Jerusalem through Chile, Brazil, the U.S.A, Scotland, England, France, Italy and the Middle East. It is partly due to this intriguing history lesson that Anglicans claim to be part of the One, Holy, Catholic and Apostolic Church. We are a true part of the Church of Jesus Christ existing historically now for over 2000 years. We value this sense of history. We know that our history includes many failures as well as many successes. But we have not sprung out of nowhere. We are not a creation of the 20th or 21st century. We have historical and spiritual ancestors.

Being made a bishop in South America was also special because of its geographical position. Jesus' command to his first apostles was to preach, teach and baptise, making disciples of all nations even to the uttermost part of the earth. Peru is about as far away from Jerusalem as you can get!

In 1992 I was present at the funeral of Bishop Cyril Tucker (ex-Argentina) in Great St. Mary's, Cambridge. I bought a new edition of E Lucas Bridges' well-known book *Uttermost Part of the Earth*. Lucas Bridges' father arrived in Tierra del Fuego in 1871 to help build the first Christian mission station in Ushuaia. It is a true mark of the Christian Church that it have an apostolic spirit—a conviction of having been sent into the unknown with the apostolic Gospel message. When I left Cockfosters in 1968, I was presented with a Spanish Bible inscribed: "If God command thee . . . thou shalt be able". This was again presented to me on Whit Sunday (14th May 1978) with an added inscription signed by

the three consecrating bishops. It is a great privilege and encouragement
to sense being caught up in something much bigger than oneself. That is
why in our prayer letter No. 25 of April 1978 I quoted the famous words
of St. Augustine:–

> For you I am a bishop, but with you I am a Christian: the first an office
> conferred and accepted; the second a grace received. As then I am gladder
> to be redeemed with you than I am to be set over you, I shall, as the Lord
> commanded, be more completely your servant.

Apostolic ministry has involved many things. Soon after returning to
the U.K. in 1988 I reread our 42 prayer letters and made this summary:

a. *Suffering is part of apostolic ministry*

It must be. It was for Christ. Mission doesn't just happen when we are
in robust health. Often it is more effective when we are broken. We
remember with gratitude Christ's suffering on the Cross, but many times
He must have strode over the Galilean hills. I think of Anglo-Argentine
Roger Vibart whom I licensed to preach in Tandil, south of B.A., who was
dead of cancer within two years. The same with Peruvian Eduardo
Walker in Lima, just two years after his ordination. I remember how
weak I was from hepatitis when I was invited to be Bill Flagg's successor
in Peru. I remember John Sutton's shock departure from Arequipa, while
working there. The illness and subsequent death of Tommy Hargrave in
new work in La Paz, Bolivia, Penny Everness's multiple illnesses in her
shanty town work in Lima. All of these, I believe, form part of mission in
a mysterious way. So perhaps we need to pray less for the avoidance of
suffering and more for the transformation of suffering in the Lord's
strange alchemy into fruitfulness and glory.

b. *Opening new work is apostolic*

It has been a great privilege to be involved in seeing new work opened
up. Sometimes it was more just keeping up with the Holy Spirit's
initiatives. In Argentina the biggest innovation had been the change of
language from English to Spanish in the Anglican Church life. And of
course, feelings ran deeply about this change of mindset and outlook. In
Peru and Bolivia, the situation was markedly different. Nearly
everything was new. The authorisation and commission for a new diocese
came from the Provincial Executive. But in both republics legal entities
had to be established, missionary teams had to be assembled, buildings
had to be acquired, either rented or built for church services and for

workshops. In Peru we had a formal welcome from the Roman Catholic Cardinal Archbishop but were regarded with some suspicion by the National Evangelical Federation of Churches. With the charismatic movement affecting some of the evangelical churches (but by no means all) and also, significantly, the Roman Church, we had a struggle on our hands to establish a viable identity. This was highlighted by our attempt to authenticate a middle way, by changing our name from the Anglican Church to the Christian Episcopal Church. This had the advantage of distancing ourselves from 'our Englishness', affirming our Christ-centredness and recognising our distinctive episcopal leadership. The decision was later revised but, at the time, it was a welcome concession to indigenise the church.

In Bolivia we were welcomed by the National Evangelical Church Federation. This was because after a number of Luis Palau evangelistic crusades, numerous people were professing conversion but not affiliating to evangelical churches. It was thought that we might be able to help among the middle class particularly, which is just what we did. We had no formal contact in Bolivia, however, with the Roman hierarchy.

Between 1978 and 1988 in Peru we grew from one to 15 churches, both in the middle class and the shanty-town areas of Southern Lima. Churches sometimes grew on the strawberry plant model. They might start in a home, a garage, a small shack. As numbers grew the house might be extended to provide a large meeting room, or an independent property was acquired and again modified, or a large hall built or rented. A third stage was for an architecturally designed church building to be erected. This was going on constantly. The last one that I inaugurated in the area called '28 Julio' still hadn't got its main door finally in place! But that didn't stop Robert Runcie, as Archbishop of Canterbury, visiting it soon after I had left! It had one of the best sewage systems in the whole shanty town, in fact perhaps the only one!

It wasn't long before new work was started in Arequipa, Peru's second city, high in the Southern Andes. Arequipa has been described as the Peruvian Rome, for its very traditional style. Eventually our central church was a beautiful architect-designed building, using the traditional white volcanic stone, typical of the city of half a million people. It was recognisably a church rather than, for instance, just a service being held in a cinema or disused carpet factory. Other churches were also founded but didn't need to be so obviously ecclesiastical.

When work began in Bolivia there was no Anglican presence of any sort. The central La Paz chaplaincy with English-language services was an interdenominational gathering. So, we basically had to start in a missionaries' rented home in La Paz in a target middle class area. We then moved to a community hall, where on Saturday evenings keep fit classes were held. Brightly coloured posters suggesting healthy diets still adorned the walls on Sunday morning! Then with a substantial Partners in Mission grant we acquired land and put up our own building. The work

Baptism in the Andes

spread to another centre in more uptown La Paz, then to Santa Cruz, then to Cochabamba and more recently to Tarija, nearer the border with Northern Argentina.

New work does involve buildings. Sometimes in Bolivia especially I longed to be able to transplant some underused church buildings from the U.K. for use in La Paz! But new work also involves assembling teams — we were well supported by SAMS and Crosslinks (BCMS) from the U.K. and SAMS U.S.A. as well. We invited missionaries from other countries to join the team as well as new recruits from their homelands. We had financial difficulties with a Bolivian-born pastor who had worked in Ecuador and who was 'given' to us by the Bishop of Ecuador. He proved to have had a previous chequered career with a Bolivian Methodist Church. We didn't check far enough back in his life and ministry. He came recommended and his gifted family of five children formed a very competent Gospel music group. Desirable but disastrous!

c. Maintaining the apostolic vision

Initiating new work is exciting, even exhilarating. It is also extremely hard going. Vision needs to be maintained. This can be achieved through a balance between spirit and structure. There are situations where structure predominates, and spirit is stifled. There are situations where the spirit is ebullient, and structure is despised. The Lord calls us to bear fruit, fruit that will remain. Organised structure helps the organism into continuity. It was Perón in Argentina and Victor Haya de la Torre in Peru who knew the value of organisation. Yet if I had to choose I would go for spirit rather than structure. Untidy life rather than ordered lifelessness!

Having said that, during my ten episcopal years in Peru I saw numerous churches of various denominations or none appear, divide and disappear! This happened especially in middle class areas. I used to say that people were like hummingbirds—they would fly from plant to plant, to wherever the word was that there was something sweet and new on offer! There was little sense of congregational loyalty.

It seemed at times that pastors and people were constantly on the move 'following the Holy Spirit' to pastures new. This was particularly true of 'our' biggest middle class church in Lima, which at one stage had to hire a large room in the local council offices, having outgrown the purpose-built extension to a building we had bought initially to house a missionary couple.

Walter Hollenwegen wrote in the *International Review of Mission* in January 1986:

For Charismatic Christians the medium of communication is:–
not the definition but the description   not the statement but the story
not the doctrine but the testimony   not the treatise but the TV programme
not the systematic theology but the song   not the book but the parable
not the articulation of concept but the celebration of banquets.

It sounds lovely and certainly spiritual but at the same time it creates a difficult atmosphere in which to build churches! Better to hire a cinema while the Spirit is with us, so that we can all move on when the Spirit seems to move elsewhere.

This affects much more than building policies. It affects the theological training of pastors; the Church's doctrinal position; the practice of baptism and celebration of the Holy Communion; the relationship with other churches, etc; the use of a set liturgy or not, in worship. Every denomination has its historical baggage. How flexible can church leaders be in holding on to genuine apostolic content and practice and accommodating positively to local culture and customs?

While in Peru a small group of us went to Hawaii for a conference organised for all the countries around the Pacific Rim! We were discussing Roland Allen's missiology — not least his book *Missionary Methods: St Paul's or Ours?*

The theological training of pastors has always been a real challenge. There was an interdenominational theological college in Lima. I and another mission partner did some teaching there. We did have two Anglican students there over the years. We did have a reasonable number of special courses of Anglican teaching on important topics. We did use every opportunity for our trainee pastors to visit neighbouring countries for conferences and seminars. We did send one English-speaking Anglo-Peruvian for a course in the U.K., but mainly theological training was done in the local situation through Theological Extension methods together with groups of lay leaders. This was excellent material, but it was reasonably basic biblical teaching.

Introducing a 'lightweight' inter-church structure for the diocese was also part of helping to maintain a helpful vision for the work. We needed to support and challenge each other rather than have a loose conglomeration of independent local churches. This needed to be set up in both Peru and Bolivia, so that eventually they were self-governing dioceses, though also members of the Province of the Southern Cone with the other dioceses of Chile, Southern and Northern Argentina, Uruguay and Paraguay.

Maintaining the vision involves keeping historical perspective. I was thrilled to be in Durban in 1985 on the spot where Captain Allen Gardiner preached his first sermon on 20th March 1835 to the Zulus, from where he left to sail to South America, for his pioneering work. It was thrilling to link up in thought with him on my many visits to Bolivia, remembering that in far more difficult circumstances he had visited and started a work in S. Bolivia in the 1850s. Thrilling also to be reminded by a Kenyan Archdeacon of the small beginnings of our work in his country, where now just in Kenya there is a province with 12 Dioceses and hundreds of thousands of Christian believers. At the Lambeth Conference of 2038 might there be a province in Peru, a province in Bolivia, and 100 L.A. bishops present representing 100s of 1000s of Christian believers?

d. *The Ministry of Apostolic Hospitality*

Hospitality!

This is a biblical command, especially mentioned for those in apostolic ministry. I don't know how many angels we entertained 'unawares' in our time in South America, but we certainly had a lot of visitors. In our four historic visitors' books which we have kept up since we got married, I notice that we had agricultural missionary Arthur Houston to stay in our house in Buenos Aires. The first night he shared the bedroom with Philip King (SAMS General Secretary). The second night with Bill Flagg (Bishop of Paraguay) and the third night with David Leake (Bishop of Northern Argentina). Hospitality, *really* welcoming people into one's home, is a great communicator of the Gospel. The Englishman's home is his castle, traditionally. Retiring to privacy and lifting up the drawbridge before putting on the kettle/telly. But being a Christian, especially in Latin America, means an Open Door, and the open door is a symbol of the Open Heart. I was personally very humbled often by the Peruvians' generosity, especially among the poor. I didn't always find it easy having someone else in the house. For example, the occasion when a person ruined my Christmas dinner by going out just as the turkey was to be brought in, and then several days later appearing at about 11 p.m. in her nightgown in our bedroom for a rather intense confession and forgiveness session! Dorothy was absolutely key for this ministry of hospitality. Hundreds of people knew from her welcoming smile and her concern for their wellbeing, that they were truly welcome and appreciated.

When we were established in Warwick in 2011, we joined the church of St Nic's. In the choir was an Indian surgeon. We invited him round for a meal and discovered that his father had been a Bishop in India and had once visited South America. Imagine the great surprise to all of us when we got out the relevant visitors' book and discovered his entry and signature from 20 years before. He had been at a Christian Conference in Lima and had come to lunch with us afterwards. Our four visitors' books are a fascinating record of the many wonderful people we have been privileged to entertain over many years.

e. Consciousness Raising is apostolic ministry

This is not just for liberation theologians! Remember that the Roman Catholic priest Gustavo Gutiérrez, the 'founder' of Liberation Theology, lived in Lima. It really is for everyone to get outside the straitjacket of his or her own small world and begin to appreciate how other people have to live. I recall three particular instances of this. On three occasions I took 20 Argentine High School and University students on a coach tour of the Chaco area of Northern Argentina. They had no previous conception of how indigenous Argentines lived in the north of their own country. It was a real eye-opener, challenging many aspects of their own lifestyle. The same happened when I took a married couple from Christ Church Cockfosters for an afternoon in Lima's shanty towns. They were on a world cruise and staying in a posh central Lima hotel. They were so shattered they sent me a cheque for £1000. Apostolic ministry involved crossing barriers, entering new worlds, relating to people who think and live perhaps totally differently from one's own experience of life. These examples quoted have to do with temporary visitors. The same challenge faced all missionaries and volunteers, who were forced to evaluate their own lifestyle in the light of having chosen, at least for a period of time, to live in another culture, speak another language and seek to understand and relate to men and women whose whole understanding of the world was foreign. I used to compare diplomatic and missionary policy on this issue of inculturation. Embassy staff don't stay too long in any one post because of the danger of becoming too assimilated to local customs. Missionary personnel, however, are encouraged to stay as long as possible and are normally better at their job the more they assimilate to local culture.

I have preached several times on the amazing words of Jesus to the 70 when he sent them out on mission (even within their own country!). They were sent out "as sheep among wolves". Not an exhilarating prospect! They were to lose many of their 'props' and norms of security and certainties. They were to learn to live precariously in considerable vulnerability. The exact pattern, of course, of Jesus' own example of leaving his eternal securities and entering into human vulnerability in a hostile environment. It is all part of the apostolicity of the church in mission.

f. *Praying is apostolic*

I believed in prayer before going to South America — you may be relieved to know! However, I returned an even more ardent believer in its importance and efficacy. For various reasons:

Firstly, because I have been stimulated by the simple, direct and unsophisticated prayer of many Christian people in South America. They really expect things to happen when they pray! They are importunate in their prayers! And sometimes they do go on about it. But these are biblical marks of prayer.

Secondly, I was persuaded to write a short book in Spanish on prayer. I shall certainly never write another book in Spanish. And if I never write another book at all I'm glad it was about something as fundamental as prayer. (May those 5000 people who bought the book continue to be real pray-ers.)

Thirdly, I was very influenced by a superb address of the former
Archbishop of Canterbury, Michael Ramsey, in Bishop Cyril Tucker's
B.A. home that prayer is "being in the presence of God with His people on
one's heart!" Like the Old Testament High Priest. How we have
appreciated the prayer support ourselves over these last 40 years. Often
we have said "someone must have been praying." Prayer brings us back
to the reality that mission is God's mission to be conducted in His way by
His chosen instruments in His perfect timing. Most of our problems are
trying foolhardily to charge ahead of Him or guiltily lag behind Him.
Prayer sets us on His wavelength, in His groove.

g. *Missionary Apostolic Motivation*

Why do people become missionaries? Henri J. M. Nouwen in his Latin-
American journal, *Gracias*, asked this question:

> Why do they leave what is familiar and known, to live in a milieu that is
> unfamiliar and unknown? There is no simple answer . . .
>
> A desire to serve Christ unconditionally
> An urge to help the poor
> An intellectual interest in another culture
> The attraction of adventure
> A need to break away from the family
> A critical insight into the predicament of one's own country
> A search for self-affirmation
>
> However, the issue is not to have perfectly motivated missionaries, but
> missionaries who are willing to be purified again and again as they struggle
> to fulfil their true vocation in life.

So, as a bishop in Peru and Bolivia for twenty years we participated, I
believe, in various aspects of **apostolic** ministry:

> A sense of joining in an historical mission
> Accepting the inevitability of a measure of suffering
> Involvement in taking up new initiatives and creating structures
> Maintaining and pursuing a worthwhile vision
> Exercising open hospitality
> Openness to cultural adaptability
> Reliance on a God who answers prayer.

Peter Atkins, Bishop of Waiapu, New Zealand, prepared in the run-up
to the Lambeth Conference of 1988 a paper entitled "The Bishop in
Mission". It covered the following ground where the principle of mission
is to be worked out in:

Liturgical order	Ministry placement and support
Synodical leadership	Moral guidance
Theological exploration	Building community

5B
A BISHOP AS A STRATEGIST: PROVINCE OF THE SOUTHERN CONE OF SOUTH AMERICA

In practice a bishop serves as a link person between different dioceses, countries and continents. He is an ecclesiastical Foreign Secretary. He should not be a diocesan dictator. To be consecrated he has to have three other bishops laying hands on him: one of whom, wherever possible, is the presiding bishop/archbishop of the province. The process of election differs around the world, but there is always due process and consultation. This has sometimes been secretive and confidential. Nowadays, as I saw recently, there can be an advert in the church press seeking suggested names.

An Anglican province has to have a minimum of three constituent dioceses. Most have far more. The Church of England has 44 in total, divided between the Province of Canterbury and the Province of York. The Province of the Southern Cone of South America had seven dioceses: Argentina, Bolivia, Chile, Northern Argentina, Paraguay, Peru and Uruguay. The geographical distances are enormous, and the possibilities of frequent meetings limited. But for church leaders, like bishops, inter-diocesan occasions are crucial, both for spiritual stimulation and for coordination in planning. Having said that, when I became a bishop in Peru my nearest episcopal colleague was some 1000 miles away! Since 1978 communication technology has transformed this situation, but all seven dioceses took every possible chance for cross-fertilization of ideas, training of leaders and sharing of resources. The older dioceses of Argentina, Chile and Paraguay have well-developed work among the Amerindians with hundreds of local churches. The urban middle class work in the cities is numerically much smaller and more recent. It is important to have both major sections of rural and urban life involved in the church. Various reasons are obvious. Anglicanism first appeared in the English language in the port cities of South America. It then made good progress in various indigenous languages and finally started to gain members from Spanish-speaking communities. Paraguayan churches have services in Guaraní and Enxet. Northern Argentina ones in Toba, Mataco (Wichí) and Chorote, and Chile in Mapudungun among the Mapuche people in the South. Otherwise Spanish predominates in Peru and Bolivia, (although Quechua is still very much alive in rural areas).

There are significant vocabulary differences between the various republics, and each historical Spanish nation has incorporated vocabulary and concepts from its own native languages. These go back thousands of years in some cases.

During the 'celebrations' for the 500th Anniversary of the arrival of Christopher Columbus in the New World, the note of celebration was definitely missing from the Amerindians, who understandably had a very different attitude to the arrival of the 'Conquistadores'. In recent years there have been considerable incidents of unrest among the Mapuche Indian people at the annexation of their traditional lands in the South of Chile. Land rights issues in Northern Argentina constitute an ongoing saga for the Toba and Wichí people. Northern Argentina and Chile now have Amerindians in priests' and bishops' orders. There has also been a German/Chilean presiding bishop of the province for some years.

Translating the Bible into the vernacular has always been a vital and strategic ministry. Finding the right way to have an indigenous ordained ministry is still an ongoing challenge. It is forgotten, or some people never realised, that it took CMS in Africa 100 years before the episcopal consecration of Samuel Crowther in Nigeria. Bear in mind that the Roman Catholic Church in Peru has had to discipline itself to ensure that at least 50% of its bishops are Peruvian or South American, and that after 500 years! We don't have the additional obstacle of the unpopularity of celibate clergy to contend with.

One problem is partially solved by internal migration. As large numbers move from rural areas to the megapolises of South America, Spanish (or Portuguese in Brazil) tends to take over traditional indigenous languages. For instance, in Lima, Peru there is hardly a Quechua-speaking church in all the capital's population of some six million. In the huge geographical area of most of Argentina, the general population have no idea that there are significant traditional indigenous-speaking people in the north of their own national territory. Some of them in the military found out in the Falklands War, when native peoples from the north were conscripted to fight in the deep south. Only Paraguay has two official languages, Spanish and Guaraní. The other countries in the South Cone Province just have the one officially. Across the vast distances of the Andes mountains there are a great number of variations in the Quechua language, traditionally that of the Incas. And geographical isolation has accentuated the differences. The official Bible Society in the Continent has authorised and produced a good number of different idiomatic versions of the Quechua Bible in order to seek to communicate effectively to very diverse groups of people.

It is true to say that the recent history of the church in South America has been turbulent. For almost 400 years the Roman Catholic Church had the continent to itself. It also at times fiercely sought to exclude non-Roman Catholics. An inquisition was set up and used in Lima. It is but a museum today. But it is hard evidence of past brutality. After the wars of liberation or independence from Spain the doors were opened and many denominations from the Old World followed the Bible Society colporteurs into the port cities and further into the countryside. Much work had been done by Roman Catholic Monastic and Missionary orders, but particularly when internal migrations brought millions into the burgeoning metropolises, the religious panorama became more complicated. Starting down in Chile, the panorama changed significantly right across the board, Protestant and Catholic. At one stage I was asked if I would be interested to approach a large Roman Catholic congregation that had turned charismatic and was looking for a new home or spiritual oversight. A couple of our pastors were very keen that we should 'take up' the opportunity of vastly increasing our numbers! We didn't.

And while spiritual effervescence was everywhere, liberation theologians were beavering away in the shanty towns, seeking to promote a people's rebellion and rising up against the State. Many believed fervently that without such an organised revolt, the poorer sections of society would never get anything near a fair deal.

I came across perhaps a mild version of this in a workbook depicting the slavery suffered by the Israelites in Egypt under Pharaoh. The whole book was profusely illustrated by Peruvian peasants suffering under the whiplash of government soldiers and law enforcement officers. It certainly was bringing the Exodus and Old Testament Scriptures up to date! I'm not sure what active official support the SPCK (Society for the Propagation of Christian Knowledge) gave to this project when an official came out from the U.K. to see how the financial grant had been used. The then Bishop of Ripon, SPCK's visiting rep., was rather taken aback!

On another occasion, when I was taking Bishop David Sheppard to one of our shanty-town churches in the midst of a desperate shortage of water, I was given a good lesson. While we were being shown round the church building with the pastor's living rooms attached, a cry went up that the water had been turned on. Everyone disappeared to fill pots, pans and tubs as quickly as possible. This was more vital than entertaining a visiting dignitary! Bishop David commented that we should be much using the biblical theme of water in our teaching and preaching. I felt chastened as I had just finished a series on the theme of law and grace in Paul's letter to the Galatians!

I will just mention three other issues, not perhaps strategic, but cultural matters that we sought to take seriously. One was the question of our official **denominational name**. Another was the question of whether ordained clergy should wear any sort of distinguishing **ecclesiastical clothes**, and the third was the question of what sort of **meeting place** was the church to have. Let's take them in that order.

a. Denominational name

Denominational name

I think it has been estimated that there are at least 20,000 different denominations of the Christian church around the world with, of course, some wonderfully exotic and impressive titles. We didn't really want to create one more! The perennial issue with the name Anglican is its obvious Englishness. It emigrates easily to countries that are members of the Commonwealth, until independence struggles arise, then they normally calm down. The U.S.A. imitated Scotland, their founder, and chose Episcopal for their name. This has the advantage of describing a distinctive characteristic of the Anglican Communion without putting all its eggs apparently in a particular cultural mould! In South America the Roman Catholic Church does use the term episcopal fairly frequently (i.e. episcopal conference) but not as a name for the church. This is normally just Catholic, not even Roman Catholic, interestingly. Another point of friction is that Anglicans claim to be part of the One Holy Catholic and Apostolic Church. The umbrella word 'evangelical' is obviously important in the South American context, while Protestant hardly registers, because of the lack of the European Reformation experience. Evangelical does cover a huge number of different forms of church life in South America including many totally independent ones. So evangelical is a good biblical word but its associations are too widespread.

In the end, rather than inventing or trying to invent the prefect name we went for Christian Episcopal. Christian clearly focuses on Christ and Episcopal is our distinctive ecclesial characteristic. Where appropriate, i.e. not on signs over the church gate, we could add Members of the Anglican Communion. This was quite painful for some of us who had been Anglicans most of our lives. But it was appreciated by many Peruvians as a gesture towards a more indigenous church. I have not made any sort of assessment of its effect. A subsequent bishop reversed the synod decision and the diocese returned to being an Anglican one! We tried.

Ordination of Juan Sedano, March 1988

Ordination of Julio Montoya and Simon Thomas, 1980

Most evangelical pastors in Peru wear suits and ties at the most, and more informal wear as well on other occasions. Protestant churches usually maintained familiar European robes. Pentecostal denominations, especially in Chile, soon moved into robes, and their senior pastors into episcopal orders and clothing. Ponchos were much used but more often for robed choirs than ordained ministers. Roman Catholic priests tended to have full regalia; though on shorter home visits they would just drape a stole around their suit.

Already in Northern Argentina the Anglican church had adopted a simple form of poncho with a red scarf printed on it. I did something similar in Peru. A sisterhood of nuns made ponchos for me and all ordained clergy wore these. They were white, as befitted leaders (the 'estancieros' rode on horseback around their farms in white ponchos). They were decorated all around with a multicoloured ribbon. This was known as the Rainbow motif. It was bought cheaply in the market. Its significance was that a rainbow had appeared on the Inca flag, recognising their dependence on the God of Creation to send rain for the harvests. The garment had therefore significance for the colonial Spanish 'estancieros' and the Inca people before that. It was also very simple, portable, cheap and cool. What more could you want? I have worn one of these Peruvian ecclesiastical ponchos in every continent of the world apart from Antarctica! Normally reception has been positive. Only Bishop Desmond Tutu mischievously commented when he asked me to preach at his Synod in Johannesburg: "It looks as if the Bishop of Peru is still wearing his nightshirt!" Well, we try.

c. *Church buildings*

Christ the Redeemer, Arequipa

It is strange being in a continent without significant numbers of church buildings. In Buenos Aires it was the bank and business buildings that dominated the skyline, not church spires. The Roman Catholic Church over the years has tended to construct cathedral-size buildings and not local churches. As urbanization spread rapidly, due largely to huge internal immigration, large areas of cities were left church-less. Many Roman Catholics had to travel considerable distances to attend a Mass. Liberation theology, of course, brought a new dynamic, and cell groups proliferated. This also happened with the Pentecostals, who would meet anywhere and everywhere, weather permitting.

25 de Julie in San Juan de Miraflores, Lima

Most dioceses in the Southern Cone had at least one English-speaking Chaplaincy church (actually there had been eleven in Argentina). This tended to be the mother church, and often was designated as the Cathedral. So, in 1844 in Lima the Good Shepherd chaplaincy church, in its third location, became the Cathedral Church of the Diocese of Peru. In Peru and Bolivia during my episcopate architect-designed buildings were constructed in Lima, Arequipa and La Paz.

The first was the Church of 27 de Julio in San Juan de Miraflores. It had developed from the flimsiest shantytown home of one of our church members, who emigrated to Lima from the Andes. Our first meetings almost had more cats, dogs and chickens present than human beings. In Lima we used a garage, private homes, sometimes with an extension. Once we hired a large public hall in the local Civic Centre, but we never rented a disused cinema, which was reasonably common practice with various Pentecostal groups. Sometimes the private house was the purchased home of a missionary family, who weekly, at least, were heavily involved in a good deal of furniture moving to accommodate the congregation. Sometimes it was the home of a Peruvian church member. This had problems as availability was not always 100%, through various family commitments. In other instances, the building was owned by the diocese, but the Peruvian pastor and his family lived at the back or on a floor upstairs.

Foundation Stone in Calacoto, La Paz, Bolivia, 1988

In Arequipa, a very religious city in the Andes, we built an impressive church which fitted into the cultural milieu. Its façade was made with white volcanic rock from the famous Misti volcano which towered over the city (see page 65).

It was important to register our presence in La Paz, Bolivia at a later stage. An impressive well-sited building was eventually constructed. I remember well digging out a hole for the symbolic foundation stone. Previous to this, congregational meetings had taken place in our pioneer missionary's front room, a Sunday rented community room, used on Saturdays for keep-fit classes, and the large drawing-room of a Bolivian family. He eventually left us and joined a group meeting in a cinema! The second church in the centre of La Paz met first in a Trade Union hall on the ground floor of a block of flats, before moving upstairs to a more salubrious venue.

In Santa Cruz we had two missionaries' homes as our first meeting places. The second of these, in Simon Thomas's home, moved to a 'galpón' or large shed in the garden, and then with an input of funds from Singapore and the ministry of the present bishop Raphael into a magnificent church building.

Throughout this period, I had been conscious of two 'conflicting' elements. One is the desire for close fellowships, for people to know each other. Therefore, numbers don't need to be large and overwhelming. In some measure this is an understandable reaction to the more common traditional Roman Catholic patterns, where church attendance could be no more than standing at the back of a large building watching Mass being celebrated, without any meaningful contact with other worshippers. At the same time, in a heavily Roman Catholic culture of some 500 years, there is an expectation of what a proper church should look like. A venue of a disused cinema doesn't necessarily meet the need! And in some countries small groups that meet in people's homes could be treated with considerable suspicion, as political cell groups. We had to be very careful about home meetings for Bible studies in Buenos Aires during times of political tension. This was especially the case with university students' groups.

5C
A BISHOP AS AN INTERNATIONAL AGENT: ANGLICAN COMMUNION

Being members of a church that is conscious of being part of a worldwide body can be problematic. The Anglican Communion is still the third-largest worldwide body after the Roman Catholic Church and the Orthodox Church, with more than 70 million members. So, the Roman Catholic Archbishop of Peru recognised us as a serious church, i.e. a historical church and not a recent upstart. But the name Anglican, evoking its English roots and colonisation generally, is more negative. For some with longer perspectives, the first Anglicans in South America were British pirates like Captain Drake! For others they were modernists/liberals, whatever, professing acceptance of women priests and homosexual practices. The Falklands War produced tensions not just in Argentina but throughout South America. Continental solidarity demanded opposition to European land claims, but often national sympathy sided with Britain against the unpopularity of Argentina itself, which at times had adopted an air of superiority to other South American countries, especially those with a more 'mestizo'—mixed blood population.

I remember being frustrated because when Archbishop Desmond Tutu was awarded the Nobel Peace Prize it was not always mentioned that he was a bishop in the Anglican Church. Most newspapers gave the impression that he was a bishop of the Roman Catholic faith. One of my most enduring memories was a journey shared with a visiting black African bishop from Tanzania. We were together in Chile and Bolivia. He caused a great sensation, both as an attractive Christian and as a black Anglican.

The viability of being a 'comprehensive church' was also a concept not easily understood or accepted in South America. Although we had long had our 'independent' province of the Southern Cone of South America, we were still beholden to Canterbury and our historical origin. When women bishops were legally consecrated in the United States there was a move for an unwelcome visit from the north to the south to enlighten us! We politely refused that time.

Among our first contributions in the opposite direction was to send first an Anglican woman, Silvia Roitberg, to the A.C.C. (Anglican

Consultative Council) and then a Peruvian Lawyer, Julio Lozano. The
motive was to augment the lay element in leadership worldwide. We also
sought as a province to influence the Lambeth Conference of 1978 to
discuss seriously the issue of lay celebration of the Holy Communion.
Our provincial theological commission under the Revd John Cobb did a
lot of research and produced a substantial paper which made it into the
discussions at the Lambeth Conference. Despite the geographical
dimensions of the issue, which affected us particularly in new dioceses in
South America, the then Roman Catholic practice of communion by
extension was deemed better and less controversial. I once sat next to a
nun in an aeroplane in northern Peru who was taking six months' worth
of consecrated elements to churches in the Andes mountains!

We were also involved in the ARCIC discussion process. This was and
is the international body composed of both Anglican and Roman Catholic
leaders seeking to move towards a united church. Our official report
sought to stress that the Roman Catholicism of South America did not
equate with European Catholicism. This made the very carefully crafted
theological statements of the ARCIC report seem foreign and unreal.
This was the continent on the one hand of liberation theology, where
issues of theological nicety were irrelevant, and social reform, if not
revolution, were paramount. On the other hand, syncretism between
animistic religion and continental and largely Spanish culture had been
living together for over 500 years. I have referred elsewhere to the
unusual but still practised human sacrifice in the Andes, where the
supporters declared that they were South American Catholics and not
Roman Catholics. At the popular level celibate priesthood and the anti-
contraception stance of the Vatican were deeply unpopular and poorly
observed.

But international connections also had their positive side. We sought
to get members travelling to other countries to visit other branches of the
Anglican Church. Our A.C.C. representative Julio Lozano never forgot
his visit to the U.K. He had a photo of himself with the Archbishop of
Canterbury. But even more memorable for him was seeing a photo of
himself on his host's breakfast room wall in the U.K. asking for prayer
support. He felt a member of the worldwide (catholic) church. How often
we had to justify the credal use of the word 'catholic', stressing that it
meant worldwide, universal and not a narrower allegiance to Rome!

By contrast I remember a conversation with a Peruvian member of the
big National Evangelical Peruvian denomination. His vision was totally

national. He was moving to Chile and he was really thrown by the idea that his denomination had no members there!

Anglicans are encouraged, with other Christians, to think globally and act locally. In our technological age we cannot be ignorant of the global scene. Even in those parts of the world that have been more isolated by geography and history before the 21st Century, ignorance must be more culpable now than ever before, and a narrow vision of the church less sustainable.

Part of the role of a bishop is to foster the sense of the universality of the Church. The bishop is a sort of Foreign Secretary to foster relationships and interchange with the other 40 (since autumn 2018 with the addition of the new Province of Chile) provinces of the Anglican Communion — that makes a lot of bishops of all shapes and sizes, languages and cultures. The tradition since 1867 is for them to meet together at a so-called Lambeth Conference once every ten years. The first met literally—but non-residentially—at Lambeth Palace, but since then numbers have grown exponentially. They have been meeting recently in the facilities of Kent University in Canterbury. In 1998 there was a core of 700 bishops present, from some 160 countries of the world. Attempts have been unsuccessful to move the venue from Canterbury to other places in the world, especially Africa. However, friction has been high on doctrinal issues in recent decades, and 2008 marked the last Lambeth Conference that attempted, unsuccessfully, to gather Anglican bishops from all the provinces. A significant number met elsewhere and did not go to Canterbury. Because of this, the 2018 conference didn't happen. However, another attempt was being made in 2020 to call all together. It does seem that significant numbers of bishops will continue to meet in a parallel conference, at a different date and location, as in 2018 in Jerusalem. I have been very privileged to attend three Lambeth conferences, in 1978, 1988 and 1998. I was only just 40 in 1978, so was one of the youngest on the block.

Only Denis Singulane of Mozambique and Hugo Pino, the Bishop of Honduras were just younger. Quite a number of bishops have never attended a Lambeth Conference. It depends on the date of their consecration and how it fits in with the normal ten-year intervals of the gatherings. Needless to say, they are incredible experiences, mind-stretching and challenging, but also hugely encouraging in sensing something of the vast complexity of the way the Anglican Church has developed around the world.

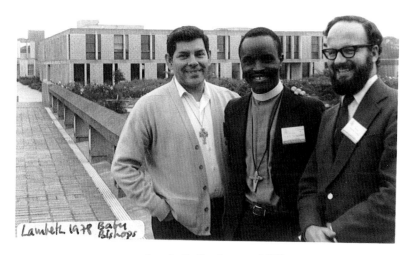

Lambeth Conference 1978,
with Hugo Pina (Honduras) and Denis Singulane (Mozambique)

Lambeth Conference 1988 (ten years later)

The universal church has always had conferences. The first was described in the Bible in Acts 15, in Jerusalem in the first century, to sort out relationships between Jewish Christians and Gentile Christians around the Mediterranean. Between 325 and 869 there were major international councils in Nicaea, Constantinople, Ephesus and Chalcedon. Then came the Lateran Council, the Council of Trent in 1545–63 and the First and Second Vatican Councils of 1869 and 1966. So, the Lambeth Conferences have a long history before 1867. However, they never pretended to be ecumenical councils of the universal church, only episcopal conferences of the Anglican Communion as part of the one Holy Catholic and Apostolic Church. Problems arose in the worldwide expansion of the Anglican Communion in the 19th Century. They were the provision of authentic episcopal ministry and the limits acceptable to genuine orthodoxy. Today we still struggle with issues of provincial

Talking over a cup of tea with the Bishop of Durham
Lambeth Conference 1988

autonomy and how to resolve conflicts caused by diversity of interpretation of theology in very different cultures.

Lambeth 1988
Speaking for Resolution 88/002
against Women Bishops on Monday 1st August – in Spanish!

The decision of the 74th General Convention of the Episcopal Church (U.S.A.) to confirm the election of a priest in a committed same-sex relationship to the office and work of a Bishop was the decisive event to fracture the Anglican Communion. The statement at the time in 2003 underlined that "what we hold in common is much greater than that which divides us in proclaiming Good News to the world." Episcopal life in the Anglican Communion has not been the same since that time, and the future remains unknown. At the time of writing, the next Lambeth Conference was planned for July 2021, but how authentic and representative of our universal membership it will be remains to be seen.

b. Highlights from Lambeth Conferences

Latin American Bishops with Archbishop Robert Runcie

As just mentioned, I was very fortunate to attend three Lambeth Conferences, in 1978, 1988 and 1998. This is unusual, as they only happen once every ten years. I was consecrated a bishop just before my 40th birthday in June, so I just got in in 1978 for the July gathering in Canterbury. That was an overwhelming induction experience. I spent some time getting the signatures of all the Archbishops and well known bishops in a copy of a book about Canterbury. I could hardly believe I was at the conference on the same basis as they were!

However, if I came as a 'baby bishop' to the 1978 conference, others came with a sense of the history of the previous two conferences of 1958 and 1968 when the importance of the continent of South America had been noted. I append now the full text of the statement issued by the bishops of CASA, the Anglican Council of South America. This was distributed to all present at the 1978 gathering.

Translation:
From the Bishops of the Anglican Council of South America

We greet our brethren at Lambeth 1978 in the name of Christ. We pray that justice, peace and joy in the Holy Spirit of the Kingdom of God will be with you. Lambeth 1958 and 1968 called our attention to the Continent of South America as a strategic area for Anglican growth. We feel obliged to renew this call with continued vigour and urgency due to the following factors:

The spiritual needs of the un-evangelised

South America continues to be a mission continent, made up of a majority of 'sacramentalised' but 'non-evangelised' peoples. In spite of the presence of the Roman Catholic Church over 400 years, and the more recent work of the Pentecostal denomination, the vast majority of the population do not belong to a church. Its enormous capital cities are among the most rapidly growing in the world and current total population is 200 million, which continues to grow as birth control is an option only open to the rich. Up to the present date there are only 50,000 Anglicans.

Our relationship with the Roman Catholic Church

We are satisfied to see a new opening on the part of the Roman Catholic Church to accept the plurality of agencies undertaking the task of making Christ known. Celibacy has put a serious brake on the vocation of Latin Americans to the ordained ministry of the Roman Catholic Church. A large percentage of priests are currently foreigners. Many South Americans have received a considerable degree of political indoctrination, although they are not aware of Christian doctrine. Our contribution to the teaching of the Christian faith is both necessary and appreciated.

True progress in the Anglican task

We have seen a response to the call of Lambeth 1968, and we thank God for the generous help already received. Church planting has increased significantly in the cities. The number of members of the Church has grown at the same rate as the population. An ever-increasing number of South

Americans are being ordained. Nine of our 15 bishops are from indigenous backgrounds. Human and financial resources have been channelled into programmes destined for the relief of suffering and the creation of employment.

The wealth we are able to offer to the Anglican Communion

This includes the already proven methods of long-distance Theological Education, church planting in urban and rural areas, spontaneity in church services, varied types of ministry and knowledge of liberation theology in its own context.

The potentially explosive socio-political situation

The capital cities of South America are real 'melting pots and barrels of explosives', to quote Arnold Toynbee's apt and colourful description. The majority of us live in countries controlled by military governments. In many areas there are clear human rights violations, social injustice and economic exploitation. We are searching for the way to support people in their needs and carry out a prophetic and pastoral ministry.

Formation of the Anglican Council of South America

This has been of decisive importance, in order to implement initial coordination of the ten dioceses which (apart from those of Argentina, Eastern South America, and Venezuela) have developed the work of the Episcopal Church of the United States of America, and the English, Irish and Australian Missionary Societies in South America. For the first time as a continent, minimal structures are in place to evaluate priorities, share resources and coordinate strategy. We give thanks for the formation of CASA and in 1974 for the historic first visit of the Archbishop of Canterbury to South America. WE ARE RESOLVED THAT SOUTH AMERICA WILL NOT CONTINUE TO BE THE ABANDONED CONTINENT. The doors are still open. The next ten years will be critical for this immense and extravagant continent, which is in a constant state of upheaval and desperate need. It will certainly figure on the political and economic map, and from the point of view of its enormous natural resources. We cannot fail in our common association in the decade 1978–1988 to present the living Christ to its people. We may never again have another opportunity such as this.

I was much more involved in the 1988 Lambeth Conference. It had been decided that it would be beneficial to organise some pre-Lambeth Conference regional gatherings of bishops. Partly so that regional bishops could relate more to each other and partly so that subjects for discussion and debate could be reviewed. We had a Western Hemisphere Pre-Lambeth Consultation in Peru in 1986! Because of the disproportion of the numbers of Anglican bishops in the area of North, Central and South America, invitees were the bishops of Central and South America and just the Archbishops of North America and Canada. We were a group of 50 people including advisers and speakers. Archbishop Ted Scott of Canada was the convenor and he and his staff did much of the organisation. However, a lot of local planning and coordination fell to me as the local bishop and I remember being totally shattered and sleeping for hours at the end! The most appreciated aspects of the consultation were 'companionship and sharing', 'participation in issue groups' and 'new information about Anglicanism in the various areas'. Strong proposals were made for full use of wide translation facilities for Lambeth and for more such regional consultations.

1986 Pre-Lambeth in Peru (Western Hemisphere)

I managed to arrange for Gustavo Gutiérrez of Liberation Theology fame to address us and for the Cardinal Roman Catholic Archbishop of Peru to visit us and bring us his greeting. We had a reasonably successful 'talent night' but the planned Latin American BBQ never materialised!

One of the suggestions from the above consultation was that the Archbishop of Canterbury nominate a bishop from Latin America to be added to the 1988 Lambeth Conference Planning Committee. That I believe is how I found my way on to the St Augustine Seminar from 16th July to 7th August 1987 in Carlisle College, Blackheath, England.

This was a small group with representatives from the 28 provinces of the Anglican Communion to continue planning for the 1988 Lambeth Conference. It was pretty high-powered! I was asked to lead a Bible Study group. Among its members were the Archbishop of York, John Habgood and Archbishop Desmond Tutu! We were given a masterly

with Gustavo Gutierrez, Lambeth 1988

overview of the expectations and subjects to be debated. Archbishop
Runcie commented that the British bishops were hoping for 'documents',
the Americans for 'an experience' and the Third World bishops for
'assistance in their poverty or their struggles'. But I believe and hope the
white domination of Lambeth Conferences is over. He also opened the
question of whether the Anglican Communion needed or wanted some
international legal appellate structure to resolve doctrinal issues. Or
would that be setting ourselves up as an additional universal church like
the Roman Catholic Church? He indicated, however, that "the 1988
Conference would be a complete failure of vision if we spent our entire
time on the identity and coherence of Anglicanism".

1986 Pre-Lambeth in Peru, with Cardinal Landazari

We produced a set of papers which served as a preliminary workbook
for the Conference. Among my contributions was a piece on poverty from
the South American perspective. Partly as a result of this involvement I
was invited to address the Episcopal Convention in the U.S.A. after the
Lambeth Conference on the whole area of social justice, commenting on
the relevant Lambeth documents. That was a pretty frightening
prospect. The U.S. bishops sit in seniority order from the front, with the

oldest and retired sitting in 'coffin corner'. I don't think any stayed awake until the end of my address!

1987 Pre-Lambeth in Blackheath, St Augustine's Seminar

In the Episcopal Convention I felt more like a fish out of water than in the Lambeth Conference itself. It was not international in the widest sense, in language or culture. Procedures were definitely North American and therefore seemed strange. Of course, Lambeth procedures must also seem foreign to those assisting in Canterbury from Africa, etc. for the first time. In 2008 the Lambeth Conference deliberately adopted some procedures following more relaxed Third World cultures.

It wasn't helpful that I had not understood the terms of my invitation fully, so for most of the time I was hungry, not having enough money to buy any substantial meals!

The 1998 Conference, the third and last one that I attended, was different again. I was still technically the Bishop of Peru, though heading to be a full-time assistant bishop in the English Diocese of Bradford. So, in a sense I was neither fish nor fowl. I certainly didn't yet feel at home with my English compatriots, but I had left my South American colleagues. At the same time together with Dorothy I was involved in doing some simultaneous interpretation from English into Spanish. This is not as easy as you might imagine it to be! Even if you regard yourself as fluent in both languages, being able to produce a coherent rendering of an address, or worse still, a rambling speech, is no mean feat and so very tiring. Dorothy achieved great things and also went once to interpret at a meeting of the International Meeting of the Anglican Communion Consultative Council in Scotland.

In my notes I found this challenging piece from an address by Archbishop Bob Runcie:-

> Does your word and your life come over *fresh* and new? Does it astonish?
>
> Does it disturb? Not just the bland leading the bland.
>
> Is it extravagant? Great promises and unlimited expectations.
>
> Does it promote joy?
>
> Does it produce love? Free us from oneself to serve others?

My prayer letter of September 1988 to our prayer supporting churches in the U.K. was rather upbeat. I quote:

The Archbishop of Canterbury's Lambeth Conference

This official bank account name accurately describes events between 16th July and 7th August. Historically since 1867 it is accurate, as the Archbishop invites to Lambeth the bishops of the Anglican

Communion (of which there are now something over 600) and in 1988 it was accurate to describe the present occupant's outstanding leadership in the face of the prophets of doom forecasting the dissolution of the Anglican Communion. As a family of churches we have moved away from the liturgical bond of a Common Prayer Book; we have moved away from the doctrinal bond of the 39 Articles and a common acceptance of the historic threefold ministry. But the historical bond symbolised in the person and office of the Archbishop remains and has been strengthened for good or ill. New 'instruments of unity' are being proposed but are of doubtful efficacy. I think we are moving towards a world federation of national churches rather than being an international communion. Despite this realistic note, the Lambeth Conference (the 12th so far) was once again a remarkable event. I have thought of the existence of the Anglican Communion as being similar to that of the unicorn! It is said to exist; claims are made about its prowess; there are masses of stories, even testimonies, but few finally are completely sure it does exist. I would judge that most of the 520 bishops present this year would testify that the Anglican Communion does exist, even if increasingly it should be included in one of Mr Ripley's series of books 'Incredible but true!'

The cross-cultural experience is an eye-opener for any parochially or even provincially minded bishop. This was instanced in the tree planting ceremony to commemorate Hiroshima Day when the Burmese and Japanese Primates were assisted by the Primates of Canada, the USA and All England. It was also instanced by the availability for the first time of simultaneous translation facilities and the use of French and Spanish in the official plenary debates. I believe my intervention from the floor in the debate on the consecration of women to the Episcopate was the first time that Spanish had been used at a Lambeth Conference. Fortunately others followed in breaking the monopoly of the English language. Whether the Western world's conference procedures can also be modified to accommodate Third World ways of doing things will have to be seen.

The parallel three-week wives' conference was greatly enjoyed by Dorothy. There were series of excellent workshops, tremendous opportunities to meet and talk, and great goings-on in the Lambeth Palace when Mrs Runcie invited the wives over. Singing and dancing was led by the West Africans with great involvement by all! And of course, they had a fuller involvement in the main Lambeth Conference itself. Ten years ago the wives were only present for one week and in separate accommodation.

Of course the international involvement often went much further than the Anglican Communion. These four photos give a sample of many conferences and congresses and other gatherings.

Global Consultation of the Forum of Bible Societies
De Bra Christian Centre, The Netherlands, April 1994

The Pope in Peru in 1985 praying for Anglicans!

3rd Assembly of Churches in Chile, Concepcion, Chile, February 1995

Protestant and other Church Leaders to meet the Pope in Lima

5D
A BISHOP AS A PASTOR: BRADFORD DIOCESE

Letter Writing

Letter writing used to be a literary art. Receiving a letter could be a real delight. Social media have now applied a brake on the flow of epistolary communication, if not a virtual stop. Norms of written letter-writing have disappeared. A modern communication might begin with the word "Hi" . . . if that is a word even allowed in Scrabble. Flourishing prose is cut back to the basics, spelling and pronunciation have become optional extras. Key national figures still have their correspondence preserved for posterity, though it is more likely to be digitalised than preserved on parchment with beautiful copperplate handwriting, as the letters of George I published recently from the Windsor Castle Library.

Diocesan Council, Bradford
Bishop's Council, Residential, Parceval Hall, May 1990

Despite the convenience of multiple e-mail communications in many dioceses there are still instances of the literary art of good letter writing. It is possible to receive a beautifully headed sheet of writing paper, personally 'topped and tailed' with a genuine flourish of an episcopal signature (though not often with the traditional Latin abbreviation of the name of the see—Justin Cantuar or Sentamu Ebor) and this even if the main content of the letter is actually typed.

Writing letters is an episcopal activity. If you count St Paul as a proto-bishop, we still have a number of his letters, forming a good part of the Bible's New Testament. While I was a bishop in Bradford (1988–1993) I wrote a lot of letters. I know how many because I have just reread all those carefully filed by my brilliant secretary Valerie Raybould. I take samples from the three busiest years. In 1998 it was 1047 letters, in 1991 it was 1654 and in 1992 it was 1328, roughly four every single day. The vast majority were on Bradford diocesan business, others to do with my EFAC responsibilities which are filed elsewhere with CMS archives.

Valerie Raybould
My faithful P.A. in Bradford, 1988–1993, who typed thousands of letters!

Bradford Letters 1988–1993

Let me give you something of the flavour of those three years from 1990–1992, opening up a panorama of the sort of situations in which I found myself helping in an episcopal role in Bradford.

A large number of letters were bread-and-butter ones . . . sorting out preaching engagements, and eventually visits to all of the 167 churches in the diocese. By 1991 there were only two (Silsden and West Bradford) where it had not been possible to fix up a visit. Over this period there were also many invitations to visit churches of other denominations, often at comparatively short notice, which proved impossible.

Others had to do with specific areas of delegated authority. Within the Call to the North in a Decade of Evangelism we had a specific Year of Evangelism, whose organisation I had to oversee. I was also responsible for feeding information into our Senior Staff meeting of all clergy wanting to come to work in the diocese.

I had to be involved in the complicated situations when parish clergy had been approached to 'remarry' divorced people. By the regulations of the Church of England at that date, they couldn't do so without presenting a detailed rationale to the bishop. I never met the people concerned, but by letter I got to know quite a lot about them through their parish priest. I then had to make a judgment whether I could support the priest in the remarriage or support another course of action. Often, I did recommend a service of blessing. But legally the parish priest didn't have to follow my advice! Some parish priests accumulated numerous couples who seemed to have heard on the grapevine that they were more accommodating than others. Not a satisfactory situation, but an attempt to put a brake on the downhill path into 'anything goes'.

A constant stream of letters had to be sent off to diocesan clergy for all sorts of pastoral reasons. These included anniversaries of their ordination, or their institutions; health and retirement issues; difficult internal issues in their work where advice had been sought or warnings needed to be issued. There was just one occasion where I had to submit evidence for court proceedings against a clergyman. This was a painful affair involving inappropriate sexual relationships. Two other cases had to do with a claim for racial discrimination against a hospital chaplain and a claim for sexual discrimination on the basis of evidence submitted to me from outside the Diocese of Bradford. I can remember getting 'pretty hot under the collar' on all three occasions. In only one case was the issue serious enough for a custodial sentence to be imposed. My testimonial letter to the solicitor did at least contribute to his sentence of imprisonment being mitigated to a considerable degree.

Over the years (1990–93) my files reveal quite a consistent correspondence with several vicars in particular. The circumstances were very different. I will just cite three examples:

The first one gives evidence that clergy come in all shapes and sizes with all the rich diversity of gifts and temperaments involved. However, the results are not always positive. Having requested an invitation to visit in one parish, I received this reply:

> Please inform me when you would like to come, or better still, just drop in. I am however, unwilling to invite you to preach on anything except a specific Episcopal visit for some Episcopal office. This unwillingness on my part is to save you from being embarrassed by the dictation of 'limits' which have to be imposed in our normal Sunday liturgies. Services here have to be strictly timed in order not to abuse the older and younger congregations when our junior church combines with the older members at the offertory. Sermons have to be within the scope of 7–10 mins. A limit which I would not wish to impose upon you, but in fairness to the congregations would be obliged to. Therefore, I invite you to be with us and look forward to your 'dropping in' to share in the great riches of our fellowship.

On the one hand this could be evidence of a very protective sensitivity for his congregation's feelings; on the other hand it doesn't show much faith in the sensitivity of a visiting bishop to adjust either his style or length of address to suit the occasion. Of course, this goes with the job, and in fact is part of the challenge and joy of itinerant ministry with different church congregations nearly every Sunday (and weekdays!) of the year.

I remember being a bit shocked when, years ago, a bishop told me he preached the same confirmation sermon every time for a year. He obviously produced the very best he could. It was always well prepared. Probably his wife didn't accompany him regularly! And then, come the turn of the year, he ditched it completely and worked a radically different approach for the next 12 months.

However, back to my slightly reluctant vicar. I got a different picture some 18 months later. I had to be in touch with the same vicar because I had received a deputation from people involved in a wedding at this church. The bride's mother and the local florist spent an hour with me complaining about their treatment. I quote from my letter to the vicar:

> Both of these people had a number of complaints about the manner they were treated by the verger and by you. They were not vindictive but felt others could be turned away. Apparently, the bride's father was constrained

> to stand up at the wedding reception and apologise to the guests for some of
> the things said in the church. So that you are clear what the issues are,
> may I just from the notes that I jotted down during the interview, mention
> a few things. They were very put out by the long harangue at the start of
> the service, which included, from their point of view, language which was
> bordering on the coarse. They were also concerned, that on a number of
> occasions, you used the term 'not my problem' when they were seeking to
> find solutions to practical issues in the arrangements of the flowers and the
> use of keys for the church. As I said at the beginning, I am more than ready
> to hear your side of the issues and I would ask you please to get in touch
> with me, perhaps on Tuesday or Wednesday of next week, to see when we
> can meet up to get this sorted.

Who would be a bishop? Certainly, occasions for peace-making and
keeping abound. Fortunately, it was only this once that I had a vicar
accused of being an 'uncouth ayatollah'!

Another vicar I had fairly extensive correspondence with over this
three-year period brings back rather happier memories. The relationship
started when I was preparing to institute him into a living in the Diocese
of Bradford. He and his wife had come over for lunch and he had brought
up his unhappiness about the taking of oaths, which traditionally feature
in the legal part of the institution of a new vicar. After our discussion I
wrote to him:

> I am very glad we had that opportunity and I hope you will forgive me
> for enclosing with this note a summary of the biblical evidence relating to
> the taking of oaths. I must admit that I have never looked at this myself
> before and found it a useful exercise. I trust that, as you look through it and
> consider your own forthcoming institution, that you will feel happy to take
> the traditional wording in the service.

Having surveyed the biblical evidence, I concluded:

> The use of the divine name in cursing and swearing is obviously
> forbidden. Christian speech is to be marked by truthfulness and
> straightforwardness. The sophisticated distinctions of Pharisaic religious
> leaders are out. But though swearing/oathtaking as a cover for lying and
> untruthfulness is out, any form of swearing as a solemn pledge in such
> undertaking is permissible.

This last point would seem to be particularly relevant in the legal part
of a public ceremony of the established church of the realm. When God's
kingly role is perfectly fulfilled oaths will be superfluous, as truth will
reign supreme. But now, given the fallen nature of the world order,
where untrustworthiness and distrust abound, where one's own fallibility

and sinfulness is not to be discounted, and where one is relating specifically to Caesar's world, it seems to me that the Christian conscience should be free to take a solemn oath of the nature of those involved in the Institution service.

I received a very gracious response:

> I appreciate you taking so much time to look into this matter of oaths. In short, you have persuaded me! If I am honest it is some years since I gave the matter any thought and it was good to be challenged on the subject. I shall be happy to go along with the usual wording.

It was a relief to me as well. No need to get the Archdeacon and Diocesan Registrar involved! This interchange was the prelude to a number of others involving the internal reorganisation of the church, which the vicar was concerned to make more dynamic. Later in my life the expression 'pushing the boundaries' became widespread. The boundaries being the grey area between the traditional shape of Anglican parish structures and the more modern flexible alternatives. The principle at issue is to be clear where the key decisions are made. Busy and active lay people don't appreciate being invited to a late evening or weekend meeting to rubber-stamp a plan or policy that has already been agreed upon by others. In the above case I asked the vicar to clarify what the function of a 'group of strategic leaders' was, as separate from the P.C.C.

The good ongoing relationship with this vicar may also have had something to do with that Institution service (referred to over and above concerning swearing oaths). On that occasion I preached on Isaiah 49:2 "The Lord made me into a polished arrow". I quote a summary which I passed on to a colleague from South America, who was just about to be ordained for work in England. I just give some of the headings:

> An arrow is the result of a lot of hard work, because of course it does originally come from the cutting down of a tree! (A reference to an unsuccessful tree felling attempt with that friend in Córdoba, Argentina.)
>
> An arrow also has to be ready for instant use, it has to be sharp, and it needs to be in good hands, and from the bow of course it receives power and direction.

Both men are continuing in good Gospel ministry.

Another vicar was a lively character who would put his strongly-held views into his parish magazine at times. There is no way that a bishop can read the monthly magazines of all the parishes in the diocese. But one way or another, he sees a fair number, and would at the very least pick up a copy on his preaching and teaching visits. On this occasion I had read the magazine and wrote; I quote

> I have been enjoying your parish magazine and I was pleased to see that you yourself had written on the subject of God. We seem to teach and preach about everything other than God, so I welcome that emphasis. However, I would just like to comment on the paragraph where you state, "The first step, I believe, is to get rid of the medieval concept of heaven, hell and judgement, and show the real meaning behind the parable of the Prodigal Son".

Quite an exchange of letters took place. I finished with the sentence:

> One of the exciting things about the ordained ministry is the tension, one hopes a creative one, between the pastoral concern of the Shepherd, the outreach and evangelistic concerns of the Fisherman, and the adventurous probing of the intrepid Explorer.

My correspondent could be very eloquent. He didn't have much time for people who gave the impression that they had got God 'taped'. He found fundamentalism in all its forms pretty obnoxious, but the following paragraph shows how sensitive he was to the, at times, overwhelming real-life experience of many people.

> I feel as if I've just been through a mangle. Nine deaths in three and a half weeks, through my visits I've been treated with great kindness by atheists, agnostics, lapsed Catholics, Methodists, Calvinists and nominal members of the Church of England. There's the lady who was looking forward to her Golden Wedding in September; an old mate of mine mourning his only son; the sudden death and the indescribable agony of the death of his six-year-old child.

He continued to write about a God who exposes himself to our suffering, opening wide his arms on the cross and is always there for us. A good parish priest is inevitably in touch with a fair amount of human suffering. As well as showing genuine empathy with his parishioners he has to deal with deep questions in his own life and understanding of God.

I was delighted to be reminded of the final sentence in my correspondent's last letter:

> All my love from the impetuous Peter of St Peter's and sometimes too the doubting Thomas of the same abode.

My last preserved letter to a vicar dates from some 18 months later and was as follows:

> Please find enclosed the cheque for £5 to pay to the young lad in the choir who is planning a fast for the Sudan. I am delighted to be able to contribute to that. Thank you for looking after me so well on Sunday. I

thoroughly enjoyed my visit, both the church, the service and the people. I also congratulate you very warmly on the contents and the presentation of your annual report. I think it is one of the best that I have ever seen. With every good wish in Christ.

Some special correspondence from 1988–1993

Provost of Bradford Cathedral, the Very Revd Brandon D. Jackson

I wrote to Brandon soon after my installation ceremony in Bradford Cathedral in February 1989. I thanked him for his warm hand of friendship to us and also his hospitality to the Revd Kenneth and Mrs Hooker from Christ Church Cockfosters. They had come up from London where he had been our vicar, sending us off for Peru in 1965.

I later wrote to Brandon Jackson, when he was appointed Dean of Lincoln Cathedral. I wrote to him in 1989:

> We were told before we left South America that the cultural re-orientation would be rather like the after-effects of a funeral, or indeed of having an amputation. I can't think we did find it as traumatic as that, partly, perhaps, because we received wise advice to look forward and not backwards. I am sure that will be your attitude as you face the new task that the Lord has given you in Lincoln.
>
> Dorothy and I are determined to have you in our home in Shipley (our episcopal bungalow as one local inhabitant calls it!). We must also have a game of squash in the Shipley Club beforehand.

Well, we did play squash, on the basis of which I wrote to him when, quite soon afterwards he moved to Lincoln. I attach his return letter to me in which he alludes to "my squash guide" — the use of squash terminology and tactics amusingly applied to the difficult task of leadership in a very conservative and restrictive ministry setting. The letter interchange became all the more poignant with hindsight when the situation in Lincoln became unsustainable. I was later to receive a letter from Brandon:

> We have been overwhelmed by hundreds of letters and cards (over 800!) all saying the same thing! *Thank you* for your love and support. The last 13 months have been pretty grim and now that it is in the public domain — which we dreaded all the more — your support has lifted our spirits enormously. We are praying that this sorry business will turn out to the furtherance of God's Kingdom here in Lincoln and beyond. How lovely to hear from you — the promise of prayer from so many folk has helped us enormously—please pray for truth to prevail.

Douglas Johnson

D.J., as he was always known, was the first General Secretary of the I.V.F. — the InterVarsity Fellowship, which over many years had a spectacular influence on thousands of university students around the world. He was a uniquely gifted person. The following letter came to me (28.12.1990) while I was in Bradford. I had been active in the Christian Union in Cambridge (C.I.C.C.U.) and afterwards had served a couple of years on the National Student Executive of the I.V.F.

It was when I was President of C.I.C.C.U. there that I visited him in his home in Cheam to talk about Christian work in the world's universities. He had an immense library classified in his own way. Books were numbered and ordered in his shelves according to the date on which he acquired them! Fortunately, he had a marvellous memory. After my visit to him and because I was soon to get married, I received a wonderful letter of avuncular advice about sex. I haven't been able to find it, but I do remember that he used a number of cricket analogies, rather like the TV show's Citizen Khan! Certainly, it was his advice not to expect or aim to hit a six off every ball!

I do wonder how many of his wonderful letters still exist. The one I copy will I'm sure delight you. Sometimes his writing is almost illegible. So I have not photocopied it, for it would lose a lot of its idiosyncrasy.

It was also very gratifying to read his very complimentary comments about the ministry of the Revd Martin Parsons, my father-in-law.

The following extract gives an example of his style:

> SO WHAT I'M COMING TO IS
>
> That you ought to regard yourself as <u>honoured</u> to be used of God as <u>President</u> of C.I.C.C.U. 1962/63 because you were one "of the faithful men" who guarded and handed on the "the Treasure" of the Gospel, the Bible and the obedience to the Shepherd's voice which is <u>crucial in preserving our religious heritage</u>.
>
> Those who have Baronetcies, Orders of the Garter, C.B.E. are nowhere beside David R. J. Evans, M.A., P.C.I.C.C.U."

Throughout the six years I served in the Diocese of Bradford I was also spending a month a year on international travel (1988–93) as the International Coordinator of the Evangelical Fellowship of the Anglican Communion. In 1990 I visited and spoke 24 times in the U.S.A., Nigeria, Kenya, Sri Lanka and Singapore. No wonder it was difficult, sometimes, to arrange the yearly cycle of engagements within the diocese. The following letters, however, had no connection with EFAC but arose from our previous 20 years' service in South America with SAMS in Argentina and Peru. There are some interesting linkups.

Correspondence with Jimmy Holme

Jimmy and Ana Maria Holme
Good Shepherd Church, Lima

I had married Jimmy and Ana Maria in Lima. A very posh reception in the Lima Jockey Club. Jimmy's brother went on to be high in the Peruvian Government (Minister of Agriculture), when he emigrated to the USA. For years he sent Christmas cards with photos of his two sons; he was always inviting us to visit them in New York. Once he also wrote to invite me to consider moving to the Big Apple to become Rector of St Thomas' Church, quite a prestigious parish. We felt no inclination or calling in fact. It was only sometime later that I discovered he had been at a boarding school in Bentham. He described it as a small village in the West Riding of Yorkshire between Skipton and Lancaster. More than well-known to me as it was in the Bradford diocese. So Lima, Peru, New York in the USA and Bentham in Yorkshire were linked together.

Correspondence with Bishop David Sheppard

He wrote to me to consult about signing up to a Peru Support Group. He had been invited to do this by the Columban Fathers who had work in Peru. They had been accused by the right-wing *Expreso* newspaper in Peru of being linked to the Sendero Luminoso, the Peruvian terrorist movement, which also had a London-based branch to collect funding. They were organising a demonstration outside the Peruvian Embassy in Sloane Street.

The letter to be sent declared

> The defence of human life and human rights in no way implies a link with armed struggles such as Sendero Luminoso. We feel that by linking human rights work with support for the armed struggle, you negate the brave and valiant work of organisations working in the defence of human life and development.

I strongly advised Bishop David against signing the letter, though he was always fearless in supporting the underdog and the cause of social justice. The viciousness of the Shining Path movement had been compared to that of the Khmer Rouge, and even the previous United Socialist Coalition before the last election in Peru was unwilling to have anything to do with them.

I don't know whether the Bishop took my advice. The Columban Fathers were also in touch with the Roman Catholic Bishop Murphy O'Connor to try to secure his support. He would also by conviction have wanted to support the work of the Columban Fathers in Peru but been wary of being associated with the Sendero Luminoso's fundraising work in London.

This letter brought to mind another one from Bishop David in which he sent me a very moving press tribute for Archbishop Derek Worlock. They worked together in Liverpool as 'episcopal twins'. I got to know them both because they visited Lima together and I had a good deal to do with organising their stay. Bishop David stayed with us in our missionary home; we didn't really have a bed big enough for him! He was drawn, of course, to the attempts of the Peruvian government to 'organise' or control the illegal land occupation of huge areas of desert in the southern part of the capital. The proliferation of 'pueblos jóvenes' (new towns) rather than 'villas miserias' (areas of poverty) as in Argentina, was an enormous headache. I secured an interview with the Peruvian Minister of Housing, after we had shown Bishop David around some of the area and the burgeoning of a cluster of church congregations. (More details of this double episcopal visit are in my book *Have Stick – Will Travel*).

Mrs Mary Tanner

Mary Tanner was the long-term, and very respected, Secretary for the Board for Mission and Unity of the Church of England. She had been invited to address our diocesan synod in Bradford on the subject of the ARCIC dialogues—the doctrinal conversations between the Anglican and Roman Catholic Churches worldwide. I had first met Mary in Peru and she had stayed in our home in Lima, which she was visiting for an ARCIC consultation, also attended by Julian Charley from the U.K. (to whom I lent a book about the birds of Lima, which he enjoyed).

Subsequent to my hospitality offer in Bradford and Mary's acceptance, I found to my horror that I couldn't be present and so had to apologise profusely and arrange for her to stay with Bishop Robert Williamson. Rather embarrassing!

Gary Harris of the Foreign Prisoners Fellowship

We met Gary briefly in Lima. He had been in prison and visited us in our home prior to leaving Peru. His letter came out of the blue. I quote

> Greetings to you both in our living Lord Jesus Christ. I have seen two of my friends who you met on your journeys—the Revd John Goode and Sylvia Dyson—they mention how the Lord has been blessing you in your ministry in Bradford.
>
> I hope that I could see you both again—how the Lord's been treating you both, as I would love to share about the work in Brazil, São Paolo. Please get in contact with me—may the Lord bless you both continuously in your work. In Jesus' grip. Shalom.

The Bishop of Tver and Kashina

I received this exuberant Easter card (see overleaf) in 1992. I can't for the life of me remember how I met this Russian Bishop! However, he addressed me as "My dear David Evans!" so we must have had some real contact. The card was of course written in Russian. I was able, through the good services of Patrick Curran, our Chaplain to Students in the University of Bradford, to reach a Miss Sharon McJury who translated its message as printed below it:

My dear David Evans!

В день Великого праздника СВЕТЛОГО
ᵞᴴИСТОВА ВОСКРЕСЕНИЯ примите мое
сердечное поздравление и братское пасхаль-
ное приветствие ХРИСТОС ВОСКРЕСЕ!

Празднуя ныне сие мироспасительное со-
бытие, принесем торжественную хвалу Спаси-
телю нашему Господу Иисусу Христу, сокру-
шившему смерти державу и отверзшему рай-
ския двери христианскому роду, поющему
Ему победную песнь и славяще Его тридне-
ное из мертвых Воскресение.

Да подаст Вам Воскресший Христос ра-
дость, здравие, спасение и во всем благое
поспешение и многих лет жития Вашего.

ВОИСТИНУ ХРИСТОС ВОСКРЕСЕ!

С любовию о Воскресшем Господе

✝ Виктор

ЕПИСКОП ТВЕРСКОЙ И КАШИНСКИЙ

3. 6684

On this great feast of Easter

accept my heartfelt and brotherly greeting:

Christ is risen

Celebrating today this act of salvation,

we bring triumphant praise to our Saviour,

the Lord Jesus Christ, who breaks the hold of death

and opens the heavenly gates for Christian people.

We sing to Him a victory song and praise

of his glorious resurrection from the dead.

May the Risen Christ bring you joy, health and salvation.

CHRIST IS RISEN INDEED!

With the love of the Risen Lord

Mr Ian Strange MBE

Dorothy and I were delighted to see in the New Year's Honours List (1992) your name for your services as a Wildlife and Conservation Adviser in the Falkland Islands. Dorothy and I quite often have cause to think of your daughters Shona and Sharon. We have very fond memories of them both and of our meetings with yourself.

We offer you our warmest congratulations on your MBE. Some day perhaps we might make it to the Falkland Islands. It is certainly one of our dreams.

Mr Strange's two daughters stayed with us in Buenos Aires for a year, while they were at school locally on an Argentine and British scheme. They increased our 'children' from 3 to 5 for that year. Mr Strange donated several of his very fine bird prints to us (mainly penguins), which decorate our visitors' room now.

However, more importantly, in 2015 we were able to visit the Falklands on a Swan Hellenic cruise, on which I was a guest lecturer. We escaped for an afternoon and were taken around by Shona, then a police officer living in Port Stanley. We also briefly re-met her father, still working in the cause of conservation with his photography and painting and prints of wildlife. He is known as the Bird Man of the Falklands, having also designed a lot of the excellent bird stamps of the Falkland Islands. Our latest contact with our 'adopted' foster daughter, Shona, was in 2017 in the Orkneys, where she had emigrated to inherit a family farm. A wonderful meeting up occasion. How small the world is!

Bishop Colin Buchanan

One of the theological subjects on which we spent a good deal of time in South America was the lay administration of Holy Communion. This arose as a very practical issue with widely separated congregations in various republics. It affected me especially with the setting up of new work in different towns in the missionary Diocese of Bolivia. Our provincial theological commission examined the pros and cons and prepared material to be considered at the Lambeth Conference of 1998. The issue can be summarised in Colin Buchanan's words:

> The need to show theological reason why the presidency of the Eucharist should be restricted to ordained Bishops and Presbyters.

Colin Buchanan was acting as consultant to John Cobb, the chair of the Theological Commission of the Southern Cone of South America. Our previous effort to influence the Anglican Communion through the Lambeth Conference of 1988 had failed. But the issue had not gone away. Should it be reactivated? Alan Hargrave from Bolivia had produced a Grove Booklet on the subject. The issue was resurfacing because of increased expectancy for a weekly celebration of the Eucharist in many churches with the declining number of episcopally ordained priests. The solution lies in one of the three following ways:

(i) Communion by extension — i.e. by carrying the consecrated elements from one place to another (impossible on the South American geographical scale, I would think).

(ii) Ordering a 'local ordained ministry' (always needs debating but is open to certain very serious objections).

(iii) A reasonably well organised and disciplined lay presidency.

It seems to me the church is driven to the third.

But at the time of writing the Church still is trying a rather confused mix of the first two options.

A pot pourri of more unusual letters

Over the years in the Bradford diocese I had a number of requests for my signature from people whose hobby was to collect autographed letters. No problem, especially when the request came from someone who stated:

> I very much admire your dedicated work for the Church of England, both past and present as Assistant Bishop at Bradford. I do wish you good health, and many more inspiring years serving both God and Mankind for a better and more blessed world for us all!!

Regular welcoming letters had to do with invitations to theatrical productions at the Alhambra Theatre. I was particularly pleased to accept wherever possible, as my sister Ruth had played the lead role of Cinderella in a Christmas pantomime years before and had her photograph adorning the wall in the theatre.

There were invitations to present prizes on various occasions: from the Bradford Area Pathfinder Leaders for example, after a five-a-side football competition.

> It was felt that your reference to having been a Pathfinder yourself surprised and impressed quite a few of our members, keeping their attention alert to the rest of your presentation speech.

Invitations came regularly from the Captive Nations Committee of Bradford (Belarusian, Estonian, Hungarian, Latvian, Lithuanian and Ukrainian representatives). These were lively and colourful occasions, though tinged with high drama in the personal stories of why they had had to leave their homelands.

A surprising invitation came from Robson Lowe, a distinguished philatelist who had picked up from Debrett's *People of Today* that I collected stamps. Also a senior director of Christie's, he was involved in regular auctions of rare postal stamps with sales in New York, Zurich, Hong King, Melbourne and Singapore. I replied

I do not think my rather humble collection of stamps depicting ornithological themes which are linked to the Bible merits such august treatment. However, I was delighted to receive your letter as a fellow philatelist.

Assistant Chief Constable of Strathclyde Police

While on a preaching visit to Scotland I had had my episcopal clothes stolen from my car. I had to preach without them! The theft was reported to the police, who later the same Sunday summoned me to the police station, where a short procession of policemen and women marched in and solemnly handed over the purloined goods. The thieves had stolen my robes' case and a rucksack from our car. Soon after turning the corner of the road they had opened both, been dismayed and/or disappointed (or afraid!). They had thrown the clothes and the Bibles into someone's garden and made off, highly disgruntled, or maybe to go to confession! They were then passed on to the police, who enjoyed returning them to me unsullied. My letter of gratitude was appreciated by all concerned.

Reg Mark of Ohmeda factory

Just after a visit to this factory of hospital equipment in Bradford, the diocese received independently a copy of the *Lima Times* from Peru with a photo of a 'vaporiser', which was part of a donation from Britain. It had come from the factory I had just visited. This was a remarkable coincidence in timing as I pointed out to the Ohmeda manager.

Apostrophe letters

I'm afraid I have had a 'thing' about the correct use of the apostrophe. I have given up now and decided that if Shakespeare could cope with a huge variety of spellings and punctuation and still produce world-class literature, then who am I to be pedantic! But it still irks me.

I just give one example, sent to a northern province suffragan bishop:

Forgive me for drawing attention, or perhaps, your secretary's attention, to the difference between the two statements that follow:

Northern Suffragan's Study Day

Northern Suffragans' Study Day

The first is what was actually written on 24th May, the second is, I hope and trust, what we are seeking to promote! The first envisages the attendance of just <u>one</u> suffragan bishop. The second plans for the possibility of all the suffragan bishops of the northern province gathering together for a study day. Excuse me for pointing it out, it is a particular bee that I have buzzing around in my bonnet, as very few people nowadays seem to get it right, failing to understand the basic rules of grammar.

A sleepy Rural Dean

May I say thank you again for your 'input' on Tuesday. It was greatly appreciated. I apologise for dropping off several times, which was not a reflection on your performance at all. In actual fact, my wife and I stayed up rather late discussing the purchase of a house which is in process. This got my adrenalin pumping and I got thoroughly awake and had hardly any sleep in the end. The rather substantial lunch was the final straw!!!

I replied:

Thank you for your comment about my input at Parcevall Hall (our diocesan retreat house). I did very much enjoy being with you and I charitably assumed that you were deep in transcendental meditation and at least had reached the Seventh Heaven, when I noticed that your eyes were closed the other day! I was truly delighted to be with you once again with members of your deanery.

Opposition to evangelism

At a recent meeting of the Church Council we had a lengthy discussion regarding the document/questionnaire produced by your committee regarding the Decade of Evangelism.

The PCC has asked me, as its secretary, to write to you regarding this paper.

We, as a PCC, wish to be assured that literature of this nature will not be made available around our village. Irrespective of the views of the incumbent, we, as a PCC, feel it would not be helpful to our mission in this parish. This is the unanimous view of the members of the PCC present at our meeting on February 6th.

I replied carefully, as the letter revealed a possible difference of opinion between the incumbent and his PCC, while also accepting that there was acceptance of a mission to the parish:

I was surprised at your letter. The Decade of Evangelism document has been widely discussed through all the diocesan structures and comes with every recommendation for use within the parishes of the diocese. However, you do have a 'veto' on its use and no one else in your area will see the document apart from your incumbent and the members of the PCC. I feel sure there must be some misunderstanding somewhere along the line, and I would recommend you warmly to invite a member of the diocesan staff for a future meeting of your PCC to hopefully lay such misunderstanding to rest.

Carol McKenna, Campaign Director of Lynx

I am very happy to make a pledge on my own behalf and that of my family, my wife and two daughters, to support the Lynx campaign against the purchase and use of garments made of fur. I do believe that if people are not discouraged from committing acts of violence against the animal world with total impunity, those same people will feel encouraged to commit acts of violence against human beings. Life is sacred in all its manifestations because it has its origin in God the Creator. Therefore respect for life is a responsibility on the part of all of us. It was Lawrence Durrell who wrote that humankind had not been good gardeners. It is our responsibility to care for the totality of creation.

The anti-fur campaign Lynx was overwhelmed by support (among them 32 bishops). A booklet was published and widely circulated.

This seemed a successful campaign and I don't regret having supported it. However, some while later the supporting C. of E. bishops were taken to task by the Archbishop of Canada, Michael Peers, who spoke up for those in Northern Canada whose whole livelihood depended on the use of fur for survival clothing! A long way from the catwalks of Paris and high fashion clothing! You can't win them all.

Blackfriars Priory in Oxford re a Christian Declaration on Trident

This was a more difficult declaration to sign up to, because it was quite detailed in its denunciations. However, a large number of religious dignitaries of many denominations did so and it was duly released to the press. I don't remember any particular repercussions.

Helen Kemp, tree hugging with Matthew Fox and creation spirituality

I had met Helen in Shipley, Bradford, where she ran a small shop selling books and crafts and promoting intuitive gardening. She taught budding recruits how to meditate before communing with the plant/spirit world and told people of the importance of hugging trees and healing shrubs with their hands.

We not only corresponded but met up and talked. I wrote to her:

When I read the article on creation spirituality you sent me, there is much I wanted to underline, much that is eminently quotable and thought provoking, much that seeks to recover a lost dimension. However, in the end, as Matthew Fox admits, it is panentheism (God is everything). For all its attractiveness on various levels, spiritual, intellectual and moral, it is, in the end not Christian. It is *so* attractive in many ways, especially in a society sold down the road to a secular, if not atheistic, materialism, that I am sure it must be basically heretical! Christian teaching has tended to swing from being affirmative of the world to rejecting it. But it has centred on the miracle and wonder of the possibility of a personal relationship with God through the person and work of Jesus Christ of Nazareth, through the influence of the Holy Spirit. As the former Archbishop of Canterbury, Michael Ramsey wrote: "God is Christlike, and in Him is no un-Christlikeness at all".

Miss C. Ralph of Settle

Thank you so very much for sending me the homemade pair of socks that I received on my return from a journey overseas. I was delighted to receive them and in fact used them almost immediately, as I took part in climbing one of the three peaks in the Dales on Tuesday of this week, when the rural deans of the Craven Archdeaconry were doing a sponsored Three Peaks' walk for the charity Committed to Caring. So your socks on my feet have already been from Horton-in-Ribblesdale up to the top of Ingleborough. Thank you again for your kindness.

Dorothy Peake of Scargill House

Thank you so much for sending me a copy of the Benedicite of the Dales which you have written. I enjoyed very much reading out the part about birds, at the evensong service at Kelbrook just recently.

It did occur to me then, and I humbly make the suggestion, that if you do go ahead and get this printed, you might do well to think about ending up the text with an invocation to men and women, however you phrase it of course, locals and farmers and tourists, and whatever, for them to praise the Lord as well. This is part of the original Psalm 148, and of course is in the traditional Benedicite as well, and seems to me might put in an 'evangelistic' note at the end, and specifically addressed to people, rather than to the created world. Just a suggestion.

May I also take the opportunity of inviting you and Michael to come and have dinner with Dorothy and myself on 7th December. I know you have a very busy life and at this short notice it may be quite impossible, however we would love it if you were available on that date.

With every good wish in Christ.

BENEDICITE OF THE DALES

Bless the Lord, all created things,
praise Him and rejoice for ever;
Bless the Lord all hills and mountains,
Bless the Lord all crags and scars
of millstone grit and yoredale screes.

Bless the Lord all sparkling waters,
becks, streams and ghylls;
Bless the Lord all rushing mighty torrents
that today are, and tomorrow are but trickling peacefulness;
Bless the Lord all falls and forces
gathering strength and power from the hills above.

Bless the Lord all birds of the air
winging your way across hill and dale;
Bless the Lord all curlews of graceful flight and
rippling song announcing the arrival of spring;
Bless the Lord all moorland grouse
running and darting through the purple heather;
Bless the Lord all oyster-catchers and peewits,
flashing black and white on land and in the air;
Bless the Lord all handsome dippers
bobbing white-throated in fast-running streams;
Bless the Lord all aptly named wagtails
running and dancing - pied, grey and yellow;
Bless the Lord all birds of prey
soaring and diving midst thermals and space.

Bless the Lord all plants of the earth
growing in harmony to enhance the land;
Bless the Lord all flowers of the north
Bird's eye primrose so clear and bright
mountain pansy, and bell flowers so tall;
Bless the Lord all trees of the earth
tall and proud or stunted, leaning with the wind;
Bless the Lord all lichens and mosses
signs of pure air to refresh the tired soul.

Bless the Lord all sheep that graze peacefully
across hills, scars and meadows with lambs close at heel;
Bless the Lord all sheepdogs as you willingly gather
and herd at the call of the shepherd.

Bless the Lord all you Dales in variety and splendour;

PRAISE HIM AND REJOICE FOR EVER!

The Secretary of State at the Home Office

I have pleasure in informing you that on Tuesday the 1st September I shall be licensing the Revd Geoffrey Peters as Team Vicar in the parish of Manningham in the Diocese of Bradford. The normal contractual period for such an appointment is five years. Manningham has a highly significant population of people of Asian culture. The Revd Geoffrey Peters, as well as speaking several languages of the Indian sub-continent, has a remarkable experience of both Pakistani and British culture to equip him in his task. We are expecting him to make a unique contribution to the cause of good relations in the city, as well as witnessing to the multi-cultural nature of Christianity, a feature that is very much needed, as we face the implications of living in a society with an increasing diversity of creeds and cultures.

I sincerely hope that there will be no problem in extending the permission for the Revd Geoffrey Peters and his family to live and work here.

P.S. At present [2020] he is Presiding Bishop of the Province of Pakistan.

He had a good ministry in Bradford but returned to work in Pakistan, where he became a bishop.

West Yorkshire Court Welfare Service

This involved an inappropriate relationship that was developing between a priest and a young lad. The priest had already left for an overseas appointment but the young lad's mother and the clergy team in the priest's former parish requested my support to insist the clergyman ceased all contact. There had been an invitation to the lad to travel overseas for a holiday. The matter had been handled well. The boy's separated mother had written thanking the clergyman for his past help but stating that it had begun to interfere with her own relationship with her son and make her other child jealous. Though intimidated she had clearly asked the clergyman to break off all contact.

Our support for her and my letter to the clergyman were, I hope, definitive in preventing escalation into a difficult and damaging situation.

Accusations of heresy!

Can I please bring to your attention the TV report *Everyman* on Sunday 19th April 1992. I cannot express in words the horror when I listened to men who are ordained into the Church of England denounce the Resurrection of our Lord Jesus. As leader and a head of the C of E you have a God-given duty to make sure that a true doctrine is preached and believed in by your ordained ministers. It is your duty to stop people from being taught this blasphemy.

So this was not an accusation against anything that I had said myself but it was a reminder that it is very much part of the episcopal task to be defender of the faith. I replied:

> Thank you for your letter. It was good of you to write and express your righteous indignation. May I assure you not only of my own orthodoxy in this matter, but also my firm intention on every occasion to make it clear that I do not believe we can 'update' or 'modernise' the Gospel of God without robbing it of its converting power. Do not be dismayed. The vast majority of Church folk also believe this.

A second example was more personal and was directed at me personally for remarks which had been published in the *Yorkshire Post* on the subject of fundamentalists. I quote from my reply:

> Your recent letter to me was a bit of a sizzler! I don't know if you kept a copy of the *Yorkshire Post*, dear brother, but there are any number of complete misunderstandings in it.
>
> I enclose for you now my original article written for our monthly diocesan bulletin. Michael Brown (in the *Yorkshire Post*) seriously destroyed the balance and intention of my article by quoting bits he wanted to, in any sort of order. He is 'notorious' in such 'misuse' of original texts. I do ask you to read my original article carefully and prayerfully. I hope you feel that it clarifies most of the accusations of your letter. I am to be away for a month now. Should you want to discuss this further, I would be only too happy to do so. May the Lord bless you richly as you hold to the fundamentals of our revealed faith and as you speak the truth in love to Christian and non-Christian alike.

A letter from 'Barney'

Barney is an Anglo-Argentine, a member of the group that meets informally to discuss better relationships between Great Britain, Argentina and the Falkland Islands (Malvinas). It is called the South Atlantic Council. It meets once a year in the House of Commons. Every two years there is a day conference with 'Kelpers' from the Falklands present, if at all possible. I attended several times and received this letter from Barney in 1995:

> It was a pleasure to meet you in Oxford and many thanks for your participation in ABC 5 (Argentine British Conference). The bi-lingual service was much appreciated. It was fitting that Felipe Noguera, who did

such an excellent translating job, should be delivering your message: he
was one of the few 'Theo-sceptics' at the conference! (a reference to my
talk). God moves in a mysterious way . . . "

To conclude, and wearing my Anglo-Argentine hat, I would like to recite
a poem created by Harry Duggan, an estanciero from the Province of
Buenos Aires, which shows how the British first arrive, then identify with,
and finally become Argentines, with the help of farming—and sport: (each
of four verses by succeeding generations)

Some talk of Alexander, and some of Hercules
Of Hector and Lysander, and such great names as these.
But of all outstanding figures, there's none compares to date
With the British pioneers who came to live by the River Plate.

Some talk of shorthorn cattle, and some of Aberdeen
Of Herefords as well, sir, the best breeds ever seen;
Of Lincoln sheep and Romney, seen grazing far and wide
They were brought out here from Britain to be Argentina's pride.

Some talk of Boca Juniors, and some of River Plate.
Of Newells and Alumni, and other football great.
As I sit in my platea, I think "Che—qué fenomenal!
The ingleses they invented our deporte nacional".

Hablan de Bonaparte, de César y Mambrú
Acá nos inclinamos por el héroe de Yapeyú
Que tomando las ideas del lluvioso día de mayo
supo implantar con sus ganaderos a caballo!

*Notice the very interesting progression of colonial Englishmen into full
blown Argentines, each stage represented by one stanza of the poem.*

Translation of the fourth verse roughly:
Some talk of Bonaparte, of Caesar and Mambrú
Here we bow before the hero of Yapeyú
Who building on the ideas of that rainy day in May
Achieved their implantation with the gauchos!

I end this section with a few brief extracts from fellow bishops, mainly
from the Northern Province, with whom I had dealings during my time
in Bradford (1988–1993).

Bishop David Hope

(to whom I wrote as follows)

I write to offer you my warmest congratulations on the good news of your
translation from Wakefield to the City of London. I have no doubt that you

accepted with a good measure of apprehension and a deep sense of the need for the Lord's grace to face London's tremendous challenges.

His reply stated:

> It has been a truly agonizing decision to make. In so many ways I am happy here in the Diocese of Wakefield, and Wakefield has taught me all I know about episcopal ministry. I would therefore value greatly a continuing remembrance in your thoughts and prayers.

I had reminded him of a lighter moment in his Wakefield work.

> You will miss the North and those of us who are working here will also deeply miss you. I wonder if we will have the opportunity of doing another charismatic conga together at any time!

(A reference to a lighter moment of fellowship at an evangelism conference!)

Bishop Jim Thompson

> Sally and I were so pleased to get your letter. We have felt tremendously supported from so many quarters, especially by the Bishops. We believe that the enormous change will do us good and I hope may even be good for Bath and Wells. Perhaps all Bishops' jobs are rather alike when you scratch the surface.
>
> Surprised by Joy! That's what it's felt like. Now we're preparing for the bereavement of leaving East London after 25 years.

Bishop Gordon Bates

When the Bradford bishopric was vacant, three names, including mine and that of the above Bishop of Whitby, were touted in the local press.

> Thanks for the list of runners in the Bradford stakes. Don't think I will risk any great sum with Ladbrokes at this stage. Let's hope the Holy Spirit has a real hand and that the going is firm and good.

None of the three named people was appointed!

Bishop Peter Ball

The late Bishop Ball has of course been much in the public eye in recent years and indeed spent time in prison. This letter reveals how so many of us had no idea of what was going on in Litlington:

> I was delighted to hear of your appointment as the next Bishop of Gloucester. I do trust that God will give you the grace to be able to continue in the real work of ministry as you explained it to me, which is very often done by the suffragan bishops, because of the extra responsibilities and strains and tensions of being a diocesan. I am aware of these at the

moment, as I have a six-month vacancy-in-see that I am responsible for. I can appreciate the difficulties of keeping one's head clear and one's heart warm.

I passed your new house the other day when visiting my parents in Seaford, and had thoughts of dropping in, but we were fairly pushed for time. I wonder if the little vicarage in Litlington will ever be put on the market? I think I could quite fancy that as a retirement home in some 15 years' time!

He replied:

I think I am far too old (60) to be doing a big job but I know that Gloucester is a lovely place and that there are lots of people who will be wonderful allies and colleagues.

Bishop Richard Hare

Our family connections with the Hares went back a long way through South America and back to Preparatory School in Seaford, where I knew Richard Hare's brother quite well. Richard was Bishop of Pontefract as a suffragan when I arrived in Bradford and was very thoughtful.

I wonder how useful the stuff was I gave you with regard to doing your accounts. You may have an IBM compatible computer by now: if so, you might be interested to know I have written a spreadsheet which handles our accounts in the way the Church Commissioners want them set out. The whole idea of actually putting pen to paper, and then getting out a calculator belongs with the dinosaurs! One need never again do any arithmetic.

Richard was known as the most charismatic bishop of the bench in my active bishopping. His down-to-earth assistance with the monthly accounts was very helpful.

Bishop Graham Leonard

Bishop Leonard was my local presenting bishop when I went forward for ordination and for a curacy at Christ Church Cockfosters in 1965.

Please accept my apologies for not having the courtesy to advise you of a meeting at which I spoke recently in London. This was the memorial service for Kenneth Hooker at Christ Church Cockfosters, where years ago I was curate. I was very honoured to have been invited to give the memorial address and was reminded of my oversight by the presence in the service of Bishop Maurice Wood, who conveyed your greetings and good wishes.

It was a good and well attended service. Being the 17th November I had the audacity to compare Kenneth's life with that of Hilda of Whitby and

Hugh, Bishop of Lincoln, at least in the question of love of souls. I think he would compare very favourably with them.

Bishop Leonard went on to join the Roman Catholic Church over the ordination of women to the priesthood.

Bishop Christopher Luxmoore

I was written to by the above, whom I had met when he visited Lima years before. He was heading up a group of bishops supporting Cost of Conscience and Forward in Faith in 1993. I was invited to join as one who would approve the appointment of Provincial Visitors to minister to those unable in conscience to accept women priests. I was just moving from the Bradford diocese to my new job as General Secretary of the South American Mission Society, based in the Chichester diocese. At that time Chichester was a bastion of opposition. South America was also opposed. In the Bradford diocese I had abstained in the official diocesan vote in our house of bishops of two. Bishop Roy Williamson was in favour and I didn't feel it right to nullify his vote by opposing.

My reply ended:

> I am concerned and committed to serve the church in the best way possible. I am aware that there are a number of evangelical groups opposed to the legislation, but who have declared their intention of staying in the C. of E. structure. I feel I must still bide my time to discern how best I may be able to help.

Bishop Lindsay Urwin

While Assistant Bishop of Chichester for a while I had the audacity to suggest through the above Suffragan Bishop of Horsham that I could help with a confirmation at Christ's Hospital, where I had been at school. My desire to do this was strengthened by the fact that I had myself been confirmed there by the famous Bishop Bell, who had also years before confirmed my mother. So I thought another generation of connection with the old school would not be inappropriate. Bishop Urwin replied:

> Thanks for agreeing to confirm at Southgate in November '96. However, I'm afraid your 'brazen' request is unlikely to receive a positive response— Bishop Eric sets the agenda for the schools' confirmations and as yet I haven't had a look in myself at Christ's Hospital. I think he rather enjoys doing that one himself. But I shall ask on your behalf for 1997.

Subsequent to this interchange of letters, of course, Bishop Bell's name has been sullied by an accusation of child abuse. It's deeply sad that such an accusation, however false, leaves a stain.

Bishop Michael Scott-Joynt

Many thanks to you and Dorothy for your letter, your good wishes and your prayers following the news of my appointment to Winchester. Lou and I appreciate your apt understanding of 'translation' (from Stratford) as a particular kind of 'cross-cultural shock', which we are just at the beginning of freshly experiencing.

I'm very interested to hear of the presence of a Brazilian priest working among Portuguese immigrant workers in Jersey, and of SAMS's collaboration with the diocese in his support: I look forward to meeting him and learning at first-hand from him and from those among whom he works, of their lives and his ministry.

Bishop John B. Taylor

An association with Bishop Taylor began when I was curate at Christ Church Cockfosters. As a teacher of theology at Oak Hill College he was technically a member of the congregation. His wife certainly was very active and we worked together with youth organisations. Years later their son Nigel got engaged to Judy Hanson, serving with SAMS in Buenos Aires, Argentina. Bishop John wrote:

We are of course delighted about Nigel and Judy, though sorry to be depriving SAMS of Judy's invaluable services. May I say how deeply grateful Linda and I are at the generous way in which SAMS has treated Judy. We quite thought she might have to return for her tying up and handing over operations at her own expense. We shall be sending SAMS a thank offering!

I do hope you and Dorothy are well and finding the work of SAMS rewarding after your spell in Bradford. I cannot conceal the fact that I am very glad you are at the helm of such a strategically important work.

In later years we came together in senior honorary roles with the CMJ (Church's Ministry to Jews), he as Patron and I as President. Now that he has passed on to glory I have stepped into his shoes as Patron.

Bishop David Sheppard

A very special letter from Bishop David, repeating his BBC Radio 4 *Thought for the Day* (9th Feb 1996) on the death of Archbishop Derek Worlock, the Roman Catholic Archbishop:

I've been watching a very special friend dying in these last six months. Watching a close friend dying brings deep human feelings to the surface. Simple trust in God becomes more important than all the theological debates. In a joint book he and I wrote two years ago, we carefully chiselled words to describe what our faith meant. We wrote 'For both of us discipleship means a living, daily experience of the undeserved love of Christ, and a confidence that beyond this life He will take us to the Father: exactly how He will do it, we do not know, but we are prepared to trust.'

The personal letter from Bishop Sheppard was special because he and Archbishop Worlock had visited Peru together while I was Bishop there. We had a number of joint meetings both with the Peruvian Roman Catholic Cardinal Archbishop, and Government ministers. It had even been possible to get Bishop Sheppard to umpire a cricket match at the Lima cricket club, though I'm sure he was personally more interested in seeing what was being done to cope with the large invasions of Peruvians from the Andes mountains region, who took up precarious residence on the sand dunes around the capital city. It was possible to get him informed about this through a meeting with the current Peruvian Minister of Housing.

Good Shepherd XI, Lima, Peru

The writing and preaching of sermons

I feel like quoting the end of St. John's Gospel which states:

> Jesus did many other things as well. If every one of them were written
> down, I suppose that even the whole world would not have room for the
> books that would be written.' (John 21:25)

Remember that Jesus' public ministry in the Middle East only lasted
for three years! John didn't know about the future use of digitalization
for the storage of information in an economical way! But books about
Jesus and sermons about Jesus have continued to be published around
the world in countless languages for 2000 years.

Millions of sermons have been preached. The huge majority have
disappeared or been rightly disposed of. Some of the greatest preachers
have had theirs preserved in collections. But mercifully not all. Because
preaching is such an important part of a bishop's life, I want to give an
overview of my preaching life and a few examples to record the huge
variety of occasions they illustrate.

For the purposes of this account I have looked through my filing
cabinet, which contained just over 2100 sermons from 19th February
1961 to the present day. I have just disposed of the huge majority
through our paper recycling facility!

These 2100 sermons have been preached around the world. In the 10
years I was both General Secretary of SAMS and International
Coordinator of the Evangelical Fellowship of the Anglican Communion I
visited an average of eight different countries every one of those years
(1993–2003). Once, in 1977, I preached in four different countries on
consecutive occasions, i.e. Argentina, Chile, Bolivia and Peru. In 1969 I
preached on the P.& O. liner *Oronsay* on the way from the U.K. to
Mexico. In 2014 I preached on the Swan Hellenic liner *Minerva* while
sailing round South America from Valparaiso (Chile) to Buenos Aires
(Argentina). I also preached once in German in Villa Belgrano in
Argentina, in a town largely colonized by German descendants from the
sinking of the *Graf Spee* in the Battle of the River Plate.

I was extremely pleased to be asked to preach in two Cambridge
University Colleges. Twice at Caius Chapel, my own College, and twice
at Queens Chapel, where our daughter had been and where her tutor had
officiated at her wedding. An invitation to Holy Trinity, Cambridge was
also very special, being the church where I had heard a wonderful
number of evangelistic sermons preached on behalf of C.I.C.C.U. (the

Cambridge Inter Collegiate Christian Union) over my four years as an undergraduate.

Other highlights would be sermons in 29 cathedrals around the world across the continents. Despite numerous visits to churches across Canada and the USA, I was never invited into any of their cathedrals. Latin America, of course, was different. Cuernavaca in Mexico, Caracas in Venezuela, Montevideo in Uruguay, Porto Alegre, Santa Maria and Resurrection in Brazil, Buenos Aires in Argentina, as of course the Good Shepherd in Peru. In Africa I preached in Pietermaritzburg (South Africa), Mombasa and Nairobi in Kenya, Enugu in Nigeria, St Andrew's in Singapore, Kuala Lumpur in Malaysia, Madrid in Spain and Sydney in Australia. In the UK I have had the chance to preach in St David's, Llandaff in Wales and in York Minster, Newcastle, Derby, Chichester, St Albans, Salisbury, Sheffield, Durham, Wakefield, Bradford, Birmingham and Coventry cathedrals.

As already recorded, a very memorable occasion was on Pentecost Sunday in 2018 when I was invited to preach and to assist in the confirmation of some 50 candidates in Coventry Cathedral. This was exactly 40 years since my consecration as a bishop in Lima, Peru. I preached on the same text that Bishop Douglas Milmine had used in 1978: Isaiah 11:2, whose words constitute a key part of the traditional Anglican confirmation prayer that "the spirit of wisdom and understanding, the spirit of counsel and inward strength and the spirit of knowledge and true godliness would rest upon you". I was made very welcome with a large cake decorated with a mitre and llama. Bishop Christopher Cocksworth 'lent' me the Coventry diocesan crozier to give the final blessing. A memorable day.

Long overseas tours with many addresses were in South Africa, Canada and the USA. Also, special presentations over four years at Spring Harvest conferences, addresses at two diocesan ordination retreats in Chester and Rochester, and talks on a pilgrimage and a retreat in Israel.

The vast majority of sermons, however, were in parishes up and down the UK, in churches great and small, as also in churches great and small in South America, especially those preached in Spanish in Argentina and Peru over nearly 20 years.

Since retirement in 2011 the pace has slowed dramatically to between 20 and 35 a year. All preachers tend to find it difficult eventually to sit in a church pew, though it is also a welcome relief from the constant pressure of preparation in a short time frame. It has, however, been an immense privilege to minister God's word in this way to many people.

I end this section by giving some flavour — either of my most used biblical passages or particularly significant occasions when I have been asked to mount the pulpit.

I have always felt challenged to preach more from the Old Testament than is common practice nowadays. The pages of the Hebrew Bible have wonderful and memorable stories pouring out of them. Of course, Jesus' use of parables and the stories associated with his incarnate life are also highly memorable. But it is not for nothing that film moguls have made hugely successful blockbusters with Old Testament characters and stories.

From the Old Testament my Top Ten would be:

The story of Gideon in **Judges 7:1–22** is a very powerful reminder that it is God who works with us in the fulfilment of His purposes. Is mission human or divine? Should the title for this story be Gideon is Victorious over the Midianites? Or God Defeats the Midianites with a little help from Gideon? It is a dramatic account.

The story of Samuel's call in the Jerusalem temple in **I Samuel 3:1–10**. The necessity of listening for and to God's voice, especially at times when 'the word of the Lord is rare' because of sin.

Passages in **Isaiah 58 and Jeremiah 31** speak of the attractive picture of the life of God's chosen people being like that of a watered garden. An oasis in a desert.

One of my very early sermons was on **Psalm 105–4**: 'Seek the Lord and His strength, seek His presence continually'.

I have often preached on **Isaiah 52: 7–10**. Three prayers for basic characteristics for Christian people: "May you have joyful voices, far-seeing eyes, but most of all may you have beautiful feet to get you out there and share the good news with others."

Genesis 3 is a mine of deep teaching about the nature of sin. This is much needed when current popular understanding is so superficial and indeed, flippant. Three of the key biblical words— transgression, sin, and iniquity can be expounded from the Adam and Eve story.

I particularly like Old Testament passages that link up clearly with the N.T. **Genesis 22:1–19** is a good case in point. The phrase "The Lord will provide" is graphically demonstrated in the story of Abraham offering his son Isaac in sacrifice and then centuries later dramatically acted out in Jerusalem (on Mount Moriah) on the cross of Jesus as the Lamb of God.

Isaiah 55: 8–11 is another passage that graphically links Old and New Testaments. My three teaching points are the transcendental Word, the creative Word and the purposeful Word. All of course exemplified in Jesus Christ, but Isaiah uses powerful images from the natural world of creative growth, of rain and snow and fruitful harvests.

A more unusual Old Testament text I have returned to on different occasions is **Judges 3:31**, where Shamgar "did what he could with what he had, where he was". He was an Israelite warrior who killed 600 Philistines with the jawbone of an ox! I linked this dramatic event to Philippians 4:13 where Paul wrote "I can do all things in Christ." I preached on this at the annual synod meeting of the Reformed Episcopal Church of Spain (in Spanish), in York Minister for the 150th anniversary of CMJ, and at the Provincial Executive Committee of the Southern Cone of South America (in Spanish) and several more! It is even more effective in Spanish: "**Hizo** lo que **pudo**, con lo que **tuvo** donde estuvo."

Asa is a comparatively unknown 9th Century B.C. King of Judah (2 **Chronicles 14, 15 and 16**). These three chapters provide a fascinating account of his life with its many successes, but sad ending. I have used this material on several occasions, not least in Jerusalem for a spiritual retreat for the International Executive Staff of CMJ. Christian life and ministry continue right to the end. A surprising number of well-known biblical figures are described realistically in that they didn't always get everything right. The Bible doesn't hold back on describing 'the warts', which became apparent in later stages of life and ministry.

Whereas Asa has three chapters about his life, Shamgar only has one verse. A very different use of biblical material for these addresses. But both were great fun to develop, and memorable and helpful for me and a good number of others, I think.

My Top Ten from the New Testament

Inevitably, though, most of my sermons, I imagine as for most preachers, have sought to be expositions of the material of the New Testament. Within that of the four Gospels, Luke's being my clear favourite.

In selecting a few sermons, I start, however, with the **Acts** accounts of the conversion of Saul from being chief persecutor of the new Christian faith, to Paul, its most famous propagator around the Mediterranean. I refer to this because it is a sermon I didn't originally preach. I prepared it in my theological topics exam and received an A–, with which I was very pleased. Later I did preach it in Caius Chapel, Cambridge as well as at the Good Shepherd Church in Lima, Peru, and at St Andrew's, Oxford. Conflating the three biblical accounts I sought to answer the two questions Paul asked: "Who are you, Lord?" and "What shall I do, Lord?" Pretty basic questions, needing clear answers.

The subject of inexplicable and apparently mindless suffering or injustice constantly rears its head. **Luke 13:1–5** is a key passage to expound and to begin to offer some guidelines. When confronted with the sacrilegious massacre of Galileans in the Jerusalem Temple and the collapse of the ancient tower of Siloam, killing 18 bystanders, what Jesus didn't say, and then what he did say, are highly instructive and challenging.

On many occasions I preached on **Luke 10, verses 17, 20–21**. Joy in Mission was the title I gave it, whether in the UK, Singapore, Canada or Kenya. There is a good deal of joy in Luke's Gospel, but this text specified that Jesus himself was full of joy, when his 72 disciples returned from their pilot mission around the towns where Jesus was planning to visit. He sensed a new chapter in his work of conquering the destructive work of the devil through his embryonic mission team.

Jesus' words "I will build my Church", from **Matthew 16:18** are well-known and not uncontroversial in their different interpretations. In many different places I expounded the text on the understanding that Jesus was not referring to the rock being the person of Peter himself, but Peter's Spirit-inspired utterance that Jesus was the Son of the Living God. That was the rock that would be the firm foundation for the universal building of the Church.

From the Fourth Gospel, **John 20:21** has often been my theme: "As the Father has sent me, I am sending you." Various necessary marks stand out in the Church's mission when this close comparison is worked out — obedience; vulnerability; authority; fullness and suffering — these are essential apostolic marks. Sometimes I spoke of mission's pattern being "Under the Father's orders, In Christ's vulnerability, and With the Holy Spirit's authority."

In **Mark's Gospel, Chapter 6:45–56** was a favourite passage. My title was "Straining at the Oars", in five basic lessons for Christian 'oarsmen'.

Obedience doesn't guarantee an effortless path through life.
Opposition is to be expected.
Omniscient Lord doesn't miss a trick.
Opening our eyes to spiritual reality is an ongoing process.
Opportunities for self-giving service abound.

In the early days of my ministry memorable titles were much in vogue. Alliteration was also much employed. Now that the attention span of an average congregation is even shorter than it used to be, such aids for the memory are not to be despised. PowerPoint and overhead projectors have probably replaced them, but maybe not in the long run. I still believe a memorable short, pithy and unusual title will survive, at least as long as a picture. Anyway, "Straining at the Oars" summarises an evocative incident on Lake Galilee with good lessons for contemporary mission.

Two passages in Romans have sparked sermons in numerous venues. Many of these were in the Advent season, the text being **Romans 13:11**, "Knowing the Time". Often I have referred to the northern hemisphere's preoccupation with punctuality as compared with a much more laid-back attitude in Latin America. Concern for correct timekeeping, however, does not normally increase an awareness of the importance of the stage of our life we have reached or the Christian understanding that human history will reach a strategic climax with the Second Coming of Christ. The Advent season with serious consideration of the Last Things in the yearly liturgical cycle of the church has faded away significantly. Men and women used to be reminded (at least once a year) of the Second Coming of Christ, the Last Judgement, Heaven and Hell. The well-known 'Doom' paintings on the walls of older churches were also vivid reminders that the Christian faith understands history to be moving inexorably to a dramatic climax.

Preaching on this text in 1997, in Maresfield in Sussex, had added poignancy because it was on the occasion of a special service to mark the restoration of the church clock and its striking mechanism. Villagers now once again could glance up at the handsome red and black decorated clock face and be reminded of the time and perhaps also the Second Coming.

Romans 14:17 is another favourite and powerful text I preached on in 1978 at the inaugural assembly of the Latin American Council of Churches in Mexico, again in 1986 at the fifth anniversary of World Vision in Peru, and again in 1988 at an ecumenical service in Asunción

in Paraguay. All these were in Spanish (the last one even with a short
introduction in Guaraní, the second official language of Paraguay).

The text reads "The Kingdom of God does not mean food and drink,
but righteousness, peace and joy in the Holy Spirit." I sought to show
that God's concern is not with insignificant religious scruples about
dietary matters, but the big issues of justice and peace, and,
significantly, joy in the Holy Spirit. Certainly in the atmosphere of Latin
American liberation theology, joy in the Holy Spirit was somewhat
overlooked, despite the huge growth of the charismatic movement across
all denominations and churches. Paul's inspired writing remains totally
relevant as he challenges us to be concerned as 21st-Century Kingdom
workers with God the Father's righteousness, God the Son's peace and
God the Holy Spirit's joy.

Hebrews 12: 1 and 2. I preached many times in both Spanish and
English on this marvellous passage. It depicts the church militant racing
round an athletic stadium with the church triumphant witnessing and
encouraging from the spectators' tiers of seats: "Run with perseverance
the race set before us,"

>Spurred on by the saints' experience
>Stripped of Satan's encumbrances
>Steadied by the Saviour's example

Again, the alliteration doesn't seem too forced. It does make it
memorable and of course, once you have got the idea or the picture in
your mind, it is very moving and encouraging.

My final choice of a well-used N.T. text is **Philemon 6**. A phrase from
Paul's short letter to Philemon about a former converted slave:

'I pray you will promote the knowledge of all the good that is ours in
Christ.'

This sermon had a number of different forms, but all to illustrate the
richness of what we are offered in Christ.

>In 1965 it was my first sermon as a new curate at Christ Church
>Cockfosters.

>In 1968 it was my last sermon at Cockfosters on completion of my
>three-year curacy.

>In 1969 it was my first sermon in St John's Cathedral, Buenos
>Aires, Argentina.

>In 1988 it was my farewell sermon in the Good Shepherd Church
>in Lima, Peru, as we left South America after 20 years.

In 1989 it was my installation sermon in Bradford Cathedral

In 2003 it was preached again in the Cathedral Church of Lima on the 25th anniversary of my episcopal consecration. Also in two shanty-town churches a few days before.

In 2010 it was not the final sermon of my stipendiary ministry as I moved into retirement mode. I decided to preach on **Psalm 73:28**, which was my very first sermon on 19th February 1961 at the Railway Mission in Cambridge, forty-nine years previously.

However, the theme is quite similar: "But it is good for me to draw near to God. I have put my trust in the Lord God, that I may declare all Thy works" (verse 28). I preached on Deliverance from the world. Drawing near to God. Declaring all Thy works.

The Philemon sermon certainly evolved over the period of 1965–2003. 'Promoting the Knowledge of the good that ours in Christ' was spelled out in 1965 as:

Full forgiveness for the past and full humanity for the future. This message was to be enthusiastically and faithfully and widely promoted. By 2003 it had become formatted differently. The good that is ours in Christ is still to be enthusiastically and faithfully and widely promoted. It is described as:

The good of being **evangelical** under the authority of the Bible

The good of being **catholic** with the vision of the universality and diversity of the Church

The good of being **charismatic**, rejoicing in the fulness of the Holy Spirit in lives of adoration and service to others.

Whether Philemon 6 will be the final text I ever preach on is as yet unknown! My thoughts at the time of writing are that I will seriously cut down from my 80th birthday in 2018. That will be nearly 57 years of preaching. Some would say it is about time he shut up! However, with many other preachers I can testify to the sense of call and commission from God to share with others the good news of all that is gifted to us in Christ. To be involved in the process of Christ, the living Word of God meeting people in need through the explaining of the written Word of God by the spoken words of the preacher remains a sacred and awesome task and joy. On the 13th August 2018 I preached at St Nic's, Warwick on John 12:21 "We would see Jesus". That's what it is all about.

Confirmations in Holy Trinity, Skipton, 1991

Confirmations

Confirmations in the Bygrave Family in Peru in the 1980s

I add a few pages about confirmation sermons, which tend to be a bit special. The first were during the ten years of my episcopal ministry in Peru and Bolivia, from 1978–1988. These were important occasions. They were important for the individuals concerned, but also ecclesiastically as technically those confirmed formed the nucleus of new official congregations. So, these occurred in many places in Peru and many places in Bolivia. I wore a simple, specially designed episcopal poncho and carried a large wooden crozier carved by a local Peruvian craftsman. The crozier divided up into three segments, which were jointed together. Later, in the UK I had the joints replaced by a screwing system and it eventually was given back to Peru to be used by Peruvian bishops.

During this time, I mostly used a simple shepherd's crook made of ash given me by the Revd John Cull of Woodchester. He had used it on his goats rather than sheep, so it had a narrow metal crook to catch a goat's hind leg rather than fasten round a sheep's neck. A disabled friend in Bradford cleverly adorned it with a cross and my initials, making the top look as if it were made of bone. This is the crook I still use today.

Confirmations in Sutton Valence School, 14th May 1995
Girl from Ghana

Confirmations in Rugby School in 2013

The second period was from 1988–1993, being the time I was serving in the Diocese of Bradford. One of these churches I preached in was celebrating its foundation 1000 years before. So the context was entirely different from the above. A number were boarding school occasions at Sedbergh, Giggleswick, Bentham and Westhouse Grove. Most, however, were in the city of Bradford itself or the surrounding towns and villages of the marvellous Dales countryside. Sedbergh produced a record 56 candidates in 1989. Numbers were lower normally, but I laid hands on some 2000 people, young and old alike, during those years. They were good local church community occasions, normally accompanied by an ample supply of 'buns'. Quite unsuitable for episcopal waistlines.

The third period was from 1993–2003 when I was the General Secretary of SAMS and travelling widely around the world. However, during those years I was an honorary assistant bishop, first in Chichester, Rochester and Canterbury, and then when the SAMS headquarters moved to Birmingham in that city as well. So I was on the rota of 'retired' assistant bishops who were asked from time to time to officiate at confirmations around the diocese. These were more difficult in many ways, because of the minimal contact with the candidates and the lack of any really close knowledge of the congregations' members. However, I officiated at 13 in 1995, nine in 1996 and four in 1997.

The fourth period, from 2003–2018, when I was Honorary Assistant Bishop of Coventry in my retirement, firstly living in Alderminster, near Stratford-on-Avon, and then in Warwick. During these 14 years I became very familiar with the annual Maundy Thursday celebration in the cathedral, where I figured with the diocesan and suffragan bishops. Sometimes there was a big united confirmation in Coventry Cathedral, when we all three appeared together. In one of these I confirmed 47 in 2005. Mostly, however, I helped out, as requested, in various parishes and particularly on a quite regular basis at Warwick and Rugby public schools. These were good meetings. I tried to meet up with the candidates, sometimes on their previous day retreat, in order not to set eyes on them for the first time just before having to lay hands on them! Numbers have diminished over these 14 years, though there were still 24 candidates at Rugby in 2019.

There have been several rather special confirmations for me. One was in 1987 when I confirmed my son Peter at Monkton Combe School. A former Bishop of Bath and Wells, John Bickersteth very kindly handed

Triple Confirmations, Coventry Cathedral, 4th December 2004
Bishop Colin Bennetts, Bishop Norman Kayumba, Bishop David Evans

the whole service over to me when he learnt that my son was one of the 43 candidates and I was on furlough in the U.K. I was still much in South American mode at the time, so I remember it all being a bit unusual and different in an English public school setting. I did of course have the traditional episcopal 'rig' (The 'Choir' outfit for the ancient Convocations of the church). This had been given me by the members of Christ Church Cockfosters in 1968 and sent out by British Caledonian Airways for my consecration in Lima. I did not acquire an episcopal ring until after returning from ten years in Peru. It seemed to be dangerously ostentatious, especially for work in the Peruvian shanty towns. But my sister-in-law, Nicky Evans, made one for me in 1988 on our return to UK-based ministry in the Bradford diocese.

Another outstanding confirmation event, indeed, safari, took place in Kenya, in the Diocese of Taita Taveta, of my good friend Bishop Samson Mwaludo. This took place in the year 2010. I confirmed 92 at one service in Tansa and then 49 the next day in Digombo. The journey between the two villages in the countryside was in a four-wheel-drive vehicle through the bush. For some of the way we were following in the tracks of a herd of elephants. The bushes beside the one-way path showed ample evidence of having been fed on and the ground had plenty of recent manure on it! Safari confirmations are, of course commonplace in Africa, especially where enormous numbers of candidates have been coming forward in recent years.

In the recently published book (2017) *Growth and Decline in the Anglican Communion (1980 to the present)* it is stated that in 1970 there were around 47 million Anglicans in the world. Their number by 2010 was 86 million, almost double. A large number of these were indeed in Africa, though often there are difficulties in securing accurate figures. After my confirmation contribution in the Kenyan Diocese of Taita Taveta, I could appreciate the gratitude of the local bishop for lending him 'my hands'.

In a different context, in the English Chaplaincy church in Dubai I confirmed four adults. This was in a special building reserved for the use of multiple church congregations on a special campus in the United Arab Emirates. Small plaques on the outside wall were the only indications of who the building was used by. The times of the different services were also recorded. It reminded me of the first chaplaincy building in the Callao dock area of Lima. This was rather tucked away out of sight. No

church bells could be rung to announce service times, as this was
restricted in the nineteenth century to Roman Catholic churches. Again,
the situation in downtown Madrid comes to mind. Here the Anglican
Cathedral occupies several floors of a large old tenement block. Fully
ecclesiastical inside, but of course no advertising bells allowed. The
ground the other side of the road from the Cathedral was leased to a
supermarket, whose back doors opened to dispose of all their rubbish
bins. It is said that Franco approved of the arrangement himself!

I think many bishops would have a special place in their hearts for
some confirmation sermons. Here are mine:

Galatians 5:25   "Live by the Spirit"
                     Keep in step with the Spirit
                     Show the fruit of the Spirit

Ephesians 2:10   "We are His" (workmanship)
                     Recapture the thrill of being creative
               Realise the truth of belonging to an international team
               Retain the simplicity of being committed.

Isaiah 43:1   "You are mine"
                           I paid the purchase price
                           I will look after you
                           I will use you.

Hebrews 12:1-2   "Let us run the race that is set before us"
                 Spurred on by the experience of the saints
                 Stripped of the encumbrances of sin
                 Steadied by the example of our Saviour.

Nearly always I incorporate in the service the following prayer which
has been one of my all-time favourites:

> O Jesus, Master Carpenter of Nazareth, who on the Cross through wood
> and nails worked mankind's whole salvation, wield well your tools in the
> workshop of our lives that we, who come to you rough-hewn, may by your
> hand be fashioned to a truer beauty and a greater usefulness for the honour
> of your holy name. Amen

I close this section about confirmation with two challenging passages:

> Each of us has a bank account credited daily with 86,400, not pounds but
> seconds. Every night it writes off as lost whatever hasn't been well used. No
> carryover to the next day. 86,400 seconds to use well every day. Don't
> misspend your life. Don't misspend your years, months, weeks, days.

May God's compassion motivate you as you see people in need.

May you be men and women of prayer.

May you catch God's vision for your life and enjoy every minute of it.

The Paradox of our Age

We have more but enjoy it less

We have multiplied our possessions but reduced our values

We talk too much, love too seldom, and lie too often

We learned how to make a living but not a life

We've added years to life, not life to years

These are days of quick trips, disposable diapers

Throwaway morality, one-night stands

Overweight bodies and pills that do everything from cheer, to quiet, to kill

It is a time when there is much in the show window and nothing in the stockroom.

Reading and writing

Bishops don't just preach sermons and write letters! They may write books, articles for magazines or newspapers, material for TV or radio programmes, talks for all sorts of social groups, addresses for spiritual retreats and conference gatherings, as well as for funerals, weddings, institutions of new ministries, etc., etc.

In order to mitigate the danger of churning out material that has been used before, it is obviously vital to ensure that there is good new input. Of course, this should come from all sorts of sources. One of them is the discipline of reading good books. I have kept a list of the books I have read since the autumn of 1968—so that's over 50 years. The person who inspired me to do this was one of the theological teachers at Trinity College, Bristol, Peter Dawes, who later became Bishop of Derby. He took time out of his lecture course on liturgy because he thought the importance of study and reading vital to ensure freshness, depth and creativity in a long ministry of teaching and public speaking. I am grateful for his insight. He did warn of the danger of spending too much time with books, rather than *the* book, The Bible. Also that thinking and digesting books (and The Book) was more important than achieving any sort of record of the number of books read. Achieving a good balance of theological books and those of a general secular nature was vital. I see from my notes that he recommended *Lady Chatterley* and other similar

---

popular novels on Saturday night or even Sunday morning to be reminded of what people might be filling their minds with! When I spoke to a Sunday Fellowship meeting of older young people at Christ Church Cockfosters during my curacy from 1965–1968, I referred to the benefit of reading sometimes the *News of the World* or the *Daily Mirror* or *Woman's Own*.

It was G. M. Trevelyan who wrote:

> Education has produced a vast population able to read but unable to distinguish what is worth reading.

R. L. Stevenson put it differently:

> People have dwarfed and narrowed their soul by a life of all work, so that they have not one thought to rub against another while waiting for the train.

After all in His infinite wisdom God means me to read because He inspired a collection of 66 writings and had them preserved and translated for us in a Book called the Bible.

In these 50 years since 1968 I have only occasionally dropped below 30 titles in any one year. Normally the annual total has been nearer 40. I have always sought to have one good theological tome on my desk. Well-known evangelical theologians feature heavily — John Stott, Michael Green, Tony Thiselton, Tom Wright and Michael Nazir-Ali, Jim Packer, Alan Stibbs and Derek Kidner in earlier days. While in South America I read the Papal Encyclicals and some Roman Catholic writers especially Gustavo Gutiérrez. I read a lot of Mario Vargas Llosa and Jorge Borges and Isabel Allende, all prolific novelists about Latin American history and culture. Also W. H. Hudson's intriguing books on wildlife, human and animal in the River Plate and Patagonia. On a lighter note I have enjoyed most of the titles of Alistair MacLean, Bernard Cornwell, Alexander McCall-Smith, Bill Bryson, Alain de Boton and J. K. Rowling. The only book (I think) that appears twice on my list is the Koran! Books on spirituality and prayer abound, as do a good number of biographies from Temple Gardner of Cairo to *My World* by Jonny Wilkinson.

Publications

Previous to this book I have written two others. The first one was in 1976, entitled *En Diálogo con Dios*. It was written in Spanish during my time in Argentina. Much corrected by Dr René Padilla, thankfully, who had commissioned me to write for university students a book specifically on intercessory prayers. It proved quite popular in a limited circulation, though I believe all the copies were sold. As well as being a practical guide to intercessory prayers, it sought to tackle the question whether what we pray actually changes God's mind. Or is it rather that through our dialogue with God we come to understand what His will is and are more likely to accept it because of the trusting relationship we have established with Him? It was Martin Luther who wrote that "the man of God is forged through temptation and in prayer." That resonates with my experience. When someone prays aloud in a group, who has made a regular practice of being in dialogue with God, you sense the reality of that relationship and indeed God's presence is more intimately felt.

My second book was written years later, this time in English in 2012. It was entitled *Have Stick: Will Travel*. This was basically an account of my numerous travels around the globe but homing in especially on the years 1968–88. This was the time when we were based first in Argentina and then in Peru. Again, the book is out of print but of course is on a 'memory stick', so can be reproduced. It was an incredible privilege to have had the opportunity to visit so many places, to have met many wonderful people, and at the same time to be doing the work to which I had been called by God and have my travels paid for by the people of God! It was in 1985 that I had my longest and toughest 'missionary' journey. I can hardly believe it now and it makes me feel exhausted. But in 110 days I visited 25 cities in 10 different countries around the Southern part of Africa and South America!

In addition to these books I have contributed over the years to various publications. The first, in 1967 while I was still a curate at Christ Church Cockfosters in London, was the well-known I.V.F. *Search the Scriptures*. This book is still in circulation today after 50 years, having gone through many editions and in 2018 published its millionth copy! My part was the study on the First Letter of Paul to the Corinthians. It may not have been fortuitous that the overall editor was Alan Stibbs, then at Oak Hill in the Cockfosters parish! 1 Corinthians has remained one of my favourite N.T. letters ever since.

In 1990 EFAC and Regnum published *One Gospel—Many Clothes*, a series of case studies on evangelism to mark the retirement of John Stott as President of the Evangelical Fellowship in the Anglican Communion. It was also a contribution as evangelical Anglicans to the Decade of Evangelism. My chapter was entitled "Evangelism with Theological Credibility" and came in the first part of the book. The case studies came from well-known speakers from around the world.

In 2005 I contributed a chapter on "Prayer and Mission" in the *Dictionary of Mission and Theology, Evangelical Foundations*. This was published by the InterVarsity Press. Mine was a modest contribution to a book of 461 pages with numerous international writers. The thrust of my article was that intercessory prayer and worldwide mission are umbilically linked. In a way it was a theological synthesis of my two books, one on prayer and one on mission.

In 2016 I was involved in providing material for the Roy Hedge Contemporary Ecclesiology series of books. The title of the book was *Growth and Decline in the Anglican Communion (1980 to the present)*. The Revd Dr John Corrie and Bishop Maurice Sinclair edited the chapter on the Southern Cone province of South America. With hindsight, as viewed now with a couple of decades' perspective I judge my contributions in Argentina to have been as one of the leaders in moving the church in Central and Southern Argentina from a series of English chaplaincies to a Spanish-speaking and increasingly national church. It was not an easy transition. Had it not happened, however, by now there would probably only have been one or possibly two English-speaking congregations surviving. In Peru my contribution was very different. We only had one English-speaking chaplaincy church. That maintains its role as a focus for ex-pat ministry, but literally a whole Spanish-speaking family of churches has grown from it. The 'original' church building is now the diocesan cathedral, the mother church of congregations in both the middle classes and the shanty towns of Lima and reaching out to other cities in Peru, especially in Arequipa in the Andes. For this growth to happen and be maintained, two things were necessary: the work and power of the Holy Spirit in promoting genuine outreach and giving vision; the charismatic movement was active in many denominations, including within the Roman Catholic Church. But structure is also needed as well as spirit. One of our local congregations grew very fast, with great emphasis on the work of the Holy Spirit. However, it did not survive to become a stable local congregation. It had too many 'humming-bird' members, who whizzed off to find nectar in other places which became more attractive, often with some new teaching slant.

We so often teach quite rightly that the Church is not a building. The people of God form the Church. But we do need a meeting place which involves money, bricks and mortar, toilet facilities and a legal identity with the Ministry of Religion and Culture. All of that involves paperwork, financial backing, personnel and hours of painstaking standing in office queues. It involves developing a pattern of corporate worship, regulations on membership and an appropriate level of loyalty and mutual support without ever seeking to establish the perfect church/denomination. Finding a middle path between spiritual vitality with enthusiastic growth and structural stability for continuity is no easy task. The Anglican Church has often been described as a *via media*. This reference is normally to a body of people who can live comfortably (?) between the Roman Catholic Church and Pentecostal denominations. That scenario could look like a bit of a compromise—looking both ways at the same time. Interpreted, however, as a *via media* giving due importance to both spirit and structure, I believe it to be a very important and healthy description.

Other writings involve the following, which again point to the focus of *my* interests:

1980   An article in the magazine of the Catholic University of Lima. This was in Spanish and was about the relationship between the Anglican Church and the Roman Catholic Church during the Papacy of Paul VI. I remember getting help with this from Anglican members of the ARCIC consultations.

1984   An article in *Mission* magazine about Roland Allen, the Radical Prophet.

1992   I was asked by CMS (UK) to give the J.C. Jones Memorial Lecture in Wales.

My theme was International Vision. It was delivered in both the south and the north of Wales. It summarized a good deal of my experience at that stage, having ceased to live in South America but still being much involved in international travel. In the Introduction I wrote:

> I doubt very much whether I am the first Evans to give the J.C Jones lecture. I am rather an International Evans, however. My father's roots were in Cornwall, but the family came originally from South Wales. I was born in Tanganyika but lived in England. I married a wife of Irish background, though again there are Welsh roots in the family history. We have two English daughters and one son born in Argentina, whose midwife was of Welsh origins from Patagonia. We served some 20 years in South America in Argentina, Peru and Bolivia and are now serving in another country—Yorkshire! So I make no excuses about my subject: International Vision.

I used this material again four years later when giving the Orange Memorial Lecture in Christchurch, New Zealand, as EFAC International Coordinator.

1996   The magazine of Trinity Episcopal School for ministry in the U.S.A. commissioned an article on Mission and the Ministry which I much enjoyed writing.

1996   A presentation of the life of Capt. Allen Gardiner, given in the Argentine Embassy in London.

My main recollection of that event was a remark from Prince Philip, who was on an official visit to the Embassy where the South American Mission Society was holding an exhibition. As I was talking about early travellers to Cape Horn being explorers who lived off 'seals' he interrupted to comment: "But you of course (including Capt. Allen Gardiner) were also after 'souls'."

2002   I did a study on the diocese as a missionary unit. This involved researching the archives of the Anglican Communion in London. Often in mission work the question is raised, not only about the minimum or desirable size to have a properly constituted local church, but also what is an appropriate size for a diocese. How many local churches should constitute a diocese? Obviously over the years political questions have influenced decisions. Cultural factors also weigh heavily. Geography plays its part, and of course the availability of money to support structure and 'full-time' ordained ministry. All of these were relevant in the area of Chile, Peru and Bolivia, as they moved from their initial one tri-national diocese into three and now more dioceses under national leadership. Now in 2019 they form two separate provinces with 10 dioceses between them.

I will mention also two other writing productions. These were printed privately but were fairly widely circulated. I was asked by my good EFAC friend the Bishop of Taita Taveta in Kenya to give some Bible Studies to his diocesan clergy conference. On one occasion I did a series of studies on Genesis 1–15 and on a second occasion a series of studies on the letter of James, entitled "On to maturity". These were distributed to all the clergy. I very much enjoyed putting these studies together and have referred to them a number of times for material in my teaching ministry.

The last course of studies I will mention here is the one I prepared and delivered on a number of different occasions on the Lord's Prayer—Living

Life God's Way. It was first given for a series of talks and discussions in the Stourdene Group of churches in Coventry diocese in the autumn of 2005. It is a wonderful pattern-setting prayer and always richly rewards everyone who returns to study it, rather than just repeat it liturgically. I quote a part from a little drama with which I sometimes introduced it:

Person	Our Father, who . . .
God	Yes?
Person	Don't interrupt me! I'm praying.
God	But you called me.
Person	Called you? I didn't call you. I was praying Our Father who art in heaven.
God	There, you did it again.
Person	Did what?
God	Called me. You said "Our Father who art in heaven. Here I am. What's on your mind?
Person	But I didn't mean anything by it. It was, you know, just saying my prayers for the day. I always say the Lord's Prayer. It makes me feel good, sort of like getting a job done.
God	All right. Go on.
Person	Hallowed be thy name.
God	Hold it! What do you mean by that?
Person	By what?
God	By "hallowed be thy name"?
Person	It means . . . it means . . . Good grief! How should I know what it means? It's just part of the prayer. (*pause*) By the way, what does it mean?
God	It means, honoured, holy, wonderful . . .

Special talks and addresses

The debate on human sexuality. My involvement in this began in my immediate post-university days. The national student committee of the I.V.F (InterVarsity Fellowship) issued a leaflet in 1963: *Sex and the Single Student*. This was a reasoned plea to preserve the sanctity of marriage and avoid the increasingly liberal approach to sexuality. It was unafraid to ask the question: 'Is promiscuity the solution?' In 1995 the theological working group of the Church of England Evangelical Council issued a more substantial publication which became known as the *St*

Andrew's Day Statement. It was an examination of the theological principles affecting the homosexuality debate. This St Andrew's Day statement was then published with accompanying articles in the *EFAC Bulletin of Easter 1997.* It was disseminated across the Anglican Communion in preparation for the debates of the Lambeth Conference of Bishops in 1998. As is well known, the controversy continues to engage a vast amount of attention. As far as the position of the Anglican Communion is concerned, the Primates (at the time of writing this in 2018) are still struggling to find a universally accepted doctrinal position or even an acceptable formula to reconcile opposite positions.

On re-reading that original university leaflet I find I still agree with its main arguments. The trust in a God who lovingly sets boundaries for sexual relationships: who provides us with moral and spiritual courage to stand against the pressures of conformity to more liberal views. I end by quoting

> Chastity is essential as a vital safeguard of marriage. Healthy and constructive relationships between the sexes outside of marriage also depend on it.

A second subject that I got involved in was Sunday observance. While acting as Diocesan Bishop in Bradford I gave the address at synod on this subject. I had preached at Christ Church Cockfosters on Revelation 1:10 on May 14th 1968 on "I was in the Spirit on the Lord's Day." By 1991 I had to begin my address rather differently:

> I was saddened to note that the low attendance at the first-ever Test Match held on a Sunday was not attributed to the possibility that some people might have been in church. It was rather assumed that they were at car boot sales, in their gardens or at DIY centres!

The Keep Sunday Special campaign was at its height and consumerist interests were strongly motivating a liberalization of Sunday trading laws. Not everyone agreed in the Bradford synod with all I said. However, five clergymen did try to persuade local stores to close. They handed formal letters of complaint to store managers at Sainsbury's in Greengates, Morrisons in Thornton Road, Enterprise 5 in Idle and Tesco in Buttershaw.

A year or so later I was invited to speak at a public debate on the title "On the Seventh Day God went Shopping". This was organized by the Christian Union of Durham University. I was invited to speak against the motion. together with the Bishop of Bristol. We lost!

In 1991 I quoted a piece from the *Chicago Tribune*, written by George Nachman, not a Christian but a shrewd observer of life. He wrote:

> One weekend recently I looked out of the window and discovered that Sunday had disappeared. Nobody had swiped it exactly, but something had gone out of the noble day. Suddenly I realized what it was: Sunday had turned into Tuesday. Out on the street, people no longer were strolling about. They had direction, a mid-week glint in their eyes that meant business. They were walking briskly in and out of stores instead of browsing quietly in the windows. The scene was as busy as your average workaday Tuesday, throwing the whole week out of gear. Now Sunday is just another day, and it appears to have lost its real purpose.

If that was an insight from 1991 how much truer is it today.

David Owen, M.P. wrote:

> As the stresses of modern life increase with mental breakdowns, higher divorce rates, greater violence and rising crime, we need to be very careful before we take any steps which could escalate and exacerbate the pace and pressure of modern life. Leisure activities for all on Sunday should be our aim.

The biblical account gives us a picture of God as interested in leisure as in labour. In Jesus' own statement we know he came to give abundant life. This is correctly interpreted as a matter of richer quality of life rather than an ever-increasing accumulation of perishable goods or an ever-increasing pace of life.

My conclusion sounds like a lost pipedream with the developments since 1991.

> Let us uphold then this vision of society in which the day of rest, God's gracious provision for human life, is given public expression for the dignity of the individual, and the proper place of work. The enrichment of family life, the well-being of society and the corporate worship of Almighty God.

It seems sad to reflect that the Jewish Sabbath and the Muslim Friday prayers seem in proportion to have a much stronger hold on people than the full Christian observance of Sunday.

In Spanish I spent a good deal of time preparing a series of lectures on Ecclesiology, on the nature of the church. Also on the Liturgy of the church, where I said

> I believe rationally and passionately in both spontaneity and planned liturgical practice in public worship.

More unusually I gave a lecture by invitation on an international summer course (August 1991), at the Complutense University just outside Madrid. In Spain the overall subject was on Fundamentalism and I contributed a paper on Protestant fundamentalisms. The first invitation had been to the Bishop of Spain. He had either been unavailable or unwilling (I never got to know) but I certainly replaced him and remember sweating profusely with a towel around my head during preparation in the heat of a Spanish summer. The notorious Bishop Lefevre of the Roman Catholic Church spoke on Roman Catholic fundamentalism and there were contributions from both the Jewish and Muslim and secular perspectives.

Other speaking commitments involved three Spring Harvest conventions at the Butlin's facilities in Minehead. These were in 1992, 1994 and 1996. Though I did preach in the Big Top and lead an Easter Sunday Holy Communion service, the main commitment was the leadership of numerous workshops and seminars, sometimes with another evangelical contributor, sometimes just by myself. Those were challenging occasions. But I think it true to say that it was a privilege to be involved in a movement where the Holy Spirit was so obviously at work, breathing life into people of all ages, whose home churches might not have been so exciting.

In 1995 I was asked to lead two ordination retreats, the first in Chester diocese, the second in Rochester, these following each other very closely. I literally had to drive fast from the Chester retreat in the north to be in time to start the Rochester retreat in the south. It was a great privilege to be able to minister to two groups of people setting out on their new life of ordained ministry in the church of God. I explained that I had been ordained for 30 years and was planning to share with them four themes that I had found helpful. So no great theological treatise on the ministry, no lengthy in-depth Scripture exposition. But a passing on of practical experience. Each of the four themes had a linguistic tag and I gave everyone a card with these on. A clear picture was also associated with each theme as a memory aid. The themes were Preaching; Holiness; Work Management; and Motivation.

A. **Contemplata or Cocta trade**: this is a Latin phrase I first read in the writings of Gregory the Great addressed to preachers. It means "pass on digested things." The sheep of Christ's flock are to be fed by the preacher. Their food needs to be well selected and personally digested by the preacher before being attractively presented to be easily digested by the hearers. If birds can do it for their chicks, preachers must do it for their congregations! The preacher's task is to feed people, to nourish their spiritual life and promote healthy growth. It is not an ego trip to produce a memorable sermon. Nor is it to impress with rhetoric, fine phrases or impressive logic. It is not to entertain, but to feed.

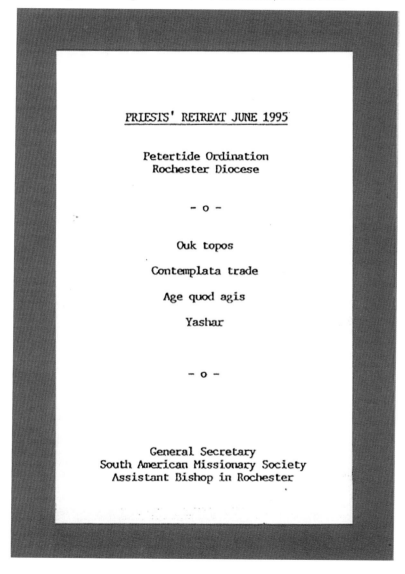

Priests' Retreat, Rochester Diocese, June 1995

I still possess a letter sent to me by the Revd Alan Stibbs of Oak Hill Theological College. He was in the Christ Church Cockfosters congregation one Sunday when I was preaching on the 16th January 1966. Graciously and very helpfully he suggested a number of necessary improvements to one of my early efforts at preaching. He said, and I quote:

> It was like a tin of condensed milk. It would have been more digestible and more attractive to the listener if you had used (say) one-third of the ideas, but as with condensed milk in use — both diluted it and given it warmth and possibly distinctive flavour, like a hot mug of 'chocolate' made with milk!

The second theme was holiness, with the Greek tag *ouk topos* or *Nullus Locus* (from Luke 2:7) meaning *No Room*. I developed the idea of the Holy Spirit being in residence in us, and there being, therefore, no rightful room for any other sorts of spirit. The flag of the Holy Spirit shall fly over our lives indicating holiness, produced internally by the transforming work of that same Spirit of holiness. I suggested seven worldly spirits that should resolutely be rejected from taking up any permanent home in our inner selves: lust, sloth, covetousness, gluttony, ambition, envy and pride. Count von Zinzendorf, the founder of the Moravian Mission, wrote about "the exclusive effort of a new allegiance." Earlier than him Henry Scougal's famous book was called *The Life of God in the Soul of Man*. So room for the Holy Spirit in every compartment of our lives and resolutely No Room for any unworthy spirits to develop characteristics of our sinful nature.

The third theme was work management. Pope John 21's saying was "Age quod agis". Concentrate on the present. The only genuine living is what we are doing at this very moment. This is the moment in time that we can either let slip by languidly or live fully and intensively. At each side we are hedged by the temptations of romantic sentimental nostalgia for the past or idealistic fanciful daydreaming about future hopes. The place of the mind, the will and discipline is central to this. If we are to plan our work and work our plan we have to "gird up the loins of our minds" (1 Peter 1:13) and allow ourselves to "be transformed by the renewing of our minds" (Romans 12:2).

I suggested three priorities for what to concentrate on. God must be first. Ordained ministers are paid not to work in the secular world in order to have time to be with God, to get to know him, to hear His voice and obey His instructions. We are expected to be expert in the divine/human encounter. People must be second. Cultivating listening to God helps us to listen to people, we are to be people-friendly, welcoming, even if we are running some computer program. The best listeners are the best communicators; one of Bishop Lancelot Andrewes' six special resolutions was never to allow too long a time to pass without being in real contact with people.

That requires planning — the third priority in enabling us to concentrate on what we are doing. Of course emergencies occur only too often, but a planned shape to a day is essential for a productive life. There can be a huge dissipation of energy, physical, mental, psychological and spiritual, because of a lack of priorities, perspective, vision, direction. We can't and shouldn't live at top speed day after day. The famous Methodist preacher Sangster's Christmas card in 1957 was entitled "Slow me down, Lord". Archbishop Benson's rule of life included the injunction "not to be dilatory in commencing the day's main work". A good P.A. will present work to the boss in different ways—the things for primary attention; secondary attention; information; reading. Not just a huge list of everything that needs to be done or you would like to do. Planning the diary, alternating periods of high intensity and planned relaxation and wisdom/discernment in being able to move from one mode to another. Age quod agis — concentrate on what you are doing now, whether it is preparing a difficult funeral message, praying about a dreaded confrontation on the P.C.C., lining up a crucial putt on the golf course, or taking the dog for a walk.

The fourth theme was purpose—based on the Hebrew word *Yashav,* which means straightforward and refers to the passage in Ezekiel 10 where the winged creatures accompanying the platform with the mysterious presence of God never swerved from their course—they went straight on. The vision of the mobile house of the deity identified a great steadfastness and clarity of direction, as it always went straight forward. I linked this with Phil. 3:10–16 where Paul testified that as an athlete he was straining every nerve to finish his course and reach the finishing line and gain the coveted gold medal. He is talking about completing a divine vocation and calling, not about fulfilling a human career. Self-effacing vocation rather than ambitious job hunting—"This one thing I do, I press on . . . " Paul said.

Going forward is very much a contemporary expression. It is pretty innocuous actually and just means in the future. It has none of the dynamism of Ezekiel's *Yashav*, the *yashav* of purposeful going straight forward—whatever. It carried together with Paul's athletic imagery the idea of forgetting the past, maybe both previous triumphs and failures. We concentrate on the job in hand without punishing ourselves with a sense of guilt or failure or dwelling in a glow of self-congratulation for the past. We forge ahead, straight ahead 'without swerving', not being tossed about like a wave of the seas, as James 1:6 has it, not being tempted off the main path into byways *à la* John Bunyan's *Pilgrim's Progress*, not allowing ourselves to be distracted by great mood swings but pressing on forwards—'onwards and upwards' as C.S. Lewis described the Christian path through the world. And it can be a strain. It does require effort. Straining is not just to do with stressful circumstances that life throws at us. It is to do with getting up early after a late night; it is to do with turning away wrath with a soft answer; it is forcing oneself to listen to an unsympathetic parishioner; it is acting with the patience of Job when a group of people don't see the way ahead as clearly as we do! It was the great missionary statesman Oswald Sanders who said there are three kinds of people: "Those who are movable. Those who are immovable. And those who move them." The frontiers of the Kingdom of God were never advanced by men and women of caution. We fix our eyes on Jesus, the pioneer and finisher of his course and we go straight forward.

I found all this a useful exercise and responsibility to put this material together. It became something of a summary of my own experience, so I used it again in 1995 at a Readers' Retreat in Parceval Hall in the Diocese of Bradford. The multilingual tags I still find helpful. In today's world people talk and write a good deal about the Wellbeing of the Clergy. These four phrases in three different languages compress important truths that can strengthen and orientate any ministry in the 21st century!

Letters to magazines and the press

Most ordained ministers are called upon to write letters for parish magazines or articles for journals and local or national press. These, of course, are of very varied value from the brilliant and provocative to the dull and predictable ... "As I write these lines you will have returned from your summer holidays ... " I have never actually been a parish vicar in the Church of England! So I have been spared the relentless approach of the monthly deadline for copy.

The nearest I came to this was during my time as General Secretary of the South American Mission Society. For ten years from 1993–2003 I was expected to produce a monthly letter; obviously the key subject was Mission, as a selection of the titles during those years underlines.

My first contribution in this genre, however, was a series of quarterly publications, written in Buenos Aires for circulation among the dioceses of the Southern Cone of South America. These were to circulate interesting news that could stimulate urban church planting. This was a new emphasis from 1969–1977.

While in the Bradford diocese as assistant bishop to Bishop Robert Williamson I was asked sometimes to contribute 'a piece' to the diocesan monthly letter. These included:

1990   Know the Time: Year of Evangelism

1990   World Cup and World Mission

1991   Receive the Holy Spirit

1991   Understanding and Faith in Today's World

1991   Facing up to Sunday Challenge

During the vacancy when I was acting diocesan bishop, after Bishop Robert had been appointed to Southwark, I produced copy for nine months on such topics as:

Electing a Diocesan

International Year

Human Sexuality

Anglican Distinctiveness

The Ideal Diocese

Do we want to be Modern?

Unanswered Prayer

Making Right Decisions

Reflections on Fundamentalism

After 'official' retirement into my house-for-duty ministry living in Alderminster in the Stourdene group of six churches there was no call to produce a regular monthly letter. However, I still have examples of the occasional letters I wrote. March 2010 produced *Euthanasia* — an investigation into what a 'good death' means, especially when we are so concerned about a good life. April 2010 produced *Anastasis* — an unravelling of the meaning of the resurrection of Jesus Christ both in First Century Greece and 21st Century Great Britain, where many still make idols of just about anyone or anything, do our own 'pick and mix' outlook on life, follow our own pleasure trail or take refuge in our own rational powers.

My favourite letter I print in full, from February 2009. It ties in with my ongoing interest in ornithology, our feathered friends:

> I wandered lonely as a cloud that floats on high above all things
> When all at once I saw a crowd, a flock of tiny *snow buntings*,
> Beside the sea, along the beach, fluttering and dancing within my reach.
> Oft when pensive on my couch I lie they flash upon my inward eye,
> And then my heart with pleasure glows and dances with those tiny 'snows'.

We haven't actually had any *snow buntings* in the Stourdene area this winter, as far as I know. I wrote the above (with apologies to William Wordsworth) after seeing these delightful little birds at Cley in Norfolk in January 2004. Bill Oddie says the flying flocks do resemble a flurry of snow, so you can imagine why my thoughts turned to them as I write these words in the midst of our deep January freeze. The *snow bunting* is a winter visitor from the Arctic Circle, normally to inaccessible mountaintops in Scotland or to coastal locations in the north and east.

What a joy it is to see an unusual bird. Or indeed an old friend like a *blackbird* or a *robin* and the annual migratory birds, with the first arrivals, the *wheatears* and the *sand martins*. Christmas cards with a bird design were rated a good second to the traditional Christian scene this year.

Birds do lift the heart and cause a flutter:
the sudden but silent ghostlike flight of the *barn owl*
the trilling crowd of *long tailed tits*
the majestic *swan* beating the air
the orchestrated symphony of swirling *starlings*.

No wonder that Jesus recommended in the Sermon on the Mount: "Consider the birds of the air".

Birds in their great variety of some 10,000 species remind us of the amazing diversity we encounter on our planet. They are evidence of exuberant divine creativity. New species are still being discovered like the *silver browed warbler* in Laos, but sadly as well, others are on the brink of extinction or have already disappeared from our world, like the *passenger pigeon*. Their adaptation to different environments and climatic systems is also amazing — *little egrets* have come to the UK and now *spoonbills* are beginning to nest here. But too often human short-sightedness and greed deny them their rightful habitats. However, it seems that Jesus didn't mean us to become eco-terrorists or even over-the-top twitchers. Several times he taught that a human being is more valuable to God than many birds (*sparrows*). In other words, attracted though we may be to the plight of starving *albatrosses* because of unscrupulous fishing techniques in the South Atlantic, we must be as much or indeed more concerned for starving human beings wherever they are. For they are formed in the image and likeness of God himself.

We are instructed to be as innocent as *doves*; to fit in with the proper rhythms of life and God's purpose just as *storks* and *cranes* know perfectly when to migrate; to find our true spiritual home in God's family just as *swallows* build their nests close to the altar in God's temple.

One of the two occasions recorded in the Bible when Jesus wept was when he was meditating on those in his day who refused to acknowledge him for who he was. He compared them to chicks who refused the offered protection of their mother hen. He wept for them in their unnatural and wayward behaviour, as he longed to gather them together. Both the Hebrew and the Greek words for 'church' have the strong idea of the gathered community.

Yes, our feathered friends have much to teach us.

When we moved into deeper retirement in Warwick in 2010, I did contribute a voluntary piece to St Nicholas church magazine. I think I must have been missing the stimulus of producing a short article on some interesting topic. I know this is the case for my brother Michael, who has been in journalism all his life and can't stop writing! And why should he? Anyway, for 14 months in 2012/13 I wrote about various topics for the *InTouch* magazine. My theme was **A Biblical Alphabet** and I had great fun choosing a subject from the Bible to go through the alphabet. So I started with Angels and went on to Baptism, Cosmetics, Death, Eschatology, Food, Genealogies, Hospitality, Inspiration, Job, Kenosis, Land, Money and Numbers. To my own disappointment I never managed to complete the alphabet, as the magazine became defunct. Whether my uncompleted series had anything to do with its demise I shall never know! If anyone wants to commission a series of 12 articles from O–Z I shall be happy to oblige!

Letters to the Press

These featured chiefly during my years in the Bradford diocese. No doubt because a bishop is a public figure. Sometimes he is asked directly to comment on a current issue. Other times he might be strongly motivated to add to public discussion on a contentious subject. Or he may decide to write off on a more laid back and humorous topic. The following give a flavour of that correspondence:

A letter to the editor of the Church Times *25/2/1982.*

I wrote to tell him that a copy of his paper had been impounded by a customs official on the Andean border between Peru and Bolivia during one of my journeys. Here is the reply from Bernard Palmer himself:

25th February 1982

My dear Bishop,

Many thanks for your letter of February 9th and it is fascinating to know that the *Church Times* is regarded as forbidden fruit by the Bolivian customs officers. Next time some snooty young English curate sneers at the paper I shall tell him that it is required in the guardhouse at Desaguadero.

Anyway I shall be delighted to print your letter in next week's issue, in which, by a strange coincidence, I am also planning to publish a major article on Anglicanism in South America—in preparation for the inauguration of the new Province in May. Actually you may have read the article already as I am reprinting it from the official news-sheet issued by the ACC. But it seemed to me so well written as to be worth a wider audience.

May I take this opportunity of enclosing a copy of the impounded edition of the *Church Times*, and you can decide which particular part of the paper may have excited the suspicions of the gendarmerie.

With all good wishes

Yours sincerely

(signed)

Editor

On returning to ministry in the U.K. after 20 years' service in South America, we were very struck by how the English language had evolved. A large number of phrases had become commonplace in our absence. Jargon was rife! I refer especially to ecclesiastical jargon. But a good number of frequently used words were common across the board. The letter was published in the *Church of England Newspaper* in 1988.

WORDS

Welcome back to good old England and to our annual reorientation course. After your time overseas you face taking quite a lot on board. Actually of course a U.K. Christian worker is rather a 'different animal'. You may now have to get into being a Sector Minister or an Executive Officer. You will be expected to have managerial, professional skills. You will be advised that there is a lot of mileage in having a support group. Sabbaticals are very much in both for you and your spouse. Of course that wouldn't be the case if you were a part-time non-stipendary parish deacon, but if you were a stipendiary team vicar working in a collaborative style you should be OK. You would have to follow the code of good practice of course. You need to take on board that you must never refer to man liturgically or you will be accused of sexist language. Women nearly became visible at the last General Synod but on a matter of procedure their appearance has been postponed. There are also quite a few more committees nowadays either standing or steering or advisory, all ready to monitor your progress to ensure you don't exceed your remit.

We advise you to go along with them or you may be faced with a major infrastructure review on your hands. Another way to avoid this would be to ensure frequent appraisals of your work by an evaluator who would come with an open agenda, or of course you could have a regular consultant, either theological, group process or management, who will soon sort out your hidden agendas. Being bland or fudging issues is definitely out, at least theoretically. As long as you know all about F.I.T.C. C.U.P.A and A.C.O.R.A. you should be on the right wavelength. Do hope you feel affirmed.

Good luck and God bless.

On 30th April 1990 I was involved in a Sunday programme on Radio 4. This basically involved an exchange of views with the then Bishop of Oxford, the Right Revd Richard Harries. This followed on from the Lambeth Conference of 1988, where the above had presented a document about relationships between Jews, Christians and Muslims. While believing firmly in the uniqueness of Christ, Bishop Harries was much happier with the concept of dialogue in, of course, an atmosphere of mutual respect. He also argued in the face of the growth of paganism in Europe that Jews, Christians and Muslims should join forces to stop the slide into paganism. I expressed the opinion that we had to go further, in the end, than exchange views in a respectful dialogue. The Christian church has a missionary mandate from Christ himself to proclaim his message to the whole world. I was 'new' to the situation in the Bradford diocese and there were some repercussions from the programme. And of course the theological issues have not gone away.

In September 1990 I wrote to the editor of the *Church Times* about an article covering the Anglican Congress on World Evangelism in Singapore. In my opinion, I said, the article did not do justice to the event, at which I had actually been present. I wrote

> I agree that attacks on 'lifeless Anglicanism' were too frequent and often made to get cheap laughs.

However, I stated that "there is another side and I hope you will feel able to publish the enclosed article."

APATHETIC, AGLOW, ABLAZE

"The Church on fire" was the title for the South East Asian Conference on World Evangelism which took place recently in Singapore with over 800 delegates from 38 countries.

By the year 2000, 58% of the world's population will be in Asia. And Asia is where the Christian Church is weakest, at least numerically. However, the Christian population of Singapore has risen from 8% to 25% in the last decade. And these churches are dynamic, have missionary vision, money, masses of young people, and excellent organisation. Of course they are over-enthusiastic and on occasions go over the top and their leadership seeks to guide them into maturity. But we write them off at our spiritual peril. They need us and we need them.

Within the course of one week two large interdenominational Festivals of Praise were held in the National Stadium with nearly 10,000 present; the Anglican Congress took place smoothly in a converted and refurbished cinema seating 2000. The congress included a banquet for 1500 people; every evening in five different locations evangelistic meetings were held in different parts of the city. The local churches were unstinting in their sheer hard work and faith and prayer and sacrificial giving.

There was a large contingent of delegates from Australia and New Zealand, token delegates from Africa and no one from either South or North America except a small group from Canada. A handful alone from the U.K. The bulk were from South East Asia and it was thrilling to see many from Malaysia. For those who like to count episcopal heads, there were 27 of us! By no means all signed-up members of the charismatic renewal.

Of course we would all prefer Christians to be just aglow with the Spirit for the Decade of Evangelism. But maybe if there are many that are apathetic, the Lord permits some of His servants to be ablaze to see if some of us can be rekindled with a spark from Singapore.

On 5th August 1991 the *Independent* published my letter about the Revd Alec Vidler in its obituary addition column.

The Rev Alec Vidler

Alec Vidler was my Church History supervisor at Cambridge, writes the Right Rev David Evans (further to the obituaries by The Rev Professor Owen Chadwick and Richard Ingrams, 30 July). I vividly remember one tutorial in his study in King's. It was a jumble of busts, books and bee equipment. I was feeling vulnerable as my fellow undergraduate had not turned up and was thus alone in this extravagant environment with an awesome personage in black and white: black shirt, white tie and exuberant black-and-white hair on his chin, his eyebrows and head.

Our subject was the modernist movement in the Roman church. I had suitably regurgitated material from his own writing. But what remains with me to this day is his teaching on an item of correct English syntax. "You *cannot* and you *will not* write ever again 'centre around', on any essay for me . . . You 'centre on'." At the time I think I resented this attention to detail. However, I have never forgotten the English lesson, though my memories of Roman modernists are more dim.

A letter to *The Times* had referred to the "unsaintly applause" during the enthronement in Canterbury Cathedral of Archbishop George Carey. Again, having been present for the ceremony I wrote to put the record straight about the "unseemly behaviour" as described by the original writer.

Unsaintly applause

From the Assistant Bishop of Bradford

Sir, the applause in Canterbury Cathedral at the enthronement (report, April 20) broke out spontaneously among the suffragan bishops as Archbishop George Carey greeted them in the sharing of the Peace. It had nothing do with the music being played.

The applause then worked down the cathedral, without those outside the door knowing why it had started. At the end of the service the "nave" congregation also broke into applause, for the same reason of expressing support for the Archbishop.

Yours faithfully

In November 1991 I wrote to the *Telegraph and Argus of Bradford* about genetic engineering.

Things have moved a long way in the last 25 years. We rejoice to have two grandchildren thanks to I.V.F. However, I believe it is still time that 'for human happiness, ethics should always control genetics.'

The Independent published my letter on *Four Weddings and a Funeral* on 27th April 1995. I was pleased subsequently to receive support from Archbishop George Carey.

On 13 October 1997 I expostulated about the conjunction of misused biblical texts to advertise the brand of Abbot Ale in a national newspaper.

Ye shall drink no wine	Jeremiah 35:6
For them hath the Lord chosen to carry	1 Chronicles 15.2
For it is written	Luke 4:8

On 10th January 1994 *The Independent* published the following letter, a contribution to a vast number of letters on the subject of Prime Minister John Major's definition of Back to Basics issues.

From the Rt Rev David Evans

Sir: Lord Hailsham's clear legal mind should be a help in the present confusion about the content of the Back to Basics programme. In his autobiography, published in 1990, he defined natural morality as:

Respect for parents' authority and one's neighbours' rights, kindness, patriotism, courage, responsible sexual behavior, respect for the environment, respect for one's own body, truth-telling, financial integrity, loyalty to friendships, tolerance of differences of opinion, openness of discussion, and forbearance to intrude into the private lives of others.

He compiled this list as a summary of the *philosophia perennis*, 'the eternal philosophy', which he expressed in the context of his own Christian faith but saw as an indispensable basis for any human community. It is a good list, far better than recent *ad hoc* ones. It is not an optional extra if we want to have a viable community life into the 21st century.

Yours sincerely,

Other speaking commitments

During the past 50 years I have married and buried many people. That of course is the normal run of events, especially for a parish priest. However, I have not had the year by year routine of ministering to people from birth to death in the life of hatching, matching and dispatching, as it has been called! But in my special 'dates to remember' diary I have at least one. and sometimes several. anniversaries marked for 214 days of the year. Baptisms, confirmations, birthdays, weddings, deaths. Many names have disappeared from my active memory. Others I can recall instantly. For instance, on 17th November 1990 I was asked to preach at the memorial service for the Revd Kenneth Hooker, who had been my first vicar after ordination at Christ Church, Cockfosters. I quote:

> I conclude with a summary, like the weather forecaster but with that alliteration that Ken was so fond of in his own sermons –
>
> Recover the true love of souls
>
> Rely on delegated divine Authority
>
> Receive overflowing divine grace
>
> Rejoice with spirit-inspired joy.
>
> What a privilege to have been able to pay tribute to a wonderful man of God.

On 1st October 1994 I preached at the wedding of David Bentley-Taylor and Felicity Houghton.

This was an extraordinary event. David was a world-famous CIM/OMF missionary among students and Muslims in Indonesia. He had already been married once for over 50 years! And Felicity was a university student worker most of her life in South America, especially in Chile and Bolivia and always unmarried, again for over 50 years. On the death of David's first wife the Lord brought the two of them together for companionship in the last years of their lives of wholehearted service. Felicity became an instant 'great grandmother'! I preached on Psalm 34: 1–5 "Exalt the Lord together and be radiant." I still have David's thank you letter from that marvellous occasion.

Marriage of David Bentley-Taylor and Felicity Houghton

On 9th September 1979 I preached at a Memorial Service in the Good Shepherd church to honour the life of the recently assassinated Lord Mountbatten of Burma. I spoke on Hebrews 6:19, the hope which is like an anchor for our lives, connecting us to the Christ whose solid worth and unique character support totally his words and promises for life and for death. Both a First Sea Lord and a midshipman, and you and I, need an anchor for our soul.

On 28th May 1982 I preached (in Spanish of course) at the episcopal consecration of the Chilean pastor Omar Ortiz in the cathedral of Asunción in Paraguay. This was a big occasion for the Anglican Church in South America. It was the first consecration of a South American national as a diocesan bishop. I preached on the text Luke 10: 17–20 and specifically on the words of Jesus: "Do not rejoice that the spirits submit to you, but rejoice that your names are written in heaven." This turned out to be quite a prophetic sermon because Omar found the move from Chile to Paraguay and the promotion from priest to bishop difficult. He was not able to complete his hoped-for work and returned to Chile.

During my time in the Bradford diocese, i.e. from 1998–1993, I instituted 65 new ministries. Always a church full to bursting to welcome

Ordination of Priests, Petertide, 30th June1991
Ken Medhurst, Jenny Smith, Anthony Atkins,
David Mewis, Bill Green, Alex Brighouse, Alistair Kaye

a new minister, with at least one bus load of faithful supporters from the previous church. Always a bun fight afterwards. Always a good occasion with legal niceties to be sorted, hopes to be raised for the future and often a sense of bereavement for those passing on their pastor to another congregation. I pick out two of these institutions:

My first one, and therefore memorable for me, was of the Revd Steve Allen in St John's Great Horton, Bradford. I preached on Isaiah 49:2 "The Lord made me into a polished arrow." I drew out a number of relevant points from this imagery: being available for use in God's powerful hands, being sharp and effective and on target to score 'bullseyes' for the kingdom. I had an actual arrow from the Argentine Chaco in the pulpit as a visual aid. This helped to focus people's thoughts.

On 5th June 1992 (my birthday), I instituted the Revd Christopher Edmondson to St Peter's Shipley. My text was 2 Timothy 4:1–5, where the biblical exhortation to Timothy was "always be steady." The picture is of a helmsman keeping a firm hand on the tiller of a ship as he steers it on its proper course. Chris fulfilled that ministry at St Peter's and went on (at the time of writing) to become the Bishop of Birkenhead. Many years later contact with him was renewed as he became involved in the 'resurrection' of EFAC in 2018.

Ordination of Deacons, 28th June 1992
Di Halliday, Terry Baxter, Tim Wright, Marc Cooper, Keith Trout, Pater Hart

In August 1968 I gave a series of talks at a young people's summer camp at West Runton in Norfolk. It was the year of the Olympic Games in Mexico, so my title for the 11 talks was The Christian Olympics. Quite soon our whole family was to be heading for Mexico. Nothing to do with the Olympic Games. We went there for three months of intensive study of Spanish, before from Mexico heading south to Argentina. Many times I have used the biblical analogy of athletics as a picture of the Christian life. Hebrews 12: "Let us run the race that is set before us" is one of the most familiar texts. At the boys' summer camp my titles were: The Christian Race: Sign On: Keep Fit: Stick to the Rules: Follow the Leader: Cheers from the Crowd: Keep Fighting: Strip Down: All Rounder: Don't Give Up: Gold Medals. I have my written notes still of these addresses. I wonder if any of the teenage boys, who would now be in their fifties, have any recollections at all of these talks. I am encouraged to think that the Holy Spirit does take biblical teaching and sometimes key catchphrases, biblical or not, and write them on our hearts in a special way. From my time in Cambridge (1959–63), I remember a phrase from a sermon by Herbert Carson: "How Much More". He was expounding the text Romans 8:32 "If God did not spare his own Son—how much more shall he graciously give us all things." Secure in the knowledge that I had received God's own Son as my Saviour and Lord, a great future panorama of divine generosity opened up to me! How much more . . . over the 60 years since I heard that sermon, do I want to testify to the Lord's generous and gracious provision for me.

Institution of David Robinson, 7th April 1992

5E
A BISHOP AS AN EVANGELICAL LEADER

(EFAC: Evangelical Fellowship in the Anglican Communion)

As mentioned earlier, it has been characteristic of my ministry, both before and after being made a bishop in the Church of God, that I have had more than one hat on at any one time. And that has nothing to do with mitres! In fact, I have only used these sparingly and only since beginning to work in the Bradford diocese.

EFAC Theological Consultation

Officially EFAC came into existence in 1961 through the outstanding international ministry of the late Revd John Stott. He was concerned to consolidate and extend the influence of evangelicals in the Church of England and throughout the Anglican Communion. He began to assemble evangelical clergy in the C. of E. through The Eclectics gatherings, before the 1958 Lambeth Conference. He also corresponded with a number of evangelical bishops around the world, especially in

Australia. The concern was the desirability for evangelical bishops from different parts of the world meeting before the Conference to consider a joint approach to the major upcoming issues. This happened on a small scale.

When the 1968 Lambeth Conference was on the horizon, an international pre-Lambeth gathering was planned. This met in June 1993 to consider "The Anglican Communion and Scripture".

I came on the EFAC scene with the 1978 Pre-Lambeth Conference held in Oak Hill College. I was a 'baby' bishop indeed. It helped me enormously before the full conference in Canterbury.

Subsequently I was invited onto the EFAC International Executive Committee as the representative Area Secretary for South America.

EFAC Pre-Lambeth 1978 in Oak Hill College

In 1987 I was at an Executive meeting in Oxford involved in preparing for the 1988 Lambeth Conference. I was heavily involved in the planning of this, to be held for the first time in Canterbury itself, at the University of Kent immediately prior to the Lambeth event. I was International Coordinator of EFAC by then and remained so for ten years, up to the 1998 Lambeth Conference. On that occasion we met in the King's School

College in Canterbury. I handed over to Canon George Kovoor in July 2003 at one of our theological consultations in Limuru, Kenya, when we also had my final (13th!) Executive Committee.

EFAC Visit to Lambeth Palace prior to 1988 Lambeth Conference

Limuru handover of EFAC International Coordinator

Limuru handover of EFAC Internetional Coordinator, July 2003
Canon George Kovoor and Bishop David Evans
Bishop Robinson Cavalcanti (Brazil)   Bishop Glen Davies (Australia)
Moderator Archbishop K. J. Samuel (India)   Bishop Anthony Burton (Canada),
Bishop Ben Kwashi (Nigeria)   Revd Michael Poon (Hong Kong)
Bishop Samza Mwalude (Kenya)

In one sense I was not functioning as a bishop specifically as International Coordinator of EFAC. However, the task brought me into contact with very eminent church leaders, including numbers of Archbishops from all around the world. I sometimes thought to myself that EFAC was a bit like an Evangelical Anglican Communion! It was built on the international ministry of John Stott as preacher/teacher and strategist. Its international coverage varied greatly. Sometimes it provided a forum for isolated evangelicals in unfriendly environments. Sometimes, especially in Africa, through its provincial Archbishop, like the late David Gitari in Kenya, it involved a whole family of dioceses.

I asked for the new title of International Coordinator for the 14 years of my work, because I saw it as that, a work of coordination between groups, who totally ran their own national programmes. The largest coordination work was for the two Pre-Lambeth Conferences of 1988 and 1998. International Executive meetings were held regularly. I bowed out in 2003 after 13 of those in various parts of the world, either as separate events or attached to other EFAC conferences like the Lausanne II

Conference in Manila, the Philippines. Sometimes we had a high technology telephone link-up normally based in Oxford. Also organized were regional theological consultations which were deliberately chosen in appropriate cultural and geographical settings. For instance, we met in Jamaica with its history of the slave trade to study the doctrine of man, "Called to Full Humanity". On another occasion we met in Mombasa to study evangelism with case studies from 11 different national and cultural settings. This was written up into a Regnum book, *One Gospel, Many Clothes,* in 1990 to mark the retirement of John Stott as President of the Evangelical Fellowship of the Anglican Communion, edited by Chris Wright and Chris Sugden.

Apart from these meetings I also travelled extensively to visit the work of different EFAC groups and minister the Word of God at all sorts of gatherings. These took me over that 14-year period to New Zealand and Australia, the Philippines, Sri Lanka, Singapore, Malaysia, Brazil, Jamaica, USA, Canada, Kenya, Nigeria and South Africa. Also Scotland, Wales and England.

Some key memories include substituting at short notice for Michael Green at a church in Singapore, where the congregation was some 2000 people. This compensating (perhaps!) for my disappointment at not preaching in Singapore's Cathedral, because of repair work—we had an open-air service in the grounds with a wooden stage, etc. instead.

I had to deliver a Latimer House lecture in Christchurch, New Zealand and a lecture on evangelism with logical credibility in Mombasa. In a three-day visit organized by EFAC Australia in 1996 I spoke at their annual conference on worldwide evangelical Anglicanism, through the lens of all the descriptive labels given to them and their respective importance. I entitled it "Personal Lament—Labels Galore" (see Appendix A, page 235).

A typical EFAC Executive meeting, this one held in Mombasa, Kenya in 1990. The people involved then give an idea of the 'world' coverage and the seniority of those involved. The Revd Chris Sugden took the photo.

In the photo from the left in the front row are:

> The Right Revd John Rodgers, USA
> The Right Revd Emmanuel Gbonigi, Nigeria
> Mrs Jill Dain, General Synod of C. of E.
> The Right Revd Ian Cameron, Australia & Chairman
> DRJE

The Revd John Stott

Archbishop David Gitari, Kenya

In the photo from the left in the back row are:

The Revd Don Irving, CEO of Intercon, Europe

The Revd David Claydon, CEO of CMS Australia

The Revd James Wong of Singapore

The Right Revd Robinson Cavalcanti of Brazil

The Right Revd Michael Nazir-Ali of the C. of E.

EFAC Executive, Mombasa, Kenya, 1990   (Photo: Chris Sugden)

5F
A BISHOP AS MISSIONARY EXECUTIVE

SAMS GB and International

This section seeks to present a summary of the ten years spent as General Secretary of SAMS UK from 1993–2003. It includes experiences as part of the SAMS International family with membership in New Zealand, Australia, Canada, USA and Ireland over that same period.

SAMS General Secrearies

Canon Philip King : 1974–1986
Bishop Bill Flagg : 1986–1993
Bishop David Evans : 1993–2003

I was the 20th since Capt. Allen Gardiner, 1844–1850

I start with a *SHARE* article I wrote in 2003 about SAMS General Secretaries.

SHARE: The Society Magazine

20 of them between 1944 and 2003—17 clergy, including 3 canons and 2 bishops. Also 3 captains, including, of course, Captain Allen Gardiner himself from 1844–1850. 2 Despards between 1850 and 1856 and now 2 Canon Suttons between 1960 and 1974 and 2003 . . .

Often I have been asked what a SAMS General Secretary does . . . if anything! I have usually replied along the lines of 'the title says it all'. Sometimes I have felt like a General in the sense of leadership and responsibility. That is right. The buck has to stop somewhere. The General Secretary is hired and can be fired by the Board of Trustees, but he/she is the Chief Executive Officer of the Society and as such has a public profile.

SAMS Executive Home Staff   We met often

SAMS Executive Home Staff
We worked hard

At other times I have felt like a Secretary, performing rather less upfront ministry behind the scenes (Let me just pay tribute to the four excellent secretaries who, over the last 10 years, have kept me afloat and going to the right church at the right weekend — Mary Rollin, Rosemary Barratt, Sue Waymark and Gillian Bamford). Whether communication is written or screened, or whether it is face-to-face in networking relationships, it is vital. Interesting, isn't it, that the United Nations has a Secretary General rather than a General Secretary. High public profile and behind-the-scenes relationships and communications. There you have it.

SAMS Executive Home Staff   We relaxed hard

Dorothy will be joining me for our last visit to South America from April 25th to May 17th 2003. We will go to Buenos Aires, Santa Cruz (Bolivia), Arequipa and Lima in Peru. Official retirement date is 5th June, but we may move out of the Selly Oak house just before that to go to the Vicarage, Alderminster, near Stratford-upon-Avon, for a 'house for duty' ministry in the Coventry diocese.

Gospel work in South America and the Iberian Peninsula has gone ahead under God during the time of 19 General Secretaries. With your continued support, I am confident it will go forward with John Sutton, Welcome your 20th General Secretary.

The attached account, sent for publication in *Newsround*, the Diocese of Bradford's paper, gives a flavour of the mindset we had on returning to work in the UK. Our missionary experiences in Latin America obviously coloured our service in the Bradford diocese and then also served as hands-on experience for the time as General Secretary of SAMS.

NEWSROUND, Bradford Diocese

Our experiences in Latin America
Our 20 years of Latin American experience has enriched us in many ways. I share briefly with you three of them.

CHANGING

In 1972 I wrote from Buenos Aires, Argentina: "We have mastered Spanish, if not perfected it, we have learned to kiss or shake hands with everyone we meet, we are used to ants, humidity, heat, hectic traffic, police carrying sub-machine guns, beggars at the door, and a hundred and one other hazards. It has been said of Latin American Christianity that "the medium of communication is not the doctrine but the testimony, not the systematic theology, but the song, not the articulation of concepts but the celebration of banquets" . . . i.e. not theology, something academic and central but something vital and dynamic. That's all rather disturbing to a Northern Hemisphere Anglican. However it doesn't mean 'being tossed back and forth by the waves and blown here and there by every wind of teaching'. It does mean discovering what is the fundamental that must be held onto and what is secondary and changeable according to culture and circumstantial needs. After all we are in a changing process in God's Kingdom; 'we are being transformed into his likeness'. I don't believe that changing process should stop throughout our life."

OVERCOMING

In 1976 I witnessed an Argentine girl student being kidnapped. Her tortured body was found four days later riddled with bullets. In Peru we had numerous experiences of the vicious spiral of violence, of life becoming cheapened, of people degenerating. Easter week spent in the Shining Light terrorist-dominated area of Ayacucho was an eye opener to suffering. It was also a shock to discover how much happens that can be kept secret for political reasons, how the truth can be distorted and how hopeless the cause of justice seems. The truly frightening aspect is that beyond the comprehensible logic of some levels of violence and vengeance we discover the 'mystery of iniquity', the sadistic darkness of meaningless cruelty and hatred. Yes, we really are in a spiritual battle. When Paul was writing to the church in Rome about not taking vengeance, he also said "Do not be overcome by evil but overcome evil with good". This overcoming is not achieved only by human effort or by united action, but by spiritual power.

PIONEERING

It has been a great privilege to be involved with many others in new work, in creating the new 27th province of the Anglican Communion, province of the Southern Cone of South America, creating a new Diocese of Peru and getting Bolivia ready for its independence, opening 14 new churches, ordaining the first 12 Peruvian priests, and to be involved in an atmosphere of spiritual expectancy and growth.

High-powered Theological Consultation in Oxford
with Vinay Samuel and Chris Sugden and four Archbishops (Tanzania and Madagascar, Indian Ocean, Wales and Anglican Church in USA)

We found this expectancy in public worship, in evangelism and in the ministry of healing. We had the sense of being on the move, which was very encouraging. I attribute this partly to the fact that in most countries of Latin America more than 50% of the population is under twenty and partly to a very direct faith in God, unhampered by institutions and traditions challenging concepts in any sphere of Christian work.

An overview of my International visits follows. This shows fairly dramatically that a General Secretary, as executive leader of a missionary society, certainly doesn't spend all his time behind a desk.

Eleven of these visits were 'full scale', roughly month-long visits to several different countries. Four were shorter visits to Spain or Portugal. The two-month visit to Australia and New Zealand was basically an EFAC invitation, but it developed naturally into a SAMS visit as well.

1st Tour	Feb-March	1994	Brazil, Argentina, Paraguay
2nd Tour	Oct-Nov	1994	Chile, Bolivia, Peru
	December	1994	Visit to Spain
	February	1995	Visit to Jersey
3rd Tour	Oct-Nov	1995	Brazil, Uruguay, Paraguay
		1995	Visit to Israel
4th Tour	May	1996	Argentina, Chile, Peru, Bolivia
	June-July	1996	Visit to Australia & New Zealand
	April-May	1997	Visit to Spain
5th Tour	June	1997	Argentina, Paraguay, Brazil
6th Tour	October	1998	Chile, Peru, Bolivia, Mexico
	March	1999	Visit to Spain
7th Tour	October	1999	Argentina, Uruguay, Brazil, Paraguay, Mexico
	April	2000	Visit to Brazil
	June	2000	Visit to Portugal
8th Tour	Sept-Oct	2000	Chile, Bolivia, Peru, Ecuador
	February	2001	Visit to Bolivia
9th Tour	Oct-Nov	2001	Argentina, Uruguay, Paraguay, Brazil
	December	2001	Visit to Peru, Brazil
	April	2002	Visit to Spain
10th Tour	July	2002	Chile, Bolivia, Brasilia
11th Tour	April-May	2003	Argentina, Bolivia, Peru

This list does not include specific EFAC visits for theological consultations around the globe, or stopping-off visits, especially in the United States and Canada when going to or from the U.K. on a furlough visit, or travel to three Lambeth Conferences and their preparation, or gathering for SAMS International General Secretaries' meetings.

As appropriate I add a few comments on the various tours as brief snapshots of interesting occasions. The reports are full of the names of SAMS missionaries, their joys and their sorrows and the state of the work in which they are involved. Sometimes there is a real problem to seek to unravel. Relating to the bishops and other national leaders is a clear priority. Seeking to assess whether we are making the right sort of contribution as an international mission agency to the growth and health of the South American dioceses is vital.

For every tour I circulated a Link Letter to our prayer supporters so they could follow me in the various countries and speaking commitments with their prayers. I quote from the second link letter 1994:

> It is a great privilege to travel, to share in stories of blessing and tales of woe. Sometimes there is a real problem to seek to unravel and there may be really difficult pastoral decisions to be made. The timetable is always exacting, the changes of climate can be dramatic, the travelling is very wearying, the constant change of faces, known and unknown, is demanding. The variation in intonation, vocabulary and culture (how many times are you meant to kiss people?) require constant attention. Several times in my diaries I came across a phrase similar to 'collapsed exhausted into bed'!

Tour 1. Brazil, Argentina, Paraguay 21st Feb–18th March 1994

The first is a document summarising five general comments on the work after five years away from South America and back in the U.K. This is followed by a report assessing the possibility of furthering SAMS involvement in the new Diocese of Brasilia.

Report of the Right Revd David Evans on his First Tour of South America,
21st Feb–18th March 1994

Half of this tour was dedicated to visiting four of the seven Brazilian dioceses plus a brief stopover in a fifth (Rio). The other half involved visits to Buenos Aires, Montevideo, Salta and Asunción. First, I want to make some general comments on the four Southern dioceses as viewed from the perspective of five years in the English Diocese of Bradford.

These are really all still missionary dioceses, because of their comparatively small numbers and fragility in countries with enormous economic and social problems. The resources available in professional backup and local finance are still limited and put local leadership under considerable strain. The Anglican Church in Buenos Aires has still to realise its potential, while other denominations have increased dramatically, and Montevideo is still in the process of establishing itself as a viable diocese.

I am immensely impressed by the total dedication of the missionary spearhead bishops and their wives who give of themselves unstintingly. They need our disciplined prayer support. They are all spiritual, ecumenical and even national figures. I believe they could benefit from more regional peer support, i.e. Buenos Aires and Montevideo, Salta and Asunción.

Future episcopal leadership continues to be a vital priority. Often, perhaps partly through 'fall-out', there is a big gap of middle management between the episcopal office and the local parish priest. Sometimes 'archdeacons' can prepare for a wider supervisory role (as in Salta) or sometimes an administrator needs to be found to bridge the efficiency gap.

Comprehensiveness. I was concerned to discern real problems in terms of the lack of a united thrust in some areas (including Brazil) where both ex-Roman-Catholic priests and more evangelical pastors exist in the same small diocese.

Challenging work

I was impressed with the amount of important Bible translation work to which we are still committed. It is obviously a need and something of a primary concern that has grown up on us, with the Draysons, Mike Browne, Tim Curtis and Bob Lunt (and Tito Lahaye) involved.

Balancing evangelism and involvement in social projects continues to be a delicate issue (Montevideo). As also the enthusiasm for new work over against the continuing support of older ones (Tucumán and Jujuy, Salta, etc). A viable diocese must have a certain number of local congregations; otherwise it cannot be a functioning diocese. In Montevideo opportunities abound to act as a N.G.O., so church planting also needs to be given good impetus. I am glad that we have been asked to strengthen our contribution to the growth of the church in Montevideo.

There is great vision in Asunción for a Teacher Training College alongside St Andrew's School. And also for the Cathedral church to have a ministry where school parents can feel at home. This is vital to capitalise on the excellent work and the long-term investment in the school.

Next I want to report about Brazil

Bishop Glauco Soares de Lima has been elected to be Primate 1994–1997. He is a moderate. I would judge that Bishop Jubal Neves will replace him in 1997, as the most dynamic Brazilian bishop, the one with an international ministry (Design Committee for Lambeth Conference 1998) and the one who knows the province best as former Provincial Secretary. He is also the one who is actively inviting support in his Diocese of Santa Maria.

The whole church continues in its 'post-emancipation syndrome', feeling orphaned rather than proceeding to adulthood after its 100 years of relationship with ECUSA. More than half of all the clergy are NSM. With 40% monthly inflation life is tough. Diocesan finances tend to rely on the renting of property rather than live income from congregations. (Shades of the Church Commissioners!) Again, as in Uruguay, there is still a long way to go to have viable dioceses in terms of local congregations, especially in Brasilia.

In Recife and Rio the bishops are not too friendly to SAMS. Both should be retiring soon. Some of the best work, however, is in their dioceses. The Meldrums and the Garcias in Olinda and Recife in the North, and the Broughtons and Edmeia Williams (Mary and Martha home) in Rio. We must not give up in these areas, where solid work has been done in the past, key people are in place and new horizons could open up. The Garcias have the biggest Anglican Church in South America, working out of an old English Chaplaincy church. 250 confirmation candidates a year. He has been invited to Swanwick 1995.

Brasilia was formed as a new diocese, carved out of São Paulo in order for the church to have a local presence in the new capital city (1960). Bishop Almir Santos, its second bishop, is very keen for our involvement and the sending of an international church planting team. The city of Brasilia has architecturally designed housing for some 500,000 and satellite 'cities' or slums, in some cases for a further 1½ million. The reasons I would bring for planning to assemble and send a team to Brasilia are as follows.

Brasilia is the newest missionary diocese, with only four full-time priests. It has a small central cathedral building and a nearby housing and administrative block to support a core diocesan team. It needs church planting ministry in the satellite cities, both middle-class and working-class and slum.

The Bishop Almir de Santos is a spiritual man, very welcoming and an expert internationally on the 360 Indian tribes in the interior of Brazil. He has a magnificent wife who would 'mother' missionaries. The Revd Luis Caetano is keen to have further staff (he is from São Paulo), the other three full timers being from Porto Alegre (and known to him as 'The Mafia'!).

I was very impressed with the NSM Guillerme Luz, an ex-Civil Servant who through initiative and enthusiasm has not only produced a huge Christian family including 2 musical groups but has also been the leading light in three new congregations which are under way. He is pure Indian, of Baptist parents, but totally integrated and accepted in this diocese's work. He would be a sympathetic 'Director of Evangelism' in the diocese to encourage missionary church planters.

Brasilia has an excellent Linguistic and Orientation Centre, run in Jesuit buildings, sponsored by the Roman Catholic Bishops of Brazil. It keeps room for 20% ecumenical members. It costs US$2,000 for 4 months and has high standards, important visiting speakers and basic accommodation for families. It would be good for Latin American Spanish speakers to go there, as well as any mission partners from SAMS.

Tour 2. Chile, Bolivia, Peru Oct–Nov 1994   *SAMS Link Letter 3*

In our 150th anniversary year, I was moved to be in Punta Arenas, feeling close to the heroic exploits of the SAMS trailblazers of the last century. Passion for souls and incredible courage and fortitude characterized their lives. We seem materialistic and soft in comparison. A plan was half mooted for the five SAMS General Secretaries to meet in Spaniard Harbour in 2001, where Allen Gardiner died in 1851.

The Anglican Marriage Encounter weekends are the main focus for church growth in the countries visited. Borrowed from the Roman Catholics by Gordon Whitehead back in the 70s this method has come into its own and bears fruit now. Seeds faithfully sown can take time bringing a harvest. The first Bolivian Anglican may return to La Paz after years in the USA. He is training for ordination at Trinity Episcopal School, Pennsylvania.

On 7th October the first regular Sunday ministry was inaugurated in Cochabamba. This is the fourth Anglican Congregation in Bolivia. Under the firm hand of Bishop Gregory Venables, the first locally resident bishop, I believe things will progress steadily. Such unspectacular growth is more honouring to the Lord than fly-by-night campaigns and the wooing of denominational travellers. The problem of 'the unchurched evangelised' is particularly relevant to Bolivia.

The return to Peru was rather emotional. So many things were happening simultaneously. The 150th Anniversary of the Cathedral Church of the Good Shepherd focused on a splendid service with Prince Michael of Kent, the Papal Nuncio, a representative of the Peruvian President and Ambassadors present.

Provincial Executive and SAMS International Executives

The church was originally called the Protestant Church of Lima and played its part in securing a greater measure of religious freedom in the first half of the 19th century. I visited my Roman Catholic bishop friend of 1984 and we prayed for each other.

The SAMS International 'executives' and the Executive Committee of the Province of the Southern Cone met uniquely also in Lima. A special document produced by Julie Wadsworth of SAMS was signed and taken back to the 12 countries represented. The relationships between national churches and mission agencies were well explored. A study was proposed of all those missionaries who had not completed more than one period of service. It was pointed out that this would include the present chairman of SAMS Ireland and the present General Secretary of SAMS USA!

Local churches, especially with no Establishment connections, are tender plants. Some are more exotic and proliferate luxuriously, others hold on desperately, while yet others die and yet their seeds bring life elsewhere. Some need the pruner's sharp knife, others the shepherd's tender care. No church exists on earth today as testimony to the original labours of SAMS missionaries in the uttermost part of the earth. But we shall meet with the peoples who came to know Christ as their Saviour at the great gathering in Heaven.

Sylvia Roitberg, David Leake and Alan Hargreaves
Provincial Executive Members
The Three Monkeys !

Visit to Spain, December 1994

This was the first of a number of visits to Spain. Two subjects stand out. The election for the next diocesan bishop was planned for January 1995 and inevitably there was great interest about the four candidates. These included Carlos López of Salamanca, Rogelio Prieto of the

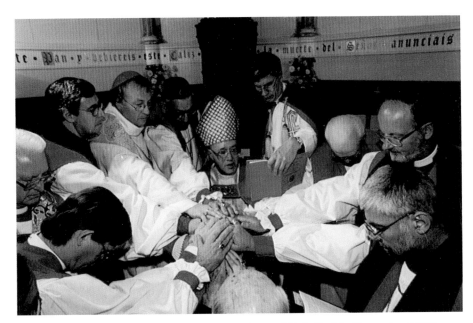

Consecration of Carlos Lopez as Bishop of Madrid, 6th November 1995

Carlos Lopez, rather more visible!

seminary and Henry Scriven, Chaplain of St George's Madrid and ex-SAMS missionary from Northern Argentina. I was delighted in November to participate actively in the eventual consecration of Carlos López by the Archbishop of Canterbury, George Carey, in Madrid.

The second area of concern was the ministry of the Revd Juan Zamora in Sevilla. Juan was the first Anglican South American missionary from Chile to work in continental Europe—at least in the modern era. This involved liaison between the Diocese of Chile, the Diocese of Spain, Crosslinks and SAMS. It was quite complicated.

Visit to Jersey, February 1995

I commissioned Alison Le Cornu (from Jersey) to work in the Madrid seminary alongside Rogelio Prieto. I also had to try to facilitate better relationships between Vivaldo and Linda Olivera and the work they were seeking to do with four to seven thousand Portuguese immigrants in part-time harvesting and hotel jobs. His ordination stemmed from the Bishop of Portugal but relationships with the Church of England (Jersey was part of the Diocese of Winchester) were not always culturally easy and finances were always a problem.

Tour 3. Brazil, Uruguay, Paraguay October–November 1995

The whole situation in Uruguay, and especially in Montevideo, was quite problematic. While normal Sunday congregational members were about 110, there were 15 foreign missionaries, two ordained Uruguayans, seven admin staff and 20 social workers! i.e. too many paid workers and just not enough ordinary Christians. An unworkable imbalance of pastoral/evangelistic work in the formation of congregations and ambitious, though highly laudable, social work programmes.

Visit to Israel

We ended 1995 with Dorothy and me going on a week's pilgrimage to Israel with a group of 40 ordinands from the UK.

This helped to give perspective to almost ceaseless travel and inevitable change.

I closed my link letter of 1995 with the following words:

We go forward with:

A deep caring for each other as partners in mission

A legitimate and meaningful belongingness with the wider church

With Dorothy in Jerusalem
Group of Ordinands of the Church of England

A name for good practice in the pursuit of excellence for Christ's sake.

We have entered a rich heritage — we must press on to fulfil our calling together as a Society and as servants of our Lord.

Tour 4. Argentina, Chile, Peru, Bolivia April–May 1996

(some short excerpts from diary)

From Santiago airport I took five different means of transport to get to Espinoza's house in Quilpué, arriving almost exactly 24 hours after leaving Heathrow.

Very tiring on the Bolivian altiplano: corrugated roads, hailstorms, bright sunshine, beautiful rural scenery, especially the campesinos in the 100–200 yards of land between the road and Lake Titicaca. Pigs snorting into the earth, sheep, goats, donkeys, cows and bulls, alpacas and llamas, chickens feeding and resting. Parties of brightly dressed women harvesting reeds, bent-double ladies digging the land, boats tied up with groups of men, giant coots, Andean gulls, glistening water. Two large open-air cattle markets beside the road further into Bolivia. Arrived in La Paz having had a bad headache for a long way on the three minibus journeys. Collapsed into bed until the next morning. Sylvia Blaxland revived me with porridge, toast and tea. She had given me 'mate de coca' for my 'seroche' (altitude sickness) the night before.

Diocesan administrator had to be dismissed for financial incompetence. Very sad record of such folk in the Southern Cone province. Large funeral for a church member Mario Pareja. He had died in suspicious circumstances with a beaten-in skull! Hushed up as an accident, but almost certainly a marital infidelity. He was one of the early Anglicans in La Paz but had moved on to charismatic groups. The Bartletts live in an excellent flat (once used by the Blaxlands from Australia). A well-known drug baron lives just across the way! Peter Bartlett is doing a good job but some of the church members continue to be very arrogant, live double lives and are thirsty for power and influence. The Holy Spirit has a tough job!

Sue Woodcock indispensable in Cochabamba at the moment. Everything hinges on her. Among many activities we had a meeting of the monthly middle and upper class women's book group. I did a presentation of the Resurrection based on *Who Moved the Stone?* A really good time and the tea and cakes were delicious! A local paper photographer came just before I had to leave for the flight back to La Paz.

Visit to Australia and New Zealand June–July 1996

Reading through my diary on this visit I was rather overcome with forgotten names and places and the intermingling of SAMS, EFAC and CMJ, and even Lambeth Conference business and contacts. My main business was to be the guest of honour speaker at the SAMS Australia Annual Commemorative Dinner (152nd Year of Mission). There were 105 present from six states, and we enjoyed:

>   Delicioso Peruano Ponche
>   Pollo Supremo Chileno
>   Barca Chocolata Paraguaya
>   Café Brasileño

Apart from multiple contacts with SAMS folk, I also went to the National Conference of EFAC New Zealand and delivered a lecture at the N.Z. Latimer House on "Labels used by Evangelicals around the World". This rather bewildering visit with visits to numerous bishops and archbishops, interviewing a SAMS Australia missionary candidate for Spain, and meeting up with the Guzmáns from Chile studying theology at Moore College, Sydney, ended with a telephone call from Japan to say I had a new grandson! I went to Japan for a couple of days, breaking my journey back to the UK.

Tour 5. Argentin, Paraguay, Brazil May–June 1997

This visit focused on two events. The first was the consecration of Humberto Axt as the second assistant Bishop in the Diocese of Northern Argentina. It took place on 25th May, Argentina's National Day. Between 300–400 people were present, representing largely the Wichí and Toba Indian churches of the Chaco. A nice touch was the presence of the General Secretary of CLAI (Council of Latin American Churches), Felipe Adolf, of German origin, like Humberto Axt himself. Since 1997 there have been many changes. Bishop Humberto has now been replaced by two Indian assistant bishops. One of the four people still in 'post' is Charles Barr Johnston, though now 'just' in active retirement. He went as a SAMS missionary in 1967 and has continued in a dedicated Bible teaching ministry to this date. In 1997 he was painstakingly and time-consumingly teaching and training 12 people individually through the How to Preach Course in the central church of Ingeniero Juárez. He is still active in 2020.

The second major event was the launching of the Bible in Guaraní, the 'heart' language of Paraguayans. This had been a nine-year ecumenical project sponsored by the Paraguayan Bible Society and the Paraguay Roman Catholic Episcopal Conference. Tito Lahaye had oversight of the translators' team. The Vice-Minister of Culture was present. The

President of Paraguay, apparently, said he would have come to the ceremony were it just half an hour! It actually lasted two hours.

After this fifth general visit to South America, I add a few reflections to my report:

There is a need to study the provenance of Anglican ordained ministers in South America. There is no central seminary and a very wide provenance from the ranks of married Roman Catholic priests to charismatic independent ministers. No wonder there is a difficulty of Anglican identity!

Bringing in a new generation of leaders to the Chaco areas of Northern Argentina and Paraguay continues to be made difficult by the culture of older leaders staying on until death. The same happens across the African continent.

There is a crucial need for literacy and other work to ensure that new Bible translations are fully used, as they come off the press.

It is nearly crunch time in Asuncion as far as middle class work is concerned. Despite the St Andrew's School ministry, middle and upper class Paraguayans are not yet coming to Anglican churches in any great numbers.

I noted down that during this 'tour' I had had meaningful talks with 87 people. A great privilege to meet so many seeking to advance the work of God's kingdom in South America, but also a great sense of responsibility to do everything possible to facilitate that mission. Not least of course by the right level of dissemination of information to be used to galvanise prayer and financial support on the home front.

Tour 6. Chile, Peru, Bolivia, Mexico September–October 1998

Every tour is different. This time I travelled to Chile via Buenos Aires from the UK with the Duchess of York, following a fatal car accident of her mother, Señora Barrantes, in Argentina. Then 23 nights in 16 different beds, leaving my pyjamas in the third bed!

I attended a Cursillo course as a full participant in Chile. Some 60 men in all. This made me realise the importance of 'movements' in promoting the growth of the church. Marriage Encounter and Youth Encounter need to be carefully led in order to integrate people into church life rather than fostering undenominational independence.

Three issues I noted in Peru were the need for a clear policy on clergy salaries and pensions. It would be good to move the Marcés family from Crosslinks to SAMS as mission partners. Juan Carlos (Peruvian) and

Penny (UK) form an excellent team and are still active in ministry today (2020). A visit is planned for Alejandro Mesco to the UK in 1999. This links with the renewed partner relationship between the dioceses of Peru and Worcester. Alejandro went on to be consecrated a bishop but, as of writing (2020) is out of favour and fellowship with the diocese.

In Bolivia I was able to note solid progress in the four centres: Calacoto and Sopocachi in La Paz and the two in the cities of Cochabamba and of Santa Cruz. All work is middle class, as per the original vision for the work in Bolivia, in order to build up local congregations and not just have highly mobile numbers of ex-Roman Catholics flitting around like hummingbirds to wherever they think they can get the tastiest food!

Mexico's five dioceses with 76 clergy are desperately seeking to establish a proper national Anglican/Episcopal identity while understandably unwilling and probably unable to cut the financial umbilical cord to ECUSA in the USA. In the two dioceses of Mexico, City and Cuernavaca, I tried to be helpful with a 12-part description of an appropriate Anglican identity. I list these now because I believe in many ways they are appropriate for all the provinces and dioceses in Latin America and Mexico:

IDENTIDAD ANGLICANA

12 points   Cuernavaca 1998

Auténtica—We are part of the One Holy Catholic and Apostolic church. Important sense of historical perspective of 2000 years.

No-Romana—Basic doctrines on which we differ from Rome. Eucharist/Pope/Salvation

Provisional—Anglican Communion, not Anglican Church at world level

Reformada—Product of 16th Century in Europe

Cultural global—Cultural aspects garnered from history

Misionera—Worldwide vision for growth

Nacional—Authentic Mexican characteristics

Vía Media—Between Roman centralism and Pentecostal independence

Ecuménica—Ecumenical movement in miniature

Bíblica—Bible reading and teaching and authority

Episcopal—Truly defining characteristic of church governance

Litúrgica—Belief in both Spirit-led spontaneity and set forms of liturgy in public worship

Visit to Spain 13–21 March 1999

There is a new spirit abroad in Spain in the Spanish Episcopal Reformed Church. This is in part because of the youthful enthusiasm of its new bishop Carlos López with the presence of new workers from SAMS UK, Ireland, Australia, New Zealand and USA. All is not plain sailing, however. I attended their four-day synod in Seville and made a presentation on mission/evangelism. The final meeting of the synod went on until 1 a.m., rather than finishing as planned at 7.30 p.m.! Relationships with the Evangelical Theological Seminary are tricky as its authorities claim that Bishop Carlos is poaching some of the best people! He has been trying to do everything at once, which is refreshing after many years of preserving a traditional reformed denomination separate from the dominant Roman Catholic Church. But inevitably there are flash points.

One of the exciting plans has been to have a Latin American group visit for the purposes of evangelism in Madrid. This proved quite difficult to implement and only met with limited success. Bishop Carlos has also secured a loan to finance a Dominican clergyman to establish a Latin American mission in the Cathedral for displaced Dominican, Ecuadorian, Colombian, Bolivians and Peruvians. In the first two months 1000 have passed through their office. I don't know what the long-term effects will be.

Tour 7. Argentina, Uruguay, Brazil, Paraguay, Mexico
9 September–13 October 1999

The role of buildings in church growth still intrigues me. In Recife, Pablo Garcia has had a further extension to the ancient English chaplaincy church in order to be able to seat 1100, with the facilities heaving with people. In another suburb Miguel Cavalcanti presides over a growing congregation (350 membership) in the converted nightclub, Babylon, on a main street. In Salto, Uruguay, the ancient chaplaincy church has been brought back into use, but the life and growth is down the road in the Holy Spirit Mission based on a Day Care Centre.

In Rosario, Argentina, the ancient chaplaincy church has a nice vicarage and new parish room, but it struggles, while in Arias, out in the comparatively nearby countryside I preached to 75 people meeting in a rented town council room. The secondary schools in Erechím, Brazil, San Andrés, Paraguay and Christ Church, Rio de Janeiro are highly successful and bulging at the seams. But the question remains, how much they have helped the growth of the churches locally. Social projects come and go, sometimes leaving unwanted buildings behind, like the Boys' Towns in Brazil. In Mexico, a ring of six churches built around Cuernavaca city, are now called the bishop's chapels. A former bishop put them up. Now no one goes. In Tucumán, the congregation is on the move from building to building. The Vergaras's house is a rented government hall. It was back to the Vergaras's house the day I was there because a key had not been forthcoming to the hall!

I am more convinced than ever that dioceses need officially to recognize two financial systems for ordained ministry. Full-time, qualified and probably itinerant, paid clergy and part-time, more locally and unpaid clergy. The ordained ministry in South America cannot realistically be an open door for a lifelong paid career. In very few places is there a solid enough base in congregational strength to support it. We in SAMS need a delicate and balanced approach between supplying paid overseas staff, ordained or lay, and helping to support up-and-coming national ministries in a non-dependence-creating manner.

Visit to Brazil in April 2000
Five-Yearly Missionary Conference and Synod

This was an important international gathering looking for significant expansion of the work of the relatively new Province. I gave an overview of the last 30 years since SAMS was invited to take part in evangelization geared to increasing church membership. I made five points about our involvement in the future:

> We believe in mission with a human face, based on the doctrine of the Incarnation of our Lord Jesus Christ. This means people, not just salaries.

> We recognize the fallibility of those involved in trans-cultural mission. They are not necessarily all prodigies! Weakness and vulnerability are characteristics of Christian mission, so we desire pastoral care for them as brethren in God's mission.

> We believe that trans-cultural mission is an aspect of the responsibility of the whole church of Jesus Christ. The Anglican Communion needs Brazilian Anglicans. Not only Brazilians in Portugal and Angola (as Portuguese-speaking lands) but in Europe, Africa and Asia. There are rumours of a Brazilian Anglican Mission Agency.

> We believe in the 'Five Marks of Mission' with personal and congregational evangelization at the heart.

> We believe interchanges of personnel for international fellowship have greatly enriched everyone involved and should be expected.

Visit to Portugal
Congress of the Lusitanian Church: 14–17 June 2000

I had to give a major address at this gathering. I had the full text printed in both English and Portuguese to facilitate genuine communication. The title was "The Christian Mission in a Changing World." (The full text is given in Appendix B, page 237.)

The challenge of the inclusivity/exclusivity debate. Human racial, cultural, denominational, liturgical inclusivity are vital and more generally accepted. But what about doctrinal and interfaith inclusivities? There must be parameters and boundaries, because of the nature of Christianity as a divinely revealed faith.

The challenge of the identity crisis. We do need to know where we are before we can have confidence in going to others and saying come and join us. We do not need to claim to be the perfect church. We will never be more than one provisional example of the one Holy Catholic and Apostolic Church of Jesus Christ here on earth. But we must feel comfortable with a working identity.

The challenge of international partnership to be active in mission, which reveals the rainbow nature of God's people, enriches our discipleship and stretches our commitment to each other across the chasms of the modern world.

Tour 8. Chile, Bolivia, Peru, Ecuador September–October 2000

I was impressed with Bishop Tito Zavala's leadership. Having powerful old-timer missionaries Terry Barratt and Alf Cooper in his patch could be a bit of a challenge.

Thirteen years later (2018) Tito is the first Chilean Presiding Bishop of the just-created 40th Province of the Anglican Communion. So others have been impressed with his leadership as well! Abelino Apeleo, Alf Cooper and Enrique Lago are also now bishops in the province after long and faithful service. Some do fall by the wayside through marital infidelity, financial mismanagement or the pull of working among Latin Americans elsewhere, particularly of course in the USA.

On this trip I was able to visit work I had not visited before or work just being started. This includes outreach among 7000 Pehuenches (Araucanian Pinetree people) in the Andes foothills in Chile; extension work in the north of Chile in Antofagasta and Arica. Santiago is roughly in the middle of Chile. Arica is 1672 km to the north, and Punta Arenas is 2180 km to the south. No wonder that the long vertical country is now a province with several diocesan bishops. In Bolivia I was thrilled to see the impressive new church building recently opened by the Archbishop of Canterbury in the second city of Santa Cruz. In Peru most of the shanty town congregations are thriving. Following the implosion of the middle-class work with three properties being sold, and the effect of the nearly five-year vacancy without a diocesan after Alan Winstanley left, much ground needs to be recovered.

Visit to Bolivia February 2001

Frank Lyons's Consecration in Bolivia, 15th February 2001
†Humberto Axt, †Bill Godfrey, †Maurice Sinclair
†Gregory Venables, †David Evans

This was a short visit centred on the consecration of the Revd Frank Lyons III (SAMS USA missionary) as the 2nd Diocesan Bishop of Bolivia.

This was 19 years after the February 2nd establishment of the legal identity of the Anglican Church in La Paz. Only I and Revd Pepe Zubieta from USA were present on both occasions.

This was a landmark event for various reasons. It was not held in the capital, La Paz. The main reason for this was the existence of the diocese's largest church building in Santa Cruz, arguably the country's second city. The Anglican Diocese of Singapore had financed the building through the ministry of the Revd Raphael Samuel (who later replaced Frank Lyons as diocesan bishop). Some 250 people attended the service, which was a good number as not many were able to travel the long distance from La Paz. The Archbishop of Canterbury had consecrated the building itself in 1991. So it came to symbolise the efforts of the whole Anglican Communion to get a new diocese under way. Though started by expatriate missionaries from various countries, it was not based on an expatriate English-speaking group of any sort. Although its third bishop was not a national or even a Latin American, Raphael Samuel was from Asia, from Penang and not white! He is still Bishop in Bolivia as I pen these lines and the work continues to grow with a largely indigenous Bolivian clergy team.

Tour 9. Argentina, Uruguay, Paraguay, Brazil Oct–Nov 2001

The outstanding highlight of this visit was a group of seven of us reaching the Allen Gardiner cave on November 10th in Bahía Aguirre, Tierra del Fuego. This was the 150th anniversary of Allen Gardiner's death, the founder of what became SAMS, the South American Mission Society. I made these three brief reflections following the visit:

A. The death of Allen Gardiner and his six pioneer missionary companions took place before a single convert had been made, before any church had been planted. However, the seed of their offered-up lives produced a harvest. Bishop David Leake spoke movingly of the 100 churches among the indigenous peoples of Northern Argentina, the Wichi, the Toba and the Chorote, who are now the spiritual harvest of those Seven. The Mapuches in Chile and the Énxet in Paraguay also owe their Christian faith historically to the events of 1851 in Tierra del Fuego.

B. It is interesting to reflect on who the Seven were—a naval captain, three Cornish fishermen, a young doctor, a YMCA waiter turned catechist and a carpenter. All members of the people of God, but without any ecclesiastical recognition or status. Their spiritual commitment was tested to the limit, faithfulness even unto death. 150 years later, seven others stood where they died—an Argentine Bishop, an Irish Bishop, an English Bishop, a North American Canon, a New Zealand clergyman, an Irish mission executive, a professional photographer, together with the landing crew of Argentine sailors. A more international group, also a heavily clerical group and a group aware of the media and photo opportunities. It is good that mission is more international today. However, is mission too dominated by clericalism? Is mission too media-conscious? Are today's mission partners in the same spiritual league of self-sacrificing commitment as the South American Seven of 1851?

C. Psalm 62:5–8 was originally chalked up on the wall of Allen Gardiner's Cave. It refers several times to God being the psalmist's rock, refuge and fortress. It forcibly struck our party that those who lay dying in that cave 150 years ago would have been unable to see anything but rock all around them. Not a picture of Christ as a rock under our feet, but a picture of Christ totally surrounding us with His presence. And of course, out of the cave, the tomb, bursts new resurrection life in the mysterious and powerful plan of our Sovereign God.

However, that visit to South America also included a three-day safari with the late Bishop John and Judie Ellison around parts of the Paraguayan Chaco in temperatures of 43°C. Memorable also was a visit with Siméa and Ian Meldrum to the infamous Olinda rubbish dump to see progress in the social outreach and church planting programme there. I wrote:

> This is an incredible work. I had an extended visit to the Olinda rubbish dump. I watched a number of the 400 registered collectors sifting through the rubbish. Often they try to work at night when the rubbish trucks unload. I saw a young, slightly pregnant woman stepping on the scales with a huge bundle of plastic bottles on her head. Some 26 kilos. She does 4 journeys a day from the dump across to the NGO. She collects enough for about 13 reales or £3. The NGO collective pays better value, cutting out the middleman, crushing the bottles in a small machine again to achieve a higher selling price. Nearby, 3 small boys pick out the bottle tops into a separate bag, which they sell. The plastic is recycled in São Paolo or even Japan for numerous products. Overhead 500 or so little white egrets fly about as they look for materials.

> Siméa knows everyone. We prayed all over the place, in homes, on the dump. Siméa sees beauty everywhere, ignores danger and violence. Some 20–30 people are murdered every weekend in greater Recife, one of the most violent Brazilian cities now. Siméa has taken the rubbish collectors' cause as far as the Senate in Brasilia to avoid a government or other monopoly, which would crush local initiatives. Her work in Olinda is being seen as a model way forward to humanise the whole rubbish industry. She is constantly on the mobile—calls from anywhere in Brazil, Canada or the States.

Visit to Peru and Brazil December 2001

Back again to South America for another visit. The main purpose was to attend a meeting of the NAME (Network for Anglicans in Mission and Evangelism) International Board. This had been set up by the Lambeth Conference of 1998 to monitor progress and act as a facilitator for the implementation of mission concerns worldwide. I found myself subsequently with the task of researching the constitutions of the

Anglican provinces worldwide to see the process of how missionary dioceses have been formed and what sort of provincial support is built into the process.

Because I had previously met Alberto Barbosa in Selly Oak, Birmingham, I had also been invited to preach at his ordination in Goiania, Brasilia on my way home! It seemed a good opportunity to meet with a lot of the Brazilian clergy assembled for the occasion.

Visit to Spain 5–12 April 2002

As a missionary society we are committed to helping the IERE (Iglesia Evangélica Reformada Episcopal) in its ten-year expansion plan. Overall numbers remain small despite the dynamic activity of their bishop Carlos López. The situation has been complicated by the huge immigrant population of one million people, mainly from Latin America. These folk are in danger of swamping native-born Spaniards in the small, very traditional IERE congregations.

The Spanish Red and the European Food Bank make food available to charitable institutions — for instance 1000 kilos of food is distributed every week at the IERE Madrid Cathedral. Immigrants have to attend a service or devotional talk before receiving their food. Organisation is good; however, the charge of 'rice Christians' cannot be discounted! Secularism has made huge inroads on a traditional Catholic culture. The ground is stony. Large-scale evangelistic methods don't work. The Billy Graham Decision Magazine organisation scrapped a million-dollar project involving a travelling van equipped to project films. 80 young people, mainly Spaniards in José de la Rinconada, failed to start a church after a month's work. Work is only 'inching forward' through long-term painstaking friendship and personal relationships.

We have agreed to continue to support the growth or planting of seven churches in three major centres, i.e. in Madrid in the cathedral, Móstoles and Alcorcón in Seville, in San Basilio and Ascensión, and in Sabadell and Barcelona. Undergirding that support is the theological education work of SEUT.

Tour 10. Chile, Bolivia, Brasilia June–July 2002

A characteristic feature of this journey was that I had a travelling companion, Bishop Hilkiah Omindo of the Diocese of Mara in Tanzania. This was a joint SAMS/Crosslinks south-to-south interchange, to be reciprocated by Argentine-born German Bishop Humberto Axt travelling with Andy Lines (the Crosslinks CEO) to Tanzania in October. This was for the Chile and Bolivia part of the journey. While in Brasilia I was part of the Indianapolis linked diocese visit with six North Americans, including their lady bishop. The different nature of the two groups significantly changed the nature of the visit.

International Company. Walking behind my black Tanzanian colleague in Chile and Bolivia, I realized I was totally invisible! The Bolivian consul in Arica told us he thought Bishop Hilkiah was the first Tanzanian ever to visit Bolivia. Everywhere people were astounded at the growth and the size of the Anglican Church in Tanzania, despite a presence of 42% of the population being Muslim. There were noticeable differences in people's questions to him . . . Bishop Abelino's careful enquiries about how he trained rural clergy and someone else's curiosity as to how often he saw elephants. Hilkiah's questions were perceptive, his summing up of people accurate and his large vision challenging. He saw the need to divide the Diocese of Chile for pastoral reasons; he was worried about the sustainability of a new residential training seminary in Santiago; he was indignant about the lack of visits by an ordained pastor to Arica (last August by bishop Tito); he didn't think that the educational institutions were clearly enough coordinated at the diocesan level; he was supportive of SEAN, which is also used in his diocese.

I interpreted for Hilkiah on many occasions in public meetings. Otherwise people loved to try their English on him. We spoke in interview sessions in some 10 classes in three schools (St Paul's, Viña, William Wilson, Chol-Chol and the Temuco School for the Deaf). In two places they had learned a Swahili song (Villa Alemana, Viña and Arica). We had good newspaper coverage in the *Mercurio* of Valparaiso, with photo prominent with San Pedro, Viña frontage, and most congregations got a blessing in Swahili. San Pedro's produced a special offering of US$1500 and Arica of US$50 for the Mara Diocese. Everywhere there was laughter and good personal relationships. After excellent meals out through others' generosity, we often just had a cup of tea and a biscuit by way of a second meal.

The *Indianapolis Company* was different. A much higher standard of living was expected, with hotels and meals and hired air-conditioned minibuses for travel. The focus tended to be on the plant rather than the people. The 'tourist element' tended to predominate because of lack of language, ubiquitous cameras and more elderly participants, who formed a cultural group making real contacts more difficult. A plan to bring all 65 clergy and their spouses to Brasilia for a conference will, I hope, disappear. It would overwhelm local resources.

Conclusion

Thank you for all your prayers. We kept well, though with headaches at 13,000 feet. The two possible setbacks were overcome. We managed to buy duplicate tickets on LAN Chile from Antofagasta to Arica at the last minute when the Peruvian airline Aero Continente was shut down for approaching bankruptcy and possible drug money laundering. We got Hilkiah's Bolivian visa in Arica from the Bolivian Consul there, who sometimes attends the Anglican Church in Arica and knew about the Sopocachi congregation in La Paz. We were welcomed everywhere. Sometimes we shared a small room at the back of an MP's home; once we had the full use of a central flat in Viña del Mar, or we were in separate nationals' homes, or a hotel in La Paz or a SIM guesthouse for missionaries. And of course, a couple of nights either on an aircraft or on a long-distance coach.

In the face of Jesus Christ, your light and glory have blazed forth to all the nations, O God; with all your people may we make known your grace. And live out your ways of peace. Amen.

Tour 11. Argentina, Bolivia, Peru 25 April–26 May 2003

This was my last tour as General Secretary of SAMS. Appropriately it was to the three dioceses in which Dorothy and I had most lived and worked for the 20 years we were in South America. The climax was the service in Lima commemorating the Silver Jubilee of my consecration there in May 1978, 25 years that had literally flown by but brought a wealth of wonderful rich experiences into our lives. 150 people from the southern area of Lima came to the Cathedral—a wonderful mix of classes and denominations and friends and church members. These included the widows of two of the men on my Episcopal Selection Committee of 1978. A huge cake and a lovely silver inscribed dish completed the occasion. I preached on the Anglican Church being Evangelical, Catholic and Charismatic!

Just a cameo of each national diocese:

Argentina

Our visit coincided with presidential elections conducted in a spirit of overall pessimism. There is a huge economic downturn, with the middle class disappearing. Many only make ends meet by having two or even three jobs. Foreigners are being kidnapped. Bishop Gregory Venables's chauffeur (actually an ex-Roman-Catholic priest, now an Anglican deacon) had been kidnapped. Sylvia, the Bishop's wife, beat the kidnappers down from US$5,000 to $1,000! He was eventually rescued, and one of the gang of four arrested.

I noted six situations in the diocese which needed to be taken forward, possibly with help from overseas. I mention just one now. Since the closure of two diocesan day-care centre buildings, we could increase contact with the well-established Hogar El Alba orphanage on the outskirts of Buenos Aires. There are 62 kids there in five buildings, with house parents. I had once half-thought of adopting a boy from there to be companion for our own son, Peter, born in Buenos Aires!

Continued contact with Argentina since 2007 has been through Peter and his family, who went to live and work in Buenos Aires for a year. Also, an unexpected invitation to be a guest speaker on a Swan Hellenic cruise liner, when we were able to meet up with a few friends from Lomas de Zamora in a posh downtown hotel, where our ship docked for 24 hours. I was also invited to take part in the 50th anniversary celebration of ABUA, the national university Christian Union movement, in 2018. Correspondence also has continued with Dr René Padilla, the well-known Latin American theologian. We were invited to his remarriage in 2017. Again, distance prevented our acceptance. Having had 30 years of my active ministry related to Latin America does make 'popping back' for meaningful occasions rather tricky and certainly very expensive! However, there have also been visits to the UK from some Argentine nationals, not least Elizabeth Birks and her husband from Lomas de Zamora.

Bolivia

Social unrest was very obvious, as in Argentina. So often this is the social backcloth to mission work in South America. There is a 24-hour strike so you can't get to that crucial Bible Study in the university or, as just mentioned, your driver has been kidnapped! In La Paz, Bolivia, a journalist reported asking a government minister, "Who is running this country? The President or the US Ambassador?" The link between the drug traffic and national and international terrorism is also one big problem. The New Tribes Mission Hostel where we stayed in Santa Cruz had a colour-coding system for levels of security risk, from green through yellow to orange and red. We were only in yellow fortunately!

I have already highlighted the outstanding ministry of Raphael and Michelle Samuel at the main Santa Cruz church. He is from Penang and sponsored by the Diocese of Singapore. I noted that he should have a long and successful ministry. As I write (2019) he is still there as the diocesan bishop! I commented also on Lico and Rosa Bascuñán and their work in the second area of Santa Cruz. Again, they have had a good ministry, not without moral hiccups, but Lico is very articulate, musical and knows his socio-political onions. It has been possible for them to return to their own country of Chile, where they are working well in the North, in Arica. I was interested to read in my report of the solid work being done in the Calacoto middle-class sector in La Paz by the Bartletts: Peter and Sally went on to head the diocese in Paraguay, where they remained until 2019. They travelled in the opposite direction to Greg and Sylvia Venables, who started in Paraguay in teaching, then went to Peru/Bolivia and finally to Buenos Aires, as Bishop and Primate of the Southern Cone.

Peru

Considerable political and social unrest actually prevented us getting overland as planned to Arequipa. The roads were blocked by a strike of transport workers. In fact we had to miss Arequipa altogether and buy air tickets straight to Lima. A great shame.

Middle-class work in Lima suffered during the five-year gap before Alan Winstanley was replaced by Bill Godfrey in 1998. This was partly because the more charismatic folk are less denominationally 'loyal'. Later the process of Catholicisation under Bishop Bill was not popular everywhere. The shanty town work was much more encouraging. Pamplona Alta now had its own fine church building with five dependent mission churches (one brick, two straw matting and two commandeered homes). Duck evangelism has largely been responsible for the growth in this shanty town valley of over 400,000 people. Dorothy and I attended and were judges at the graduation ceremony of the 20th Duck Project in a community centre. Six groups of women presented six different duck dishes. We had to taste and judge all the dishes, which came with alcoholic accompaniment! There were folk dances, and we both had to dance the very traditional 'Marinera' with two professionals. A really incarnational event with churches and local authorities involved and many people's family budgets helped through the duck-breeding scheme.

It was particularly good to go to the 27 de Julio Church, which I had been able to consecrate just before my time ended as bishop in Peru years before. A successful day-care centre and Christian academy had helped its growth. There were 60 at the evening service in Villa El Salvador. There are significant young adults at this church, led by Juan Carlos Marcés (still active in the diocese in 2019 as Vicar General), some of them ex-gang-members.

Amy Griffis's MBE for Service to the British Community in Peru

Other events included a dinner party at Bishop Bill's house for old friends; a tea party at Pat Bygrave's house for 'Ancient Brits'! Attendance at the National Interconfessional Committee I used to chair was a special surprise. We must have added pounds to our 'avoirdupois' with all the meals in homes and restaurants! The climax of course was the 25th Anniversary service itself in the now Cathedral Church of the Good Shepherd in Miraflores.

The journey home to Birmingham from door to door took 27 hours. Three of these were spent in Lima Airport for security reasons. Another almost three were in Madrid on a stopover. But five were spent getting from Heathrow to Selly Oak!

5G
A BISHOP AS AN ASSISTANT: RETIREMENT IN UK

What's in a name? Bishops in Birmingham, 2002
An Assistant Bishop, a Suffragen Bishop, a Diocesan Bishop
a Flying Bishop, an Assistant Bishop
l to r: David Evans, John Austin, Mark Souter, Andrew Burnham, Tony Dumper

A Flying Bishop is a fourth species! A different animal! Created to serve over a wider area than a Diocese by an Archbishop, in order to minister to the special needs of those unable to accept the ordained ministry of women in his area.

An assistant bishop's role is very flexible. Basically it means that a diocesan bishop has another pair of episcopal hands to assist him in the parishes of his diocese. Where there are a large number of confirmations for instance, these are shared out between the diocesan, the suffragan and the assistant bishop(s). An assistant bishop can also be called upon if the diocesan is ill or some clash of diaries occurs. Even a diocesan can't be in two places at once! Sometimes a retired assistant bishop may be called up to continue in some specialised ministry when he has moved into his retirement house. Most continue to minister in local churches when they are invited to do so by the incumbent. Many appear at big diocesan occasions and national consecrations, which normally take place either at York Minster, Westminster Abbey or Southwark Cathedral. And there are biannual meetings for retired bishops with the Archbishop of York.

My episcopal trajectory has been a long and unusual one. It started off as Diocesan Bishop of Peru, without the more usual first step of being a suffragan (No. 2) in a diocese. But overseas bishops have a different context in which to work and often have to create a diocese or develop one from a small structure. This was the case in Peru. I was then asked to accept responsibility to initiate a diocese in Bolivia at the same time. The 'original' diocese had been Chile, Bolivia and Peru. Bolivia only had an interdenominational chaplaincy church with English services for expatriates. There was a lot of prospecting and contacting to be done.

On return to the UK my role as bishop was different. I was officially called a stipendiary honorary assistant bishop. In 98 cases out of 100 assistant bishops are retired and their work is unpaid and entirely on a voluntary basis. At the time (1988) only Newcastle and Bradford had such 'weird beasties'. The two of us had had episcopal experience overseas and were serving in new territory in the UK, in the same way that a diocesan bishop and his suffragan were on the Church Commissioners payroll. The big difference, of course, was that the 'buck' stopped with the diocesan bishop.

Subsequently and after 1993 I had various different dioceses where I was on the books as assistant bishop. These were all very much in an honorary role but provided some wider profile, which was particularly useful while I was General Secretary of SAMS. Based in Maresfield from 1993, I was Assistant Bishop of Chichester, Rochester and Canterbury at the same time! My commitments in Chichester—actually the diocese in which I was resident—were more numerous than elsewhere. They were normally confirmations in 1994. In 1995 I had four confirmations in Chichester, four in Canterbury and five in Rochester. In 1996 it was nine confirmations in Rochester, in 1997 two in Chichester and two in Rochester. Two other services were also memorable. One was in Rochester when Bishop Michael Nazir-Ali asked me to consecrate an extension to a burial ground. This is a marvellous service, if you have a good sunny day. It involves a robed choir and congregation walking in procession around the new territory singing as lustily as possible. On this occasion with the rivalry of local blackbirds! Burial grounds have traditionally been correctly hedged in with legal requirements out of respect for the persons whose mortal remains are being interred. Each of my different episcopal licences over the years refers to this task. For instance in my licence of 28th January 1994 by the Bishop of Chichester, Eric Kemp, the wording was:

> We authorize and empower you upon our request or the request of the Bishops of Horsham or Lewes or either of them, to administer the rite of confirmation and the rite of ordination, to license, to institute and to consecrate churchyards and cemeteries and extensions thereto.

The legal wording does differ from diocese to diocese and there is a distinction between an episcopal licence and an episcopal commission. But I will spare you the details of that!

Understandably ecclesiastical niceties are not always observed and there can be confusion in nomenclature. I rather like the following — a letter sent to *The Times*, published on December 24th 1997. The heading was the work of *The Times* newspaper!

Good Evans

> Sir, I note with interest in today's Church News the appointment of the Right David Evans as honorary Assistant Bishop of Birmingham.
>
> I am grateful the right David Evans got the job rather than the wrong David Evans or even the left David Evans.

Yours, as the Right Reverend,

DAVID EVANS

Nowadays different practices are observed with the disposal of mortal remains. Cremation is extremely common, and most people do not have a problem with this. It is one solution to the huge increase in population, soon to be 70 million, with full cemeteries in many urban areas. Disposal of the ashes is then the next question to arise. Niches in walls or small graveyard burial of the urns are common. But so too are scattering ashes in gardens of remembrance, with perhaps a rose tree as a visible reminder. Ashes are also scattered in favourite countryside places or the sea or in people's gardens. Other people even keep the ashes in their houses and sometimes have them made up into an ornament for the mantelpiece.

Many ceremonies nowadays are devoid of any Christian content and secular/humanist officiants continue to multiply. I have only attended one such ceremony, which I'm afraid made me very angry. The traditional funeral master of ceremonies sympathized with my reaction.

The concept of resurrection was totally transformed, from the hope of a better and transformed incorruptible ongoing life of the human being, to a pious expression that the mortal remains of the cremated person would help the daisies grow more strongly, or the tree's roots be strengthened. The perspective was one of goodbye to a person finally disappearing into the bowels of the earth rather than a joyous, though future, reuniting with the loved one in an incorruptible and eternal life of heavenly bliss.

The selection of 'prayers' and meditations for the crematorium service suggested in the book on the internet managed to avoid any reference to the historical resurrection of Jesus Christ from the dead and his promise to raise his followers to a new and fuller life with him.

I must take you back now from churchyards and cremations to another responsibility that I was called on to exercise as an honorary assistant bishop. This time it was as Assistant Bishop of Rochester and Assistant Bishop of Canterbury. The two contiguous dioceses were to share a diocesan officer with oversight to develop social work programmes in both areas. So it was appropriate, though not, of course, strictly necessary, to have an episcopal figure from both dioceses. Leadership does have a good deal to do with visibility. The written liturgy for the service indicated clearly a dual role for the person whose double ministry was being officially instituted. But the presence of two bishops, one from each diocese, confirmed the fact of this more unusual appointment. Bishops do need to be released from centralised activities, either office-based or large-meeting-focused, to be seen by the people. It is one of the reasons for the popularity of pilgrimages and/or prolonged episcopal visits to different parts of the diocese. I felt this even as an honorary assistant bishop.

In Bradford I made it an aim to visit for Sunday ministry every single church building as soon as I could. It took some time! By 1990 I'd visited 96 churches. By 1991 the total had risen to 161. This left just six for 1992, which eventually I managed to 'nail'. One was difficult because it only had occasional services in the summer season. The other was difficult because the incumbent was not exactly over the moon with the prospect of a visiting bishop to preach at ordinary Sunday worship. But by early in 1992 I had visited all 167 places of worship. During this time I was a 'full-time' stipendiary assistant bishop, so it was appropriate to try to get around everywhere.

This was not the case after leaving Bradford. From 1988–2002 when based as General Secretary of SAMS in Birmingham, I took some half dozen confirmations a year. The pattern changed again from 2003 up to 2018 as Assistant Bishop of Coventry. The majority of confirmations were in Bolton Grange School, Rugby School and Warwick School, with some big centralized services in Coventry Cathedral with the diocesan and suffragan bishops. On occasions we were confirming 50 people each in such joint services. Numbers at Rugby School kept to a consistent number between 27 and 22, but at Warwick School they fell from 15 to 4 by 2013. As Assistant Bishop of Coventry I also took some deanery confirmations and more recently a number of local confirmations, either in my old stamping ground of the Stourdene group of churches, or in and around Warwick.

Martin Fawley and Bishop Roy Williamson's chauffeur
"Gaping Gill Descent", Dales

For many people a bishop is associated with a cathedral, although of course he only visits to preach on a few occasions in a year as diocesan. His 'Cathedra' chair sits in the cathedral building but he is very rarely there. Most people associate a bishop with confirmations. That certainly is when many people have a chance to see one 'close-up'!

Since returning from South America the following more unusual confirmations remain in my mind:

In 1987 I confirmed 43 boys at Monkton Combe School, including my own son, Peter. This was at the kind invitation of the then Bishop of Bath and Wells, John Bickersteth.

Confirmations at Sedbergh and Giggleswick Schools were big occasions. I visited both on a number of occasions. Sedbergh was famous for producing rugby players, especially a former English Captain, Will Carling, though I didn't confirm him!

In 1995 I confirmed four people in Holy Trinity Dubai at the invitation of the English Chaplain, Dennis Gurney.

The highlight of my confirmation activity has to be in April 2000 when I was in East Africa in the Diocese of Taita Taveta, Kenya on EFAC business. On the 29th I confirmed 92 Kenyans in Tausa and then 49 the next day nearby in Kigombo—a total of 141!

On 8th June 2003 I confirmed ten people at Christ Church Cockfosters. Again, this was particularly moving, because it had been my training parish from 1965–1968 as a new curate. I had returned several times to preach as the church was incredibly faithful throughout our 20 years in South America and prayed for us regularly over that time.

Over the last year or two I have, on invitation, confirmed three individuals, all in the southern Archdeaconry of Warwick. One was an old friend, a 93-year-old farmer in Alderminster, who I persuaded to join his wife at the Communion Table, rather than stay in his pew. He had been let down decades before by a clergyman who had not put him forward for confirmation.

A second was a very switched-on young man in Ilmington in 2015, who was about to embark on a career in the USA. He was very keen to go as a publicly acknowledged Christian.

And the third, in 2017, was a lady in her middle years in Shipston-on-Stour with a horrible past history in her family, who had come to a releasing experience of God's grace. She was keen to mark her conversion in a public way. Her new local church was the best place to do this, partly because of a mobility problem. She gave a short, but powerful, account of her pilgrimage from the struggle of life to peace through surrender to Christ.

All of these were at the request of the diocesan bishop.

Assistant Bishop Mark II. 2003 – present (2020)

Installation in 2003 in the Stourdene Grop of Parishes,
and Assistant Bishop in the Diocese of Coventry, by Bishop Colin Bennetts

I became 'just' an assistant bishop in 2003, though for the next seven years I was 'half-time' as a house-for-duty priest in the Stourdene group of churches. After 2010 and until 2020, at the moment I am still Assistant Bishop of Coventry, though now living in Warwick, without any statutory responsibilities in a parish. That changed a bit when I was asked by the Bishop of Coventry, Christopher Cocksworth, to become Chaplain to the retired clergy. There were three of us and our ministry was to back up that of the parish clergy in preventing retired clergy and their partners/spouses/widows from feeling neglected across the whole diocese. This was in excess of 200 people, counting husband-and-wife teams, and during this time numbers increased as different 'varieties' of ordained people came on board, especially those coming into retirement (unofficially) from non-stipendiary ministry. The catalyst in those years was the publicity achieved by cases of abuse, sexual or otherwise.

Safeguarding assumed huge proportions and no clergy person was allowed to function in any way without ongoing post-retirement in-service training. Unfortunately this was rightly seen to be a necessary safeguard and therefore obligatory for all. It did seem to be a disincentive to some who wanted voluntarily and without any fuss to help out in taking the odd service, during a sudden illness, interregnum or holiday/sabbatical period. Many situations, however, especially where Holy Communion celebrations were concerned, had to be duly authorized by the proper diocesan authority.

Having the initials PTO (Permission to Officiate) after your name in the Diocesan Directory or in *Crockford's Clerical Directory* itself has become the distinguishing indication of legal availability for retirement ministry! The church papers regularly update the statistics. Some clerics of the more academic variety might end up with the identification 'The Revd Canon Dr Joe Bloggs, PhD, MA, PTO'!

My own experience of retirement ministry has been a happy one. I have enjoyed an annual number of confirmations to help out the two Coventry full-time bishops. Many of these have been in public schools—the largest number in Rugby School over the years. A big sense of occasion and in 2018 nearly 1,000 people present between the two consecutive services on a Sunday morning.

I have deputized for the diocesan bishop on a variety of other occasions. Preaching his sermon at a past archdeacon's funeral, who was my predecessor as Chaplain for the Retired. Representing the diocesan by leading prayers in Tamworth Parish Church for a big multi-diocesan commemoration of the 1100th anniversary of the death of Lady Æthelflæd (daughter of King Alfred), Queen of the Mercians. I dedicated the new chapel windows at a Civic Service in Warwick School with the Mayor and her full Council in splendid medieval dress.

Non-episcopal requests for ministry largely came from my local Warwick team ministry (with six churches) and other local churches where I have had some personal contact with the vicar, who, for whatever reason has asked for my help. I have basically enjoyed these, especially as I have got to know some of the people. I have no administrative or authoritative issues to deal with. I just have to check I get the dates right and turn up at the right church at the right time! Not always as easy as it sounds! Preaching is down to about 20 times a year at the moment, and I can only expect it will continue to diminish. I have

resolutely not taken on any of the occasional offices, as they are called—
baptisms or weddings or funerals — they can be a source of income of
course. The few funerals I have officiated at latterly have only been for
relatives or very close friends.

Otherwise I have sought to be a faithful member of my local church
of St Nicholas, Warwick, carefully avoiding any controversial issues
and deliberately not taking sides with any particular group in the
congregation.

Feldon Valley Golf Club
The Annual Past Captains' Plate

I have much enjoyed my hobbies. I took up golf in my retirement and
15 years later (at 80) am still going—though not quite so strongly. I have
won cups, captained the Seniors' section of Feldon Valley Golf Club,
invented a number of appropriate 'Graces' for golfing occasions, and
basically thoroughly enjoyed myself in the company of some 100 other
senior golfers.

I have also spent a good deal of time in philately, based at the
Stratford-on-Avon Philatelic Society. Again, I have displayed collections,

Happy Birthday, David

To my favourite brother-in-law (I was his only one)

Here's a golfer's prayer specially written for you ...

Lord, as I stand here by the tee.
I have three things to ask of Thee.

First, let my drive be quite precise,
With not a hint of pull or slice.
But if this prayer must be denied,
Then use th' event to quash my pride.

Next, if my partner boasts a lot
Don't let my temper flare up hot,
But rather let me bite my lip
And not indulge in gamesmanship.

Please Lord, do not take it amiss
If my third, timid, prayer is this:
Just once, before my life is done,
Lord, let me hit a hole in one.

love and best wishes,
David

been chairman and got to know a small group of some 30 people quite well. Over the years I have built up quite a good collection of Kenya, Uganda and Tanganyika (pre-independence) stamps. But even more so a display of Birds of the Bible stamps which I have exhibited as far away as Cambridge. A more sedentary hobby, but also highly enjoyable. Though I am sad that, as yet, I have not been able to interest any of my children or grandchildren. Indirectly I even had one of my former possessions displayed at an exhibition at the Royal Philatelic Society in London!

My ornithological interests dovetail happily with the botanical interests of Dorothy, and we travel around the British Isles together ticking off birds and flowers! She is a real expert (though she wouldn't admit it!). I am not a 'twitcher', one who will travel any distance to see rare birds, when advised by phone that one has arrived on some isolated promontory after an Atlantic storm or, more frequently, strong winds from the Siberian direction. If one happens to be around when I am in the area, that's fine. I have certainly enjoyed ticking off the less common birds on the normal British list. There are still quite a few I haven't seen. For instance, goshawk, black grouse, ptarmigan, capercaillie, whinchat, redpoll and hawfinch. However, I have seen quite a few of those listed by Bill Oddie in his *Birds of Britain and Ireland* as 'rare, escaped and localized birds'. These include the bar-headed goose, red-crested pochard, Egyptian goose, spoonbill, white-tailed eagle, red-necked phalarope, Cetti's warbler, Dartford warbler, crested tit, golden oriole, chough, little egret and ring-necked parakeet. Some of these in recent times have become 'common' in local areas, like the ring-necked parakeet in Richmond Park. Just in the last few years spoonbills have been appearing, but I still have not seen a hoopoe or wryneck.

What I have seen was a Stella fish eagle. This was over my golf course in 2018. Together with my playing partner we spotted this very large bird flying fairly high. We knew it was not a buzzard or a red kite. Both of those are quite regular. We guessed it looked like a fish eagle from its size and 'jizz'. Reading *The Times* the next day I learnt that a Stella fish eagle (from the Far East) had escaped from Warwick Castle's birds of prey exhibit! It flew around the skies of Warwickshire and the Midlands for a few days. It then decided the supply of fish was better at Warwick Castle, and returned! I have put it on my list as a temporary escape!

Ornithology is a good, healthy hobby. It gets you to see some spectacular scenery, to experience every sort of weather. Often you are encouraged to do some very early morning rising to hear the dawn chorus, etc. In its more advanced stages it does make a good telescope desirable, rather than just binoculars. I have never felt the pull of bird photography, so a good pair of binoculars satisfies me. There is, however, a great camaraderie between bird watchers. Folk with powerful telescopes are normally quite ready to share them with those less equipped, in bird hides at reserves or on cliff tops or sea watches, etc. This has enabled me to spot species I would never have been able to identify accurately even with my binoculars.

Bird watching is not, however, chasing after elusive species and adding another tick to one's year or life lists. When on a bird outing, I do keep a list of the day's sightings, even the so-called common birds. 60 different species would be a very good tally. A trip to Ireland produced 72 and to the Orkneys 83. A holiday in Suffolk 87 and a summer holiday in Devon and Kent 113. In our Alderminster Vicarage garden we totalled 44 over the years. Here in Warwick we are just up to 29.

But sometimes it is not the number of different species spotted that brings delight to the soul. It is the sheer number of birds seen. In 2018 we went for a couple of days to North Norfolk, where I was blown away by colossal numbers, all seen in one site at the same time. This was at Snettisham, on the southern edge of the Wash. At the right migration time of the year, at the correct state of the incoming tide over the mudflats, you can see thousands of birds in a bonanza, a cornucopia that really blows your mind away. The backbone of what we saw was a huge flock of 50,000 knot (a middle-sized wader), which had just flown south from the Arctic to spend the winter feeding on British mudflats. These performed a number of stirring, swirling sky dances like the starling murmurations off Brighton pier, or over the Severn estuary. But they were not alone. They were competing for food with several thousand shell duck and oyster catchers and hundreds of bar-tailed and black godwits and black-headed gulls, sanderlings and turnstones. Nearby, on the fields were 500 pink-footed geese and hundreds of Canada and greylag geese. For the keen-eyed there were also golden and grey plover and sandpipers. Stalking around among them, little egrets and a few long-legged spoonbills. Quite amazing. An ornithological spectacular. A very different experience from deciding whether you have seen a ringed plover or a little ringed plover (size difference is 7.5 inches to 6 inches!). The little ringed plover has a golden eye ring, the ringed plover doesn't.

So ornithology as a retirement hobby for an assistant bishop is very rewarding! I have also combined my philatelic interests with my ornithological ones, by adding a theological component! I have an extensive collection of stamps which depict the birds of the world found or referred to in the Bible. In the 2003 Stanley Gibbons *Special Thematic Catalogue* it states that "there are now 2,900 different bird species depicted on stamps." In total we are talking about over 17,200 stamps. And that catalogue was issued 15 years ago. My plan is not to try to collect every such stamp. But, rather to illustrate each biblical reference with attractive and appropriate stamps, not necessarily just from the Middle East, although Israel itself has produced some very beautiful ones. For an example, both Leviticus chapter 11 and Deuteronomy chapter 14 have a list of bird species it was forbidden to eat—a total of 19 species. These include black vulture, red kite, raven, screech owl, gull, hawk, hoopoe etc. All these birds are scavengers. The prohibition was of course for hygienic reasons. So my collection has two pages with examples of these 19 forbidden species.

My most recent philatelic venture involves stamps illustrating collective nouns for birds. Most people are familiar with 'a murmuration of starlings' but would be surprised to know that there are between 100 and 200 such collective nouns. Some popular well-spread species have several such descriptive words used in different locations around the British Isles. Crow, for instance, can be a horde, a hover, a mob, a murder, a muster, a parcel or a parliament. On the other hand, skylarks are only designated by the word exultation. Anyway, it opens up another way to present bird stamps in an attractive format.

Talking of collective nouns reminds me that in January 2012 Ann Treneman wrote a parliamentary sketch in *The Times* about 'We all do God now'. She referred to the role of bishops in the House of Lords, and I quote:

> In the absence of any other collective noun, a congregation of bishops sat in a row, white robes circling like giant petticoats, crosses heavy on chests, opinions dancing on lips.

A congregation of bishops? Not so! On subsequent days five letters were published with the following suggestions: Bench of bishops, Bevy of bishops, Diagonal of bishops, Surplice of bishops, Fianchetto of bishops— even a Lack of bishops! I added a short letter as follows:

> I suggest 'fizz' as a suitable collective noun for bishops. The reason is that episcopal is an anagram of Pepsi-Cola.

MINERVA

5 intrepid golfers on the Southernmost Golf course in the world at Ushuaia
Submit their unique discovery of the following endemic

BIRDIES

1. Raised Brow albatross in summer plumage.
2. Harped (on about) Eagle
3. Great Sand bunker
4. Thick necked Rough
5. Blue footed Bogey
6. Dogleg Tern
7. Handicapped Finch
8. Megallanic Driver
9. Putting Bird
10. Green Warbler
11. Stymied Duck
12. Buggie Tryant
13. Tee Sparrow
14. Stableford Leaftosser
15. Holeinone Dipper
16. Pin Penguin
17. Scratch Owl
18. Up and Downland goose
19. Wandering Tattler
20. Sharpbilled Treehunter
21. Bluecapped Puffedleg
22. Parred Owl

These sightings were verified by the F.G.P.O (Fuegian Giant Petrel Office)

T.E	Early Bird Globetrotter
P.C	Scruffy Pratinole
J.L	Great Rhea Rosebeak
M.E	Silver Haired Stemcelll Eater
D.E	Wandering Red Bishop

Authorized by the Joint Argentine Meat and Chilean Agricultural Boards

11th Feb 2014

DavidRJEvans .

Golf and Ornithology

My most outrageous mixing of hobbies, however, was during my spell as a guest speaker on board the *Minerva* cruise ship with *Swan Hellenic* when we sailed from Valparaiso in Chile round Cape Horn to Buenos Aires in Argentina. We had a real ornithologist on board, Mr. Tim Earl, who introduced passengers to the very rich seabird life of the South Atlantic. I joined in as often as possible. Halfway through our trip we had a day's land excursion in Ushuaia, Argentina. Instead of going on the planned excursion, five of us (not the five guest speakers) landed in order to play a round of golf on the southernmost course in the world, on the outskirts of the town. It was great fun. Afterwards I had the idea of composing an imaginary list of birds spotted during our outing on the golf course: all uniquely described with a mixture of golfing and ornithological phraseology. This was duly posted (with permission) on the boat notice board for the delight or otherwise of the 350 passengers!

The verification of the different species was duly signed by:

T.E. Early Bird Globetrotter (Tim Earl the ornithologist)

P.C Scruffy Pratinale (Dr Peter Cattermole, the planetary volcanologist)

J.L. Great Rhea Rosebeak (Rear Admiral John Lippiett of the Royal Navy)

M.E. Silver Haired Stemcell Eater (Professor Sir Martin Evans, Nobel Prize for Medicine)

D.E. Wandering Red Bishop (Missionary in South America for some 30 years)

Being an assistant bishop is not a full-time occupation, as you can see. It can be great fun!

6
FAMILY AND FAREWELLS

Many people's experience of a bishop's ministry is seeing one on some episcopal occasion, very probably in a church building. But bishops don't just live in church buildings nor are most of them single. A bishop's wife and children are in fact more involved in the life of a bishop than in that of other professions and jobs. Especially if the bishop in question packs up the family home in the UK and flies them off to the Southern hemisphere for 20 years!

For one thing education takes place in a foreign country and is probably in two languages. Growing up in two cultures is both a challenge and an enrichment. There are big advantages and big losses. Flying off from the UK to spend the winter holidays in the sunshine of Peru is a clear plus. Separation from the wider family network, especially the grandparents, is an obvious loss.

Our children, Hilary, Caroline and Peter, in 2000

Our three children, Hilary, Caroline and Peter, stayed with us throughout our time in Argentina from 1969–1977. This of course was prior to my being made a bishop. They all attended a bilingual school throughout that time. For the last years in Buenos Aires we lived together as a family in an Anglican vicarage built very near the railway line which took trains to the southern regions of Argentina. A short ceremony saluting the Argentine flag was a daily routine at school. All the children became bilingual, sometimes like Anglo-Argentines with a mixture of both languages at once. This depended on which word came to mind first and which seemed the most appropriate and expressive. Spanglish was the 'official' name for this linguistic hybrid. Right up to the present date when we are together, some Spanish or Spanglish words occur in our conversations!

After we had moved to Peru and after I became a bishop in 1978, we still lived for several years in an Anglican Chaplaincy house next to the church building, which was destined to be 'upgraded' to a cathedral in due course. The children still went to bilingual schools: Hilary and Caroline to San Silvestre and Peter to Markham. However, there were fewer children who spoke English in their own families with their parents and Hilary especially had lost significant Argentine friends. She it was who brought up the option of moving to an English education in England. This option seemed more realistic, as a girl cousin was already at a suitable boarding school. Once Hilary had moved her formal education to the UK, the other two almost inevitably did the same as they moved into their teens. One advantage of this was becoming familiar with UK education and acquiring qualifications for university grants. Overseas missionary children can be treated like the children of diplomatic families, but we didn't need to resort to that route. However, considerable time and energy was needed to gather together financial grants from charitable trusts for school fees. We experienced great generosity from various society sources. Our comparatively low missionary allowance qualified us almost straight away!

There did seem to be a preordained inevitability about this huge disruption of our family life. Grandparents in the UK also came up trumps with the one school holiday a year when the children didn't fly out to join us. However, there was a big emotional cost incurred by this prolonged separation and disjointing of family life. This was felt especially by Dorothy. Letter-writing was the only way to seek to bridge the gap, as we are thinking about those long-off days up to 1988, when mobile phones and social media communication were either non-existent or beyond the normal missionary budget. Airports became synonymous with tearful goodbyes, although of course they were also counterbalanced by happy reunions.

Towards the end of our time in Peru we had a moving experience with one of our Peruvian pastors. He was just experiencing the absence of one of his sons, who had had to go away to do his military service. He came to us and confessed that he was realising only now what we were experiencing as English missionaries in Peru with our children miles away for long periods. Eventually this disjointed family experience was one of the reasons why Dorothy and I left Peru and South America to return to a UK-based ministry.

I have not questioned the children about the pros and cons of their experience of these years of family life. There have obviously been advantages and disadvantages of a boarding-school life. There have been sorrows as well as joys, pluses and minuses from their point of view. We do rejoice however that all three of them, as 'missbish kids', have gained university degrees, have well-paid successful professional careers and have produced 10 grandchildren between them in their happy marriages.

As I write these words one grandson is on a three-month gap-year visit to South America. Both his parents will be visiting him there in either Peru or Argentina. Our son and his wife also spent working time in Argentina, the land of his birth. Our other child, Hilary, with her husband and four children, now live in the USA, so international travels continue for all concerned. Now, of course, the world is smaller, communications are transformed in speed and it is easier to sense connectivity. However, I expect most of us still would opt for closer living conditions and the easier development of family relationships. At the same time family reunions and visits become more precious and special, and we certainly avoid any sense of possible monotonous routines or exaggerated sense of obligation.

One obvious consequence of our children's time with us in South America is their awareness that the world is a big place, but visitable. Hilary now lives with her family near Baltimore in the USA, after living in both Japan and Switzerland. Caroline has always worked in London, but in her several jobs in Human Resources for international law firms has often visited Australia and many other countries en route, including

China. Peter has worked in Argentina, Italy and Ireland, and commutes regularly at present to Germany. However, on different occasions they have all been with us to take tea at a Buckingham Palace Garden Party! All this may sound rather grand and exciting, but each family has also shared in different ways with painful issues in the bringing-up of their children. Being part of an 'episcopal' family is no sinecure for an easy trouble-free life, either for the parents or the children. But it has certainly been a rich human experience on many levels for all of us.

Buckingham Palace Garden Parties

Farewells (1969–2010)

Farewells can be tear-jerking occasions! They also mark important transitions from one sphere of work to another. In our case this often involved moving from one country to another or even one continent to another. There is always a farewell sermon or address. Sometimes this seeks to summarise the concluding ministry. Often there is also a memorable parting gift. This may become increasingly precious—like the Spanish Bible, beautifully inscribed, given us when we left Christ Church Cockfosters after our three-year curacy. Ten years later it was further inscribed and dedicated to us on my episcopal consecration in Lima. It is in my study with me now after 51 years.

The first tear-jerking moment for me, however, came in 1969 in Southampton.

I was standing on the deck of a P & O liner on my way to language and cultural studies in Cuernavaca in Mexico. Dorothy, ill with yellow fever, was staying in the UK with our two daughters. My parents and my sister Ruth were on the quayside waving farewell for our first four-year period of service in South America. Ruth did a little jig to relieve the pressure of just arm-waving. It provoked a flood of tears in me, which I couldn't stop! Tears always accompanied farewells. Often they were for children departing for another term in the UK while we stayed in Peru. Or they were when we said goodbye to our respective parents in the UK and sometimes wondered whether we would ever see them again. They were all blessed with long life, well into their nineties, except for Dorothy's father, and he was only just short of his 90th birthday. We need not have worried. They all did stalwart work in looking after our three children in the school holidays over Easter, when they did not fly out to join us in the sun.

My third farewell memory comes from the time we left Buenos Aires to travel overland to Peru. The Anglo-Argentine Bishop, Richard Cutts, had a party in his house in B.A. for the diocesan clergy and their wives. Before handing over a number of commemorative presents, which I still have, he recited an appropriate and quite long passage from Martín Fierro's famous gaucho poem. But he read it in an English translation! Our main ministry in B.A. was encouraging the congregations to move from the English language and culture into Spanish. And here was an Anglo-Argentine bishop using an English translation of Argentina's most famous gaucho poet! I didn't think there was a message intended in this; in fact I'm sure there was not. The two presents I still have were a cowhide wastepaper basket and a cowhide umbrella basket. Both in excellent leather and very handsome. Both still in use in my study and by the front door. The umbrella basket now also holds a squash racquet, a Nigerian chieftain's stick, a northern Argentina Wichí arrow, my father's white walking stick and a deer-antler-handled walking stick from Scotland.

The fourth farewell, completing our time in South America, was in May 1988. I copy my farewell letter for the *Good Shepherd News*. This gives an overview of our time in Peru, especially viewed from our involvement with the English-speaking chaplaincy work.

Letter from our Bishop
Dear Everyone:

I'm glad that I shall have the opportunity to say goodbye officially and personally to many of you on Whit Sunday May 22nd at the 10 a.m. service. I feel very happy to be able to preach at the Good Shepherd on my last Sunday because as you know it was there everything began for me in Peru.

I first preached on the 17th January 1971 at the Good Shepherd but that was while on a visit from Buenos Aires to an International Student Conference. My 'trial' service was on the 13th March 1977 and I was instituted as the 21st Chaplain in August 1977 and officially continued as such for six years until 1983.

From May 14th 1978 I doubled up as bishop and chaplain with the Revd. Wilbert Kelly helping as Assistant Chaplain. It was about then that I got called the 'Flying Bishop', as both I and the congregation realized that part of a bishop's job is to be sort of ecclesiastic Foreign Minister. Within the country I have enjoyed memorable visits to **Arequipa**, to the Macon project personnel in the Colca Valley as well as the faithful English group in the White City; to **Cusichaca** near Machu Picchu to minister to Ann Kendall's group of amateur and professional archaeologists; to **Yarinacocha**, near Pucallpa, to visit the Summer School of Linguistics' work and to **Ayacuch**o in Holy Week on a visit of solidarity to those suffering in the emergency situation.

Outside of Peru I have visited every country in South America except Guyana, and also Panama, Mexico and Cuba in the Spanish-speaking area of Central America and the Caribbean. Further afield there have been 3 visits to Canada, 16 to the UK, 3 to the USA, 1 to Israel, 1 to Spain, 1 to Ireland and 1 to South Africa. In all I have preached in 16 countries and visited 5 more. So I think the title 'Flying Bishop' does fit!

Coming a little nearer home, so many names and faces come to mind as I think of the changing congregation at the Good Shepherd, many who have passed on to be with the Lord, many others scattered around the world and others still faithfully present. Allow me to mention some present names and forgive me if I don't mention yours, because the list must be abbreviated. I remember Pat Bygrave, John Cox and Barry Alcock at my chaplain's interview in '77; Jack Harriman, Billy Bygrave, Mary Nickson on my Episcopal Selection

Committee; Amy and Don Griffis on multiple occasions including family weddings, funerals, baptisms; Helen Doig seated at her organ for innumerable services and weddings; Peggy Massey's deadline for *Good Shepherd News* material; Eileen Wilson, Fred Buchner, Grace Ashworth, Bob and Dora Collins, Ken and Eleanor Eckett, Eddie and Ann Howarth and many more. And Marando and Simeón, whose work at the Good Shepherd has been so outstanding over the years.

Marando and Simeon,
who kept the Good Shepherd Church buildings and garden shipshape in Lima

Dorothy and I feel tremendously enriched by our time in Peru and through our connection over 11 years with the Good Shepherd. We sincerely thank the Lord for you, for your love, generosity and patience. We hope to take with us an updated address list of ex-Good Shepherd members, at least in the UK, to drop in to see them some time.

And of course as soon as we can announce our UK appointment we will let you have our address and will be genuinely delighted to receive a phone call or a visit from you. With me I take my bishop's crozier generously donated at my Consecration by the 1978 Good Shepherd

Congregation. It will be a frequent reminder of you all as I use it in the UK. And a reminder that it is the Lord Jesus Himself, risen, ascended and seated in Glory, who is the Good Shepherd and Bishop of our souls. Praise Him.

Your former Chaplain, nearly your former Bishop and always your brother in Christ.

David Evans

When we left Peru and Bolivia, we collected quite a number of commemorative plaques from different churches. The Peruvian ones were mainly from our own leather workshop in the shanty town of Pamplona. The Bolivian ones were pewter plates suitably engraved. As we have downsized into our present home, they have grown more prominent. Each one, leather or pewter, brings back memories of the foundation and establishment of the various congregations. But the *coup de grâce* was a gift from the Church of the Good Shepherd in Lima. This was given at a farewell party the day before we were leaving by plane for the UK. It was a total surprise—a very handsome silver filigree mitre—not quite full-size, though nearly . . . quite delicate and beautiful . . . but a great headache to know how to transport it! I certainly wasn't going to try to wear it. That also is still in my study. We got a glass-and-wood case to house it while in Bradford. Whether it was given me because the English-speaking congregation thought I wasn't a proper bishop without a mitre, I don't think I shall ever know. And what our children will eventually do with it, I also don't know.

When we left Bradford diocese after our six years there, we had a wonderful farewell service in the Cathedral, with the choir singing a Rutter evensong. Their main present was a lovely music centre with excellent loudspeakers. A very talented woodworker had fitted it into a case so that it could be housed in a bookcase, and the diocesan crest had been carved in its front. We still have that in our sitting-room in Warwick.

I transcribe also my last sermon of 20th June 1993 from Bradford Cathedral and my farewell speech to the diocese at the reception afterwards. Between them they give an overview of our time in the north from 1988–1993.

Farewell Sermon—Bradford Cathedral   20th June 1993

Isaiah 52:7–10 is my text. In my installation sermon I quoted St. Augustine's famous words,

> For you I am a bishop but with you I am a Christian. The first an office conferred and accepted; the second a grace received. As I am gladder to be redeemed with you than to be set over you, I shall, as the Lord commanded, be more completely your servant.

One of the most important ways to serve is to pray. I pray for you three things.

May you have beautiful feet

I well remember sniggering at my prep school while our music mistress bravely sought to get us to sing Handel's inspired rendering of Isaiah's words: "How beautiful on the mountains are the feet of those who bring good news, who proclaim peace, who bring good tidings." Beautiful feet. Some of you may have to spend time with a chiropodist. I don't expect most of us would list our feet as one of our greatest attributes. Can you see it on a CV? Or your church representatives insisting in their job description of their desired new vicar . . . must have beautiful feet.

And yet in the way that Isaiah writes, our feet become a splendid symbol for the willingness and the commitment to get out there with the Good News of the Gospel of our Lord Jesus Christ. To get up out of our seat—from in front of the telly perhaps—and get out to where people are overcome by bad news, violence, foreboding and death. How beautiful are the feet of those who bring the Good News, the best news that any radio or TV network could ever broadcast, that God the Father has offered us eternal life, on the basis of the life and death of His only Son Jesus Christ and through the active work of the Holy Spirit.

It is not just on the mountains that such feet are beautiful. Or the fells as we would say here. It is also in the Dales. It is in every one of the 171 buildings where I have been privileged to preach in these last years: Keasden, Stanbury, Halton West, Dalehead, Ravenscliffe and Western Estate, to mention some of the lesser-known ones. However, Isaiah certainly was not thinking about the activities of a full-time stipendiary assistant bishop in the employment of the Church of England. He was writing of *all* those who take the message out.

Whoever gets the Good News delivered to those who need it, those are the ones who have beautiful feet.

It may be loving pastoral visits, it may be a special effort, like the Love Bradford campaign in the city, or the march of the 1000 men in the rural areas, it may be presenting the message through the music of a Freddie Mercury, or the traditional vibrations of a Lambing service, it may be a pilgrimage.

The vital end result, however, is that there are new Christians who thank God that their path has crossed with ours. And we normally have the responsibility to do the walking. How beautiful on the back streets of Bradford, in the boardrooms of city businesses, in the leafy suburbs and towns, in the remote rural communities as well as on the famous Three Peaks, are the feet of those who bring the Good News.

May you also have joyful hearts

Verses 8 and 9 of Isaiah 52 are full of joy.

"Listen! Your watchmen lift up their voices; together they shout for joy." Every ordained clergy person in the Church of England is compared to a watchman. So I suppose this could be a picture of the Chapter meeting of the clergy, or the deanery synod. Your watchmen lift up their voices, together they shout for joy. I like that. It should be a foundational mark of the Chrch of Jesus Christ. Joy. It is the fruit of the Holy Spirit. "Love, joy, peace", wrote Paul to the Galatians. We speak about love and peace. I certainly hope we don't miss out on joy. Joyful gatherings should characterise the meetings of the Christian Church. Our central service is the Eucharist Celebration. When Paul was correcting the congregation in Rome for getting issues out of perspective, he wrote: "For the kingdom of God is not a matter of eating and drinking, but of righteousness, peace and joy in the Holy Spirit." This should be how you can recognize the hand of God at work in society. Righteousness yes. Peace yes. But also joy in the Holy Spirit. Isaiah put it even more dramatically in verse 9: "Burst into songs of joy together". We are pretty cerebral in the northern hemisphere. That doesn't mean we are brainy necessarily! It does mean that we have a tendency culturally to overdo the rational.

It is being widely canvassed even in the most surprising circles that we need more experience. When people talk about authority, they refer to the normative authority of the Bible, and the balancing authority of Tradition and the use of Reason. But experience is also vital.

When we stand at the Pearly Gates, we will not be given a written intellectual test to be classified for entry into different parts of heaven.

The test is: Do you know God? Have you experienced Him during your life on earth? Has the joy of the Holy Spirit been yours? Now, this joy is not a hyped-up thing. It is a deep experience that bubbles up irrepressibly as from an underground spring. I say that very deliberately because life is not naturally all joyful. Life involves pain.

I think the most pain I have experienced in the diocese has been in the marriage breakdowns. Clerical marriage breakdowns are likely, humanly speaking, to approximate to the national average for breakdowns, which is heartrending.

We all need to pray for and care for each other more than we do.

There are some special pressures on the clergy role in our society today. But however bad and depressing the panorama, this must not undermine the Church's calling by God to be a joyful people.

We are congenitally not of the doom and gloom brigade. We are commanded to be joyful together. I understand there is a North American Gospel music group called Mighty Clowns of Joy. I like that. Why, we are even told to be joyful givers. I hope you have discovered that 90% of your income can stretch further than 100% when you give 10% to God's work. It is more likely to be affluence than poverty that stifles joy.

But the exhortation in Isaiah to "burst into songs of joy together" was directed to "you ruins of Jerusalem" and sometimes we may well naturally feel more like ruins than brilliant demonstrations of the glories of the Bride of Christ or the Heavenly Jerusalem. But we are to be joyful.

May you have international vision

"The Lord will lay bare his holy arm in the sight of all the nations, and all the ends of the earth will see the salvation of our God" (Verse 10). When Isaiah wrote these words he knew that God wouldn't act in a corner. His decisive intervention was to be for all, and all were to be informed.

I'm delighted that we have Bishop Ephraim with us today from the Sudan, and to have heard him at Synod yesterday. Today many are also remembering the ongoing need for effective international solidarity with Southern Africa, to see apartheid finally ended. Yes, all the ends of the earth will see the salvation of our God.

I'm delighted to have been called to concentrate on the international mission of the church for the next few years. Yes, there will be yearly visits to South America and also Spain and Portugal. Some of these will be very poignant. Perhaps the consecration as bishop of people I ordained in Peru or Bolivia or ministered to during their university careers in different countries of South America. Certainly visiting the highest capital in the world in Bolivia, La Paz, where I laid the foundation stone for the first Anglican church there some seven years ago. But also, through SAMS, helping a Bolivian woman travel to India for missionary work. Also, two Chilean families to go to Spain to work in the diocese there. Also, bringing key people for work experience in this country, who will no doubt bring refreshment and enthusiasm and creative ideas for the decade of evangelism in the UK.

But perhaps even more than these things, or certainly as well as these things, to be a constant episcopal gadfly with others in the voluntary missionary societies of the Church of England to remind us all that the church that lives to itself dies to itself. It is only as we live out and keep constantly in our minds that we are members by grace of God's international family, that we can be saved from parochialism, and avoid the danger of losing our Catholic and Apostolic nature.

I am delighted that the diocese now has a Links officer. I think I would have preferred the title of World Mission Officer, though that does sound a bit grand, especially in our post-colonial era. I have no doubt that the Church of England still has its part to play in world mission. Perhaps it will play a good part in the re-evangelisation of Europe. Many of the Honorary Canons of our cathedral are named after famous Celtic missionaries who took the Gospel not only right across our diocese, and our country, but also across Europe.

If Isaiah's vision was international in the 8th Century before Christ, and it was, how much more should ours also be unashamedly so, in 1993 and beyond.

Conclusion

Dorothy and I have been very privileged to be allowed to live and serve among you for the last four and three-quarter years. We have been enriched. We have learnt a lot. We have loved being here. We have loved the diocese, city and Dales. We have loved you, both Yorkshire-born and bred, and offcumdens. As we go south, we wish you well. We want to hear of your continued health in the years that lie ahead. That health will have a lot to do with having . . .

BEAUTIFUL FEET   JOYFUL HEARTS   INTERNATIONAL VISION

Farewell to Bradford Cathedral   20th June 1993

My brief on coming to the diocese was to prevent Bishop Roy having a second heart attack. As he was promoted hale and hearty to the enormous Diocese of Southwark, I can't have failed completely! My second brief was to hold the fort in the vacancy until Maidstone could move to Heaton. Despite a complete change of infrastructure and nomenclature, and the Church Commissioners' bombshell about financial cutbacks, I think the diocese was still recognizable, if not even in good shape, to welcome its eighth diocesan bishop. So from darkest Peru to darkest Tunbridge Wells, via the shining lights of the Diocese of Bradford.

I do want to thank you all very much for being here this afternoon. I know just how many other things are going on. Thank you for your generosity in welcoming us into the diocese, putting up with us and now sending us forth in such a splendid way. We have enjoyed splendid services in this lovely cathedral, not least our daughter's wedding. Many thanks to our Provost and choir. A big thank you to Bishop Roy and his senior staff for their daring faith in taking on a bishop from Peru. And a big thank you to Bishop David for the gracious way he accepted me with the diocese. He could not have been more helpful and understanding during these last nine months.

I must be one of the most licensed (not licentious) bishops around. Five times at least.

Once to act as Bishop Roy's assistant bishop

Once to act as Bishop Roy's commissary during his sabbatical

Once to act as Archbishop John's commissary during the vacancy-in-see

Once to act as Bishop David's commissary before his enthronement

Once to act as Bishop David's assistant bishop until the end of June.

One of my fondest memories is of a visit with a group of members of St John's Thorpe Edge to the rural parish of Gisburn. We were shown round a pig farm. The farmer was explaining the whole process of pig farming to us, as urbanites and townies. He was proud that everything was done on the farm except the actual slaughtering, and he explained that for that he took the pigs to the local slaughterhouse. To keep the interesting conversation going I asked, "And how often do you take them there?" Back came the reply, "I only takes 'em once".

My other favourite was the induction service for John Birbeck at

Hurst Green and Great Mitton. As I walked up the aisle at the end of a long procession a loud whisper was clearly heard from a member of the congregation: "That's the biggest crook I've ever seen." I do actually have a very large crozier of Brazilian mahogany carved in Peru, but from the pulpit I asked the whisperer to clarify whether he was referring to that, or to me.

My new job is to be General Secretary of SAMS. It is interesting how words get put together. Is there any difference between a General Secretary of a Missionary Society, and a Secretary General of the United Nations? Are we meant to be generals or secretaries? However, I expect it won't be very different from the episcopal task of seeking to lead, but in a spirit of service.

Hopes for the future include

Visit Bradford diocese as my job is an itinerant one. Au revoir—not farewell forever

Be involved in thinking and working for the present and future role of the Church of England in the world mission of the church

Renew contact with many friends throughout South America in situations of desperate poverty, spiritual exuberance and growing indigenous leadership

Retire to Yorkshire one day!?

Farewell from SAMS in South America

(Translated from Spanish)

Dear Companions in mission,

I am writing these lines from my old study in the vicarage for the chaplain in the garden of what is now the Cathedral Church of the Good Shepherd in Lima, Peru. I have just been preparing three sermons for three of the Lima churches. Perhaps my last sermons in Spanish! I am preaching on Philemon verse 6: "That we may be active in sharing our faith, so that you will have a full understanding of every good thing we have in Christ."

Dorothy and I have been highly privileged to spend 30 of our 38 years of ordained ministry life (up till now) in close contact with Latin America and the work of the South American Mission Society. Our lives have been hugely enriched from having known and worked with national brothers and sisters, missionaries, home staff and SAMS supporters throughout these years. From the bottom of our hearts we thank our bountiful God for all of you.

With Monseigneur Javier Ariz in Lima, Peru, at my farewell

During this last tour in South America, through Argentina, Bolivia and Peru, we feel full of gratitude for the grace, the faithfulness and the patience of God in fulfilling his mission. The truth is that he pursues his mission purposes in spite of us! We have wanted to be pure instruments in his hands but often that has not been the case. Realistically we remember failures, sins, errors and tensions. However, we also gratefully recognise growing congregations in Lomas de Zamora in Buenos Aires, Argentina, Santa Cruz and La Paz in Bolivia, and Arequipa and Lima in Peru.

Dorothy and I assure you of our support and prayers for the future and of course 'our house will always be your house'.

The Vicarage, Alderminster, Stratford-upon-Avon, CV37 8PE

Farewell from SAMS in the UK

This happened in two phases. There was an informal buffet in London, at which the SAMS Trustees said farewell.

To this were invited some London-based guests, representing different mission agencies: Bishop Mano Rumalshah from USPG and CEFACS, Bishop Michael Nazir-Ali and Canon Tim Dakin from CMS. Also a Rep

Farewell from SAMS in Birmingham, 17th June 2003

from the Archbishop of Canterbury representing PIM of the Church of England. The main farewell was at the SAMS General Council meeting on 17th June in Birmingham, when the Society's President Bishop Maurice Sinclair spoke and the official handover to my successor, Canon John Sutton took place.

PIM Farewell

Sec. of PIM John Clark
Gen. Sec. of CMS Diane Witts
Gen. Sec. of BCMS Roger Bowen

Farewell from Alderminster

We had six happy years in Alderminster, near Stratford-upon-Avon for our retirement ministry of four days a week, house for duty. The six years since our welcome and installation by Bishop Colin Bennetts in Pillerton Hersey had flown by.

We had good numbers from the six rural churches in the benefice. We had a tent in the vicarage garden and an imaginative liturgy was put together by the new incumbent, the Revd Kath Vickers. On display and illustrating the themes were:

      a Cross and Bible—giving thanks for faith
      a bowl, towel and Teddy—for love and service
      wildflowers and bird food—for the beauty of creation
      a loaf and a golf club—for community and fellowship.

Also a highlight of this (last) farewell in 2010 was the surprise I gave to Dorothy. We travelled the last two miles to the gathering in Ettington in a splendid horse-drawn carriage! I had made friends through pastoral visiting with the owner of this very handsome form of conveyance. He hired it out for weddings, but he also renovated carriages and had had connections with the Duke of Edinburgh and at least one Indian Maharaja, who kept a silver carriage in the UK for his convenience. So, rather a grand finale in a rural multi-parish benefice in Warwickshire. I think they would have approved of it in Peru and Argentina.

The ordained ministry of the Church of England has as one if its distinctive features the practice of regular moving on from one parish to another. Days are long past when vicars had the legal right to stay in one post all their lives. They became very much part of the local landscape and frequently officiated through services of baptism, marriage and burial for whole families. They became embedded and often were experts in local history, flora, fauna, etc. etc., and wrote erudite books. Those days are long gone. Modern parish ministry is much more mobile, as indeed are the populations of town and country. The official 'cure of souls' is given for a set period of years only and then reverts to the diocesan authorities to be handed on to another. So all personal friendships created in that geographical parish come to an official end and the shepherd is moved on to care for another flock of sheep or of course into retirement, where he or she is not meant to live too near to the last parish served.

If you add in, as part of a life's ministry, a period of overseas service, as we had for 20 years in two different countries, with the Andes mountains in between them, then many, many people inevitably slip from one's memory. Social media can now of course overleap even the highest mountain ranges, but meaningful human relationships need time and space to deepen and mature. This is not always possible in a peripatetic ministry. The compensation is the privilege of meeting a rich diversity of people from totally different backgrounds in totally different cultural settings.

I close this section with two addresses. The first, the short thank-you speech at the Stourdene group of churches farewell garden party. The second, my farewell sermon, which, you will see, had reappeared on various occasions, in various forms, since it was first given in September 1968.

My famous TV star wife with a team from The One Show!

'Speech' at farewell party in Ettington   31 July 2010

In our 46 years of married life we have never lived anywhere longer than we have in the Alderminster vicarage—seven years. On the other 10 previous occasions people have always managed to get rid of us quicker before!

It has been a very happy seven years for us, despite the fact that we have written off two cars—I crashed one in fog, Dorothy another on ice. I had a TIA and Dorothy broke her hip. On a more positive note, three more grandchildren arrived to make a total of eight.

Above all, we have been so privileged to meet many lovely people— some now already in heaven—others of you still part of the church militant here in the Stourdene group. Visiting you in your homes, meeting with you in church services, and social events, has been a real joy. Spared admin and finance issues has been a real bonus, so golf, chickens, gardening, ornithological, philatelic and botanical hobbies have been enjoyed. Time for teaching and preaching preparation, time for visiting non-churchgoers to remind every person in the six villages that each has a God-given soul.

Farewell to Stourdene Group   Psalm 73:28

It is good for me to draw near to God. I have put my trust in the Lord God, that I may declare all thy words.

This was the text of my very first sermon/talk in September **1960** in a small Railway Mission chapel near Cambridge almost exactly 50 years ago,.

I have a good filing system. I have that sermon still. I also preached on Psalm 73 in **1968** at Christ Church Cockfosters where I was curate when first ordained. The title was The Home of Mr and Mrs Self-Satisfied and the home of Mr and Mrs Faithful Christians.

Basically the same sermon I preached in **1971** in Holy Trinity Lomas de Zamora in Buenos Aires, Argentina. In **1980** at a university student conference in Peru I preached in Spanish on Psalm 73, on the individual's time of daily private devotion—Quiet Time with God.

And it was this verse of Psalm 73 the Holy Spirit brought to my mind on Thursday this week, thinking of today, as a period of 50 years of preaching comes to an end.

A very brief comment on those three phrases:

It is good for me to draw near to God: This speaks of communion with God, which is our great privilege and joy. It is good, it does us good to draw near to God and commune with Him.

I have put my trust in the Lord God: This speaks of our commitment to God. Each person putting his life for time and eternity into God's faithful hands. I did just that at Cambridge 50 years ago and have never regretted it.

That I may declare all Thy words: This speaks of our calling to make known the words of God. The inspired message of the Bible and supremely the good news of the Word made flesh, incarnate in Jesus Christ, the Saviour of the World.

By God's grace I am still happy to subscribe to the truths of Psalm 73:28:

Communion with God
Commitment to God
Calling to declare God's works

Moving On – From One 'Job' To Another

In some areas of life this can be quite straightforward. There is a clear career structure. As long as you have basic skills and the ability to learn and change, then the sky is the limit! Though not everyone can occupy the top jobs. There are various 'ceilings' which may involve gender issues, not wide enough experience, lack of intellectual ability, etc. etc. but if you live long enough, have a degree of luck, perhaps, and are willing to work hard, jobs tend to materialize. People are always dying, retiring or going higher up the ladder. Not everyone has a silver spoon in their rucksack, but most move from one job to another or are promoted within a large organisation. Not everyone wants promotion! Even with a bigger pay packet. Dedicated teachers don't always want the headteacher's job. It has usually less teaching and more administration. Some quail at the thought of speaking in public. Some don't want responsibility. Others always have their sights set on the top job. They will take every opportunity for in-service training. Or are keen to travel the world, even if in a not-too-well-paid job.

Becoming a bishop in Peru was a comparatively easy process. It was not even officially a diocese until three months after my consecration. There were not a host of hopefuls eager to have oversight of Paddington Bear's home territory. There may have been more things going on behind the scenes than I knew about, but I was offered the job, and I felt it right to accept. As a family we had moved from Argentina to Peru, knowing that an episcopal candidate would be needed, and so it proved to be.

Funnily enough it was even easier when we moved from Peru, South America, to Bradford in S. Yorkshire. Again, as a family, we felt the time had come for a move. There were education and family concerns with our three children, all eventually in the UK. I felt I had made my contribution in getting a diocese organized, legal and growing. So on our previous visit to the UK I was advised to have a short interview, at my request, with the Archbishops' Appointments Secretary in Westminster. So I did and went back to Peru. Some time later I received a phone call from Roy Williamson, the Bishop of Bradford, asking me to come to be a full-time assistant bishop in his diocese. Right out of the blue! I remember, while still on the phone, trying to get Dorothy to find Bradford on a map of England, being myself such a southerner! That was it basically! Having had a heart attack at a meeting of the General Synod, Bishop Roy (without a suffragan in his diocese) needed episcopal help. It had been decided earlier not to create any more suffragan bishops. Therefore someone already in episcopal orders was needed. A recent precedent was that of the late Bishop Bill Flagg, who had also served in Peru, and gone to be an assistant bishop in Liverpool with Bishop David Sheppard, so I said yes!

Later the move from Bradford to be General Secretary of SAMS, whose headquarters was in Tunbridge Wells, was much more drawn out and complicated. Bishop Roy Williamson had been translated to Southwark and I was left in temporary charge of the Diocese of Bradford, with due documents signed by the Archbishop of York. My name appeared in the list of runners for the episcopal stakes in Bradford, but that was just newspaper headlines. Eventually after some nine months David Smith came from Rochester to take over, and my stint as diocesan and assistant bishop came to an end. I was to move away! But where to? It took some time. I actually said no to six different offers! Before accepting the General Secretary job with SAMS!

The following letter to Bishop Bill Flagg illustrates this period of uncertainty:

Wednesday 27th January

Dear Bill and Marj,

Thank you very much for your letter of the 26th January received today. It is good to have a clear outline of plans for your future and we rejoice with you in this. It certainly looks as though you are going to be kept busy and I know that Pat [Harris] must be delighted to have the benefit of your experience in so many spheres in his diocese.

Dorothy and I continue to covet your prayers. Our own future is still veiled in mystery. It doesn't get any easier as it inevitably is the topic of conversation with just about everyone we meet. The Church Commissioners have extended our contract until June 26th, by which time I shall just have had my 55th birthday. We feel we have something to offer the Church still. It seems we need patience and faith in this period of uncertainty and enforced waiting. It is harder in some ways having had a very busy year as acting diocesan and being 'in the know' to feeling now rather on the sideline. We do value your prayers.

Yours ever in our Lord

(signed)

The first invitation was to consider the prestigious Church of Christ Church in New York! This came via a Peruvian whom I had married in Lima, brother of the Peruvian Minister of Agriculture. Interesting but way out!

Secondly, I was approached by David Lunn, the Bishop of Sheffield, to replace the retiring Suffragan Bishop of Doncaster. This was rather nearer the mark and we went on a visit to have an informal chat. It did not prosper. I think the bishop may have been trying to speed up the usual protocols, which are as strict for suffragans as for diocesans.

Bishopthorpe, 12th June 2017
Retired Bishops' Gathering

Thirdly, a kind letter from the Bishop of Derby, offering the possibility of an evangelical living in one of his churches. Peter Dawes had been on the staff of Trinity College, Bristol when I was a student there.

Fourthly, a letter from Canon John Moore of CPAS (The Church Pastoral Aid Society) to replace retiring Ian Savile as Patronage Secretary. This seemed quite interesting, partly because it was John Moore who had officiated at our wedding and because Martin Parsons, my father-in-law, had been heavily involved in Patronage work with the Charles Simeon Trust, which looked after some 150 churches across the Church of England.

The fifth attempt to find the next and right sphere of service was from the patrons of Muswell Hill in North London. We went for an interview but didn't feel it was for us. They didn't think so either!

Finally, in the sixth instance, news came of a vacancy in the role of General Secretary of SAMS. We applied on 1/3/93 and were accepted after interview on 22/3/93. So full circle! After quite a bit of heart-searching I had begun to wonder whether we were unemployable? In the end it did seem to us that the continuation of nearly 20 years' experience in South America and seven years working in an English diocese had equipped us for the job for a 'go-between' for South America and the UK.

So some very different experiences. Less problematic in every way was after the ten years at SAMS as General Secretary, because it just involved retirement ministry. The norm is that a retired bishop is offered the title of honorary assistant bishop in the diocese where he resides, by the diocesan, who will call upon him when he has a particular need. He also normally receives a P.T.O. (Permission to Officiate) for diocesan-wide preaching and ministry at the invitation of the parish or diocesan clergy. Retired bishops can also be asked to participate in the consecration of new bishops: they get invitations to Buckingham Palace Garden Parties once every two years, and the Archbishop of York hosts a day event at Bishopthorpe for those who can make the journey and enjoy meeting up with past colleagues.

Having said that, on the episcopal front, by far most of my time was spent at grass-roots level, as an assistant priest in the Stourdene group of churches. This was hugely refreshing. A reminder of what the ordained ministry is really all about. Teaching and pastoring God's people without any constant travel to distant parts and participating in the day-to-day life of local communities.

6
EPILOGUE

I am reminded of a short article I wrote in my ordination year while at theological college in 1962. Back to basics, in fact:

My Ordination Year 1963   Contributed by David Evans

> So you are going into the church?
>
> Going to be a minister, then?
>
> Turning your collar round, I hear.
>
> How nice. I'm sure you will do well.

I expect most young men in training for the ordained ministry have their patience tried on numerous occasions by similar remarks. How grateful Dorothy and I are that your concern and interest go deeper than this and that you are supporting us in your regular prayers as well as with financial help during these two final years of training. My ordination should be in September of this year, which means that I now have two full terms to complete at Clifton Theological College, before moving up to London to a first curacy.

As this is now my ordination year I feel increasingly grateful to God for the definiteness of the call to the ministry which He gave me at the end of 1960. It is a great joy to find the particular vocation prepared by the Lord, and of course this is a privilege enjoyed by every Christian, for God has good works prepared before the foundation of the world for every person, who by faith in His Son has committed himself or herself to a lifetime of service and worship. One Greek word expresses both the idea of service and worship, teaching us that there is to be an integrated wholeness about our Christian living. It is no doubt easier for the ordained minister to be conscious of this wholeness, but the New Testament does not limit it to him alone. In our modern secular world it is one of the exciting and testing challenges to Christian men and women to work out the implications of the Christian faith in their places of work and in their spheres of relaxation and entertainment. The secularist can rightly mock the person whose Christian faith is confined to a small closed pigeon-hole of Sunday observance.

In an Ordination charge at Durham Bishop Lightfoot once said, "What is your diaconate but an intensification of the function of ministering which is incumbent on all believers alike? What is your

*Marking VE Day's 75th Anniversary, 8th May 2020
for our street party outside our house in Warwick*

*Almost 42 years since 14th May 1978 in the Cathedral in Lima, Peru
42 years in Purple and counting!*

priesthood but a concentration of the priesthood of the whole people of Christ?" A person is called and set apart in order to intensify his activities and concentrate all his attention on the growth and well-being of Christ's church. The same actual tasks lie before every member of the congregation, but the minister has more opportunity to devote himself wholly to them. In the Ordination service itself I shall be reminded: "Have always therefore printed in your remembrance how great a treasure is committed to your charge. For they are the sheep of Christ, which He bought with His death, and for whom He shed His blood."

2 Corinthians chapter five teaches that "we have this treasure (this time the Gospel of the glory of Christ) in earthen vessels, to show that the transcendent power belongs to God and not to us." The minister is specially responsible for both the treasure of the Lord's people in his parish and the treasure of the Gospel of God's power. He must understand and love both these treasures and devote himself to the task of ensuring that the one treasure, the Lord's people, understand and love the other treasure, the Gospel of God's power. This is a glorious task but it is also a large one, which every ordinand can only view with a sense of personal unworthiness. Please pray that the Lord will so control Dorothy and myself that this full knowledge of both people and the Gospel may increase in us and so equip us for the Lord's service.

DAVID EVANS

APPENDIX A

'Personal Lament'—Labels Galore[1]

If all ecclesiastical labels were abolished, I wonder if we would have an identity crisis. In China, even denominations were scrapped by political decree and only the Christian Church as such was officially recognized. In many parts of the Christian world there is an obsession with labels. It used to be sufficient to describe oneself as an evangelical Anglican or was it Anglican evangelical?

Putting my cards on the table, I am happy to be called an evangelical Anglican. *If* I had to choose between the two epithets, I would have to choose evangelical, because by its very nature it seeks to stand for the essence of the Gospel itself, although of course in practice with considerable development into an entire sub-culture offering services, events, festivals, concerts, conferences, magazines, books, merchandise, record companies, mission organization, training schemes, holiday clubs and celebrities. At the same time, I want to hold on to Anglican because of, I believe, a not unworthy loyalty to a particular section of the One Holy Catholic and Apostolic Church which is part and parcel of my own particular history.

However, today the label mania goes further and in our supermarket world there are numerous brands of evangelical Anglicanism on offer. We are all aware that historically there are strong Puritan, Pietist and Revivalist strands in the evangelical label, which have produced a list of so-called evangelical distinctives in the past, such as the necessity of conversion, the responsibility of evangelism, the authority of Scripture and the centrality of the atoning work of Christ on the Cross.

It is widely acknowledged that there are some 12 tribes within Evangelicalism (Evangelical Alliance's *Who do Evangelicals think they are*) and in recent years we have been seeing a flow of books fine-tuning definitions and producing an ever more confusing number of labels. When I returned 8 years ago to England after 20 years in South America, I found many of my friends and contemporaries were Open Evangelicals, others were Charismatic Evangelicals. More recently, in 1995, a book was published: *The Anglican Evangelical Crisis*, edited by Melvin Tinker, contributed to by 12 authors, 3 from Australia, 1 from Canada, 3 from USA and 5 from the UK. Part of its thesis is as follows:

---

[1] Presented at the EFAC Australia Conference, 26–29 June 1996

As evangelicalism has continued to grow numerically, it has seeped through its older structures and now spills out in all directions, producing a family of hybrids whose theological connections are quite baffling: evangelical Catholics, evangelicals who are Catholic, evangelical liberationists, evangelical feminists, evangelical ecumenists, young evangelicals, orthodox evangelicals, radical evangelicals, liberal evangelicals. Liberals who are evangelical and charismatics who are evangelicals. The word evangelical, precisely because it has lost its confessional dimension, has become descriptively anaemic. To say that someone is an evangelical says little about what they believe. And so the term is forced to compensate for its theological weakness by borrowing meaning from adjectives, the very presence of which signals the fragmentation of the movement. **David F Wells** *No Place for Truth* Eerdmans, 1994, p.134. Though the term is not used, I detect a desire for a return to a robust evangelicalism.

In 1996, Nigel Wright's book, *The Radical Evangelical*, published by SPCK, has a first chapter entitled, "In defense of labels" and he goes on to justify his own choice of the adjective 'radical' in an extremely attractive and challenging way. Just previously Dave Tomlinson produced his book published by Triangle entitled, *The Post Evangelical*. He sums up his thesis in these words:

> To be post-evangelical is to take as given many of the assumptions of evangelical faith, while at the same time moving beyond its perceived limitations (p.7).

Many of us might wonder at the looseness of the first part of that sentence but perhaps sympathize with the desire to interact on a more positive level with theologies and perspectives and spiritualities which do not come from evangelical sources. There is in this book a desire to be free of narrow-mindedness and dogmatism, a yearning for more creativity and new fresh spirituality.

But throughout we have either an obsession with labels or their use and multiplication to describe a panorama of change. Is labelmania evidence of evangelical fissiparism? Is it evidence of narrow party spirit? Or is it evidence of an evangelical comprehensiveness that mirrors the Anglican comprehensiveness normally associated with our denomination? Is it good, bad or indifferent? How far are you prepared to go spiritually with the addition of adjectives to describe your commitment to Christ? And if you think labels are helpful, how many of them do you need to describe the width and depth of your understanding of the Christian faith?

APPENDIX B

The Christian Mission in a Changing World[2]

To address you on this subject I want to acknowledge three conscious sources of contribution. *Firstly,* my own involvement with one of the 11 Church of England voluntary mission agencies, SAMS, which incorporates the Spanish and Portuguese Church Aid Society. I joined SAMS in 1968 and served for 20 years in South America and have now also served for seven years as its General Secretary. *Secondly,* the 1999 book, *What is Mission?* by Prof J. Andrew Kirk, Dean and Head of the School of Mission and World Christianity at Selly Oak College, Birmingham. And *thirdly, The International Bulletin of Missionary Research* of October 1999 and an article by Ted Ward in *Repositioning Mission Agencies for the Twenty-First Century.*

1 *Missio Dei*

The title given to me for this lecture presupposes a particular interest in the changing world in which we are to conduct Christian mission in a responsible and sensitive way. However, we must also start from the basic premise that Christian mission is *Missio Dei*. If it is not the activity of God, then it is not Christian mission. Christian mission can degenerate into a private part-time hobby, a professional livelihood for those who are paid to do mission, or an academic interest. Therefore we must never lose sight of Jesus Christ's mission commission recorded in John's Gospel "As the Father has sent me, so I am sending you." The apostolic activity of the church is mandated by Christ, and patterned on His own activity as the One sent into the world to give historical evidence of the Father's love for fallen humankind. Mission must therefore always be characterised by costly obedience, incarnational vulnerability and spiritual empowerment. Put in another way, we can even go so far as to say that "there can be no theology without mission and no theology which is not missionary." (*What is Mission?* J. A. Kirk, p.11). If the *Missio Dei* focused historically on the person and work of Christ, as the Sent One, the missionary par excellence, then mission should always have a human

---

[2] Presented at the IVth Congress of the Lusitanian Church, 14–17 June 2000, Vila Nova de Gaia, Porto.

face to reveal the presence of God in the needs of the world. Mission is about people, people who send, people who go and people who receive, in a dynamic partnership patterned on that of the Triune God. Having, I hope, pressed home this fundamental point, I want to survey briefly some of the ways that mission in a changing world has recently been described.

2 The Changing World

a **Dr Andrew Kirk** devotes pages 56–184 of his book to "Contemporary Issues in Mission". He lists seven which he states are correct applications of the whole subject of Christian mission masterfully systematised in David Bosch's magnum opus, *Transforming Mission*. Kirk lists: cultural sensitivity with all the issues of correct inculturation and contextualisation; justice for the poor; the encounter with world religions; the need for peace building in a world of violence; the care of the environment and the nature of sharing in partnership. These seven areas are the ones where he sees the Christian Church engaging at the beginning of the 21st Century.

b **The Anglican Communion's** official documents on mission in our changing world added a fifth characteristic mark to our understanding of mission. In *Mission in a Broken World*, the report of the ACC.8 meeting of 1990: To strive to safeguard the integrity of creation and sustain and renew the life of the earth was added to the more traditional marks:–

  i.   to proclaim the good news of the Kingdom;
  ii. to teach, baptise and nurture new believers;
  iii. to respond to human need by loving service;
  iv. to seek to transform the unjust structures of society.

c **The Church Mission Society** of Great Britain spotlighted four areas in their Bicentenary mission statement. They are committed to mission on the margins of society, mission in the cities, mission in interfaith circumstances and mission in a materialistic world. **The United Society for the Propagation of the Gospel** describes three challenges they face as they approach their Tercentenary in 2001: reconciliation work, reciprocal mission and community development.

d The article referred to already in *The International Bulletin for Missionary Research* speaks about the effects of mass technologies for the communication of the Gospel, the challenges of sustainable structures in the Two-Thirds World, the question of financial transparency and accountability. All three of these have shrunk the world out of all recognition. Communication technology is already making some of our traditional mission work strategies appear to belong to the age of the dinosaurs!

I do not intend to do more than mention these specified areas of concern as evidenced by the various documents I have just quoted. What I do want to do is pinpoint three more underlying challenges that face all of us.

3 Three Contemporary Challenges

A. The Challenge of the Inclusivity/Exclusivity Debate

In the world of mission debate the term inclusivist has become the policitally correct word to describe the attitude of the church towards the world. The position frequently stated is that the Church of Jesus Christ must be inclusivist. Often this may not be too closely defined, which can lead to a chaotic woolliness about the message we are seeking to communicate, and a sentimental openness to all and everything, which cuts the whole nerve of and motivation for meaningful mission. I want to mention seven different areas where the term inclusivist is being applied today and suggest that five of these are legitimate and two are not.

i **Human inclusivity.** This involves the gender issue and the sexuality issue. We believe the Gospel is to be presented to all of humankind in its sinful state and that the doors of the church must be open for all.

ii **Racial inclusivity.** The church must be committed to reflect the 'rainbow' nature of humankind both in its universal outreach to men and women of every race and in its internal local membership.

iii **Cultural inclusivity.** The church is committed to inculturation and contextualisation in its universal mission. It does not believe in a monochrome ecclesial culture, though it needs much wisdom to discern what can be affirmed and what needs to be confronted in any particular culture.

iv **Denominational inclusivity.** We are involved in the ecumenical movement as we recognise fully the existence of other expressionssof the Christian faith, quite apart from the different expressions of the Christian faith within the Anglican Communion itself, which as you know has been described as an ecumenical movement in miniature. We are not sectarian, denying any spiritual reality for other expressions of Christianity.

v **Liturgical inclusivity.** The days of a *Book of Common Prayer* in common and regular use in the Anglican Communion around the world or even within one province have gone. We believe that cultural diversity and also human psychological needs lead naturally to different patterns of worship and in principle we accept the rightness of this.

These five areas of inclusivity strengthen and enrich us in our mission in a changing world where we are constantly confronted with immense pluralities. However, there are two further areas of possible inclusivity which endanger the vitality of our mission and even remove our motivation for mission. I refer first to

vi **Doctrinal inclusivity.** This area is dominated by the postmodernist denial of absolutes in issues of truth. The concept of the once-for-all revelation of authoritative truth has evaporated and is frequently replaced by the norm of the individual's experience of what is regarded as true for him or her. So we are faced with an unprincipled, unregulated doctrinal comprehensiveness where almost anything goes. Can one expression of the One Holy Catholic and Apostolic Church, i.e. the Anglican Communion, survive, if in practice it stands for opposite and unreconcilable doctrines? In one sense it can be said that it has already survived enormous differences and harboured great varieties of doctrinal interpretations. Many Anglicans may have been uneasy but in the past there has been an appeal to the primacy of the authority of Scripture. In recent times there has been a subtle and perhaps dangerous shift to the appeal to the so-called Lambeth Quadrilateral (The Holy Scripture; the Two Sacraments; the Three Creeds and the Historic Episcopate). Even this bench mark, never intended to control orthodoxy within Anglicanism, seems unlikely to put a brake on intolerant liberalism. In the area of doctrinal inclusivity we must be principled. We are to be subject not to emotional or cultural factors but to the Word of God written, which remains the normative revelation for us of the final authority, which is the Living God Himself. The world may be changing but there is a right and proper sense in which the Gospel of God promised through His prophets in the Holy Scriptures regarding His Son (Romans 1: 1 & 2) does not.

vii **Interfaith inclusivity** in its most generally accepted sense, means that salvation is available in different forms through all the different world religions. Through increased communication facilities, through increased mobility of peoples from one country to another, we are all faced with a confusing multiplicity of ideas and methods of salvation in different cultural dresses. One result of this plurality of cultural options has been to undermine our grasp of the uniqueness of Christ as the Saviour of the World. This does not make us rigid exclusivists. We believe the Judge of all the world will do what is right, in the famous words of Abraham. But we have to be guided by revelation in the person and work of Christ and take with the utmost seriousness the missionary mandate given by Christ to His body, the Church.

So it is important that we are inclusivists in at least five important and far-reaching ways, presenting a welcoming and attractive face to the world. But in doctrinal and interfaith issues we tend to be more exclusivist, believing that there are parameters and boundaries, because of the nature of Christianity as a divinely revealed faith, involving matters on which it is inappropriate for humankind to be guided solely by its own cultural and historically conditioned personal opinions.

B The challenge of the identity crisis

Wherever I have been in recent years there has been talk of the identity crisis, as synods have been debating Anglican identity in Brazil, in the Southern Cone of South America, in Mexico, etc. etc. I'm sure it is a relevant issue for you in the Igreja Lusitana Catolica Apostolica Evangelica. Each of those four adjectives has a historical rationale to do with the establishing of an identity. Looking more widely, however, we can see that there are many reasons for concern about identity.

a It may arise from an existential and legitimate psychological need. As it does in the life of most teenagers growing into adulthood, so it happens in the life of a church.

b It may arise from the present distrust of authoritative institutions, not least amongst the younger generation, creating a lack of loyalty to any one particular denomination. Modern people are more prepared to learn about and to go 'where the action is'. This is ultimately unsettling to the desire for the security of an identity.

c Sometimes Anglican identity is a problem because in any one place quite a number of Anglican clergy have not been born as Anglicans and have even come into the Anglican church as pastors from other denominations. This can be enriching but it can also undermine a clear sense of belonging and identity in leadership which affects everyone.

d A concern for identity may also represent a totally legitimate process of moving into a more autoctonous and national expression of faith. The more culturally foreign any denomination is through its founding fathers, the more unsettling a period of proper inculturization can be.

e Concern for identity may also come from confusion and distress and even righteous indignation about unacceptable developments and contradictory teaching or practices in another part of the Anglican Communion. This again can undermine one's sense of belonging and may evoke the feeling, 'I don't want to be associated with a particular person or particular teachings, regarded in some cases as heretical'.

Now the question of identity is important for mission and even more so in a changing world. We do need to know who we are before we can have confidence in going to others and saying come and join us. We do not need to claim to be the perfect church. We will never be more than one provisional example of the One Holy Catholic and Apostolic Church of Jesus Christ here on earth. But we must feel comfortable with a provisional identity. This is vital spiritually because ultimately we are to be ready to lose our identity, as the seed disappears into the soil of the world, where our mission takes place. If we are commanded to be prepared to lose our life, we must surely be prepared to lose a particular identity label. And of course our ultimate identity and security is in Christ Himself. Our life is hidden with Christ in God and one day we shall see Him as he is and be made like Him for ever. I cannot envisage ecclesial labels in heaven. Identity will be Christlikeness. Meanwhile ecclesial labels have relative historical value, as long as we live out their positive potential, allow them to motivate us to mission, refuse to use them as excuses for inaction and inward-lookingness and as long as we are ultimately prepared to sacrifice them into the greater reality of the universal Church of God.

C. The challenge of international partnership

Partnership in the mission of the Church is first and foremost with God Himself—we are His partners—He is in partnership with us. That fundamental international partnership must influence all relationships between human partners, and it very rarely does. Too often international partnerships are conceived of in purely financial, business terms. Or we think in terms of senior and junior partners. Colonial and paternalistic attitudes are alive and well in the 21st Century. Control rather than trust follows all too easily the handing over of resources, whether financial, personal or strategic planning. Achieving a genuine partnership of equals in interdependence in the Universal Church of Christ is hard. The primary responsibility for mission is for the local body of believers. However there is no local expression of the church that is exonerated from the responsibility and privilege of both sending and receiving help from the world-wide church. More than reciting the Nicene Creed, this reciprocal movement teaches us the international nature of the Church of Jesus Christ, especially when it involves people. If mission is potentially from everywhere to everywhere, from everyone to everyone, then it needs to be incarnated in exchange programmes, in people of different races, languages, cultures being moved around the world in every direction, helping local communities to know their membership in the Universal Church of Christ.

In 1992 I had the honour of giving the J. C. Jones Memorial Lecture in Wales. I spoke on International Vision, based on the text of Genesis 13:14. God commanded Abram "Lift up your eyes from where you are and look north and south and east and west." I believe that is a right and valuable thing for every church to do, be it a local congregation, a diocese or a national church. As John Wesley said, "the world is my parish." It is certainly in our changing world of increasing globalisation a perspective for which Jesus prepared us in the inauguration of His Kingdom on earth. As the Father sent Him, so He continues to send us sometimes in body, but always in mind the spirit to those beyond.

So we face three particular challenges in our part in the *Missio Dei* in the changing world of the 21st Century.

The challenge to be inclusivist, to present an attractive face to the changing world but without distorting or watering down the Gospel of God, the core authoritative message which must be communicated in word and deed to a world which lives either in breathtaking poverty or unbelievable affluence—but with spiritual emptiness.

The challenge to be confident of our eternal identity in Christ, so that we concentrate on the essentials, spend our time and resources gladly in the work of Christ's Kingdom, so that individual hearts, families, societies and nations can be transformed, "and we will in all things grow up into Him who is the Head, that is, Christ." (Ephesians 4:15).

The challenge to be active in international partnership in mission, which reveals the rainbow nature of God's people, enriches our discipleship and stretches our commitment to each other across the chasms of the modem world, looking expectantly for the time when all the kingdoms of this world will be handed over to God by Christ, "for God was pleased to have all His fullness dwell in Him, and through Him to reconcile to Himself all things, whether things on earth or things in heaven, by making peace through his blood shed on the Cross". (Colossians 1 :20).

The Right Revd D. R. J. Evans
General Secretary of SAMS
Assistant Bishop of Birmingham

Questions for Group Discussion

The Christian Mission in a Changing World

1 We need knowledge of and sensitivity to the changing world around us. But does this legitimise changing our message?

2 What would be the three key priority areas for Christian mission in the role of the Lusitanian Church?

3 Do you agree with the presentation about inclusivity?

4 Is the Lusitanian Church responding to the challenge of international partnership?

APPENDIX C

Some Archiepiscopal Correspondence

Lambeth Palace London SE1 7JU

15th May 1990

Dear David,

       I am most grateful to you for your help for my
forthcoming visit to Latin America. I am on the verge of
leaving and only have time for a brief note of
acknowledgement.

       Lima comes at the end of what looks like a pretty
arduous tour so your prayers for my stamina will be more
than welcome!

       I am most interested in what you say about Mario Vargas
Llosa. I gather his chances are minimal but I will keep in
mind your connection with his family.

       Thank you for the briefing and the work that you have
done for us. I shall look forward to giving your greetings
to your old friends.

Yours Ever

Robert

The Rt Revd David R J Evans
30 Grosvenor Road
Shipley
West Yorkshire
BD18 4RN

From the Archbishop of Canterbury, Robert Runcie, who had asked me to
give him some sermon material before his visit to Latin America in 1990

Lambeth Palace London SE1 7JU,

23 September, 1998 .

Dear David

Thank you very much for all you did to help the Spouses' Programme in the Mission and Evangelism Presentation. Right from the beginning you had a vision with Peter Price of the way forward, and although with your other commitments much of the spade work was handed over, I know that you were there supporting it. It was a very worthwhile Presentation and was just right for that point in the programme when the spouses were rather tired and needed to have a much more visual presentation, and not be bombarded with too many words. This Presentation was exactly that and held our interest in a very exciting way. So thank you for all you did to enable that to happen.

With Love
From
Eileen

Mrs Eileen Carey

The Rt Revd David Evans
12 Fox Hill
Birmingham
B29 4AG

From the Archbishop of Canterbury's wife, Eileen Carey, to thank me for my part in preparing material for the Bishops' Spouses' Lambeth Conference in 1998